Excellence in Internal Communication Management

Excellence in Internal Communication Management

Rita Linjuan Men and Shannon A. Bowen

With foreword contributed by industry leader, Keith Burton

Excellence in Internal Communication Management

First published in 2017 by
Business Expert Press, LLC
222 East 46th Street, New York, NY 10017
www.businessexpertpress.com

ISBN-13: 978-1-63157-675-1 (paperback)
ISBN-13: 978-1-63157-676-8 (e-book)

Business Expert Press Public Relations Collection

Collection ISSN: 2157-345X (print)
Collection ISSN: 2157-3476 (electronic)

Cover and interior design by Exeter Premedia Services Private Ltd., Chennai, India

First edition: 2017

10 9 8 7 6 5 4 3 2 1

Printed in the United States of America.

*To all who have experienced ineffective internal communication
management; may this book be your comfort in knowing how
things should be done, even when they are not.*

Abstract

This book integrates theories, research insights, practices, as well as current issues and cases into a comprehensive guide for internal communication managers and organizational leaders on how to communicate effectively with internal stakeholders, build beneficial relationships, build ethical organizational cultures, and engage employees in a rapidly-changing business and media environment. Solidly grounded in theories of organizational communication and behavior, public relations, leadership, moral philosophy, and business management, this book shares insights about current workplace topics including employee engagement, trust, change communication, new technologies, leadership communication, ethical advising and decision making, transparency and authenticity, and measurement. Mechanisms underlying best practices of internal communication are explained. Data-backed strategies and tactics in enhancing internal communications are discussed. We offer valid scales for use in internal communication assessment. The book concludes with predictions of the future of internal communications research, theory development, and practices.

Keywords

change management, employee communication, employee engagement, employee relations, ethics, future of internal communications, internal communication, internal publics and stakeholders, internal relations, leadership, measurement and evaluation, organizational communication, organizational culture, social media, structure

Contents

Foreword

Clad in black anodized aluminum and gray-tinted glass, the iconic Mies van der Rohe-designed IBM Plaza rises like a sentinel along the Chicago River. In the early morning hours, shafts of sunlight sprayed into empty cubicles and offices, tracing along carpeted hallways that a week earlier teemed with people. Now, everyone on the floor was gone—victims of a major downsizing spawned by the earliest re-engineering project in American business.

In the wake of the employees' departures, the floor was cluttered with the personal artifacts of their work and "I-Bleed-Blue" careers at IBM Corp. Huge wheeled dumpsters filled with bulging manila file folders and computer printouts sat in silent testament to the corporate carnage that had taken place. The IBM leader accompanying me stopped to examine a few of the files and shook her head as we moved down the hall.

"It's funny", she said, unemotionally, in assessing a critical challenge business leaders face during a change process—communicating clearly to cut through information overload. "Today, we're 'gagging on data and starving for information.'"

And so, it began. The year was 1992, and the re-engineering of IBM was like the first orchestral movement of an Aaron Copeland symphony that would carry me forward through more than 25 years of successive waves of corporate change.

We are still enduring change related to corporate restructuring, downsizing, post-merger consolidation, and the growing globalization of great corporate brands: In 2015, global corporate merger and acquisition activity of $4.7 trillion eclipsed all prior years. New generations of employees have ascended to put their imprimatur on corporate cultures and the values that guide their beliefs and behaviors. And, developments in technology—the global dominance of smartphones, the introduction of text messaging, VoIP services such as Skype, apps like Snapchat, Twitter, and Facebook, and multiplayer games, to name only a handful—have resulted in revolutionary changes to the way we communicate in the workplace and how we interact with friends, family, and society.

In our 24-7/365 worlds, where work can be unrelenting and unyielding, we are still gagging on data and starving for information. Just ask the frontline managers and supervisors at the ExxonMobil refinery in Torrance, California, who at one time said they receive more than 100 e-mails a day, wade through overnight voice mails, and participate in multiple teleconferences and meetings that consume their days before they can finally turn their attention to their direct reports. Or Facebook's millennial employees, who have all the social and digital tools and streams of data any new age worker could ever imagine, but long for seasoned, experienced managers more advanced than "twenty-something" who can provide critical context and leadership for their work.

"What does *good* look like?" Alex Thursby stared down his glasses, as he asked this question in his conference room at the National Bank of Abu Dhabi's headquarters in the United Arab Emirates. Through the windows behind us, the late-afternoon sky was a pinkish gold and the sun was beginning to bow to the waters of the Persian Gulf. "That's what I want to know", Thursby continued. "What *does* good look like?"

The CEO of NBAD was driving a new strategy that would fuel the bank's expansion in the West-East corridor, from the Gulf Region into India, the Philippines, Indonesia, Malaysia, and China. Strategic employee engagement would be critical to his strategy, and the ebullient Australian executive wanted his corporate communications team to know *and* adopt best-in-class practices that would help educate, inform, and align his employees with the strategy.

Not only did our global consulting team show him a clear, measurable strategy through qualitative research and by applying proven models, we delivered a program that enabled employees representing more than 30 ethnicities and a multitude of differing cultures to coalesce and expand NBAD's footprint in key commercial hubs across the West-East corridor.

Excellence in Internal Communication Management is all about laying the foundation upon which *good* must be constructed. Co-authors Dr. Rita L. Men, University of Florida, and Dr. Shannon A. Bowen, University of South Carolina, are gifted educators helping light the path in employee communication for academic leaders, graduate students, and professionals in corporate communication, human resources, finance, labor relations, and management consulting fields—all those seeking greater understanding, knowledge, and insights regarding this critical discipline.

In the chapters to follow, you'll discover and, in some instances, re-discover academic research and theory beneath the art of our work. You'll have an opportunity to consider the origins of employee communication; the evolution of our craft; the roles of audience segmentation, internal communication channels and tools; the importance of building trust and acting ethically in our work; using existing measurement models and evolving new methods that gauge outputs, outgrowths, and outcomes; and envisioning the future of our work where *good* will continually be tempered on the forge of the truths we face in the marketplace, in the halls of academia, and in society.

We face business challenges more dramatic than at any time in our history, including:

- *Structural challenges* related to the globalization of companies and the ascent of matrixed leadership models.
- *Workforce challenges* tied to information overload, the fast pace of the workplace, finding skilled workers, generational differences, morale issues, and a failure to recognize the contributions of frontline employees.
- *Media challenges* related to bad press, misinformation, the consolidation of global media, and "Citizen Journalists" who are at the core of Andrew Keen's *The Cult of the Amateur.*
- *Product challenges* related to recalls, shortages, quality issues, distribution problems, and the need for applying new, more innovative technologies.
- *Marketplace challenges*—competition that is ever-changing, everywhere, as well as our ability to quickly read and respond to fast-changing customer needs.

Over the next five years, more than 21 billion information devices will be installed globally, dramatically influencing how we engage others. For U.S. children, minorities will become the majority by 2020, and millennials will be the dominant generational group, easily eclipsing Generation X and Boomer employees. Forty percent of all large U.S. factories have closed their doors in the 2000s, and 5.7 million manufacturing jobs have been lost, mostly to overseas markets. As its middle class rises and costs increase due to a higher standard of living, countries like China, too, will lose jobs to countries in Southeast Asia like Myanmar, Cambodia, Laos, Thailand, Vietnam, Indonesia, and the Philippines—bringing even greater competition in that geographic region based on low labor costs. And regrettably, we should expect to see a continuing, growing gap between the rich and the poor throughout the world.

There will be critical questions that our leaders must answer:

- "What about corporate culture?"
- "Why require codes of ethics if no one follows them?"
- "Empathy is in short supply among managers. Why is that?"
- "The world is going to university, but does it really matter when jobs aren't available? Why train or educate people when we cannot hire or advance them?"
- "What happened to pay raises?"
- "Where does work end and work–life balance begin?"
- "Why do CEOs say one thing but act differently when it counts?"

In 1992, when we created for IBM the first, omnidirectional, receiver-based model for employee communication tied to research, metrics, and integrated streams of information, we could not have anticipated changes like those referenced earlier. And, more change surely lies ahead.

While our model has endured time, I believe the model destined for 2020 will be:

1. driven by analytics, business performance, outcomes, and strategy socialization;
2. steeped in discussion, dialog, and debate;
3. optimized to enhance the organization's ability to communicate with its internal stakeholders;

4. boundary-less, platform-agnostic, integrated, "democratized," multi-way with peer-to-peer channels; and

5. segmented and targeted for influence, engagement, and social prowess.

It's been written that we're not defined by our past; we're prepared by it. Prepare yourself by looking back and looking forward through the narrative of our co-authors as well as through other rich resources available. Beyond *Excellence in Internal Communication Management* and the body of research and experience it draws upon, I would also invite you to visit one of the world's best repositories of information on organizational communication—the Organizational Communication Resource Center (OCRC), found on the Institute for Public Relation's (IPR) website, www.instituteforpr.org/organizational-communication-research/. I chair the IPR's Commission on Organizational Communication and Dr. Men has been an important contributor to the OCRC since its inception under Dr. Bruce Berger, professor emeritus, University of Alabama, and one of the true thought leaders in employee communication.

I leave you with one final story. While in Seattle, Washington, for work with Boeing Corp. a number of years ago, I paid a visit to the global human resources leader, Jerry Calhoun. As we sat down, Calhoun, who later led HR at Ford Motor Company under CEO Alan Mulally, looked at me for a long time before speaking. Then he shook his head as he said, "This is the last time we'll ever meet here in the corporate office." Thinking our firm had been fired before our engagement began, I asked for clarification.

"Real work is done out in Renton and in Everett, where people build our aircraft and other products", Calhoun said. "That's where you need to be."

I've never forgotten this conversation. Like J.M.W. Turner, arguably Britain's greatest painter, who lashed himself to the mast of a ship to observe the foundering of the *Ariel*, a paddle steamer that would sink in a squall after leaving Harwich in 1842, I have forever been "strapped to the mast"—destined for client locations in the field that allow me to observe leaders, managers, and employees to see how communication works where real work is done. Let me encourage you, too, to get beyond your office or classroom to see and observe people where they work.

In closing, I want to thank to Drs. Men and Bowen for inviting me to collaborate with them, to review their work, to provide feedback on *Excellence in Internal Communication Management,* and to use these words to lead you into this book, as we seek to understand "What does *good* look like?" I wish you well as you journey on.

With best regards,
Keith Burton
Chicago, Illinois.
May 31, 2016

Acknowledgments

The completion of this undertaking could not have been possible without the endless support, kind and understanding spirits of the authors' family members, friends, and mentors. We also would like to extend our deep appreciation to Keith Burton, an industry leader who reviewed our book and offered tremendous insights and real world examples to help keep our manuscript grounded in professional practice. Our thanks are also due to the editor of this volume, Dr. Don Stacks, who offered excellent and thorough feedback on our book and has guided us through the book writing and production process. We also owe our thanks to The Institute for Public Relations' (IPR) Organizational Communication Research Center and its former Chief Research Editor, Dr. Bruce Berger, for offering invaluable research insights for this project. Finally, we thank you, the reader, for your time and the faith you have placed in us for this journey into the best practices of internal communications.

Introduction

This book examines the role of internal communication, internal relations, and employee communication from a perspective of relationship building through engagement. This work is solidly grounded in the excellence theory of public relations with its emphasis on two-way symmetrical communication (i.e., research and dialog), organizational communication and behavior, leadership theories, and business management geared toward competitive advantage, ethics and moral philosophy, employee engagement, and organizational effectiveness. Although incentive and reward systems are discussed as well as training programs for on-boarding employees, we do not seek to include all of human resources (HR). We see HR as a distinct yet a complimentary function, overlapping in some areas with employee communication.

In the best or ideal sense, employees can be ambassadors of the organization. They can provide information from the front lines of an organization, as well as represent it in the communities in which they work and live. We recognize that, in the real world, not all organizations view employees as a strategic asset, let alone a primary source of competitive advantage. However, leveraging the power of employees who are engaged and motivated with commitment toward organizational goals is an often-untapped source of competitive advantage. This book offers original research and solid theory on how employees can become the best asset of an organization through the lens of *strategic internal communication and relationship management*.

We undertook researching and writing for a number of reasons. Although symmetrical systems of internal communication are one of the primary components of creating an excellent organization, it is often an area that is overlooked, little understood and researched, yet assumed. We thought that a detailed exposition of the research laying the groundwork for knowledge in this area was long overdue. Public relations managers are often tasked with internal communications, yet there is little research or strategy to drive those efforts. We include new, original, academic research. We discuss important long-standing and emerging issues of employee engagement, change communication, leadership, culture and ethics, communication channels including enterprise social media, and measurement and evaluation. Those new insights are based on a solid grounding in theory. We hope that it provides an essential resource in helping internal communications become an essential contributor to organizational effectiveness.

This book can be an invaluable resource to MBA students, advanced public relations classes, organizational communication instructors, HR courses, scholars in public relations and organizational communication, and professionals all across the world who seek to enhance their employee communication programs. Though the volume includes research and theory, we have conscientiously tried to simplify, clarify, and decrease our reliance on academic jargon, so that it is accessible to professionals and students alike. Chapters are concise because we realize your time is valuable and we want to help make the most of every moment you spend with this book.

Several thanks are in order. Keith Burton, an industry leader and the author of the foreword to this volume offered numerous insights and real-world examples throughout the book to help keep our manuscript grounded in professional practice. His compelling foreword provides a rich insight into the professional world of internal communications, and enormous thanks are due to Keith. Don Stacks has been a patient and thorough editor who always encouraged us to do what was best for the quality of this book, rather than the expediency of its publication. We would like to thank the Arthur W. Page Center for Public Integrity, who funded separate grants for each of us to do some of the book's original research. We also owe our thanks to the Institute for Public Relations' (IPR) Organizational Communication Research Center and its former Chief Research Editor, Dr. Bruce Berger, for offering invaluable research insights for this project. The IPR site is also the home of an excellent resource, the 2013 *Dictionary of Public Relations Measurement and Research*, by Stacks and Bowen that we referenced throughout this book.

Lastly, we thank you, the reader, for your time and the confidence you've placed in us in your journey into internal communications.

With gratitude,

Shannon A. Bowen, Surfside Beach, South Carolina, USA, and

Rita Linjuan Men, Gainesville, Florida, USA

May 28, 2016

CHAPTER 1

The Evolving Practices of Internal Communication

Internal relations are comprised of communication—both by an organization and interpersonally. Communication is one of the most prevalent activities of any organization (Harris 1993). Communication is needed to coordinate activities among individuals and teams, especially as an organization grows in size or complexity or spreads across borders. Communication coordinates direction from top management and helps employees understand the vision, mission, goals, and objectives of an organization to keep them moving in that direction (Bowen in press). Internal communication, which has been called employee communication (Grunig and Hunt 1984), employee relations, internal relations (Bowen 2005a), or internal communication (Grunig 1992), has expanded both in importance and scope over the past decades.

Research shows that effective internal communication is critical for the success of an organization. First, internal communication keeps employees informed on a daily basis regarding their job, organization, and environment. Internal communication helps employees make sense of the organization, its strategies, and policies. Moreover, internal communication helps organizations acculturate their employees by instilling corporate values and beliefs; it builds trust, shared identity, and loyalty that spurs engagement (Berger 2008; Jiang and Men 2015; Men 2014a, b), and thus greater effectiveness. Furthermore, internal communication connects employees, builds relationships, and strengthens a sense of community and belongingness. Similar to a machine, internal communication ensures that the organization continues to run smoothly. It plays a vital role in important processes such as decision-making, socialization, values, and organizational change management (Berger 2008).

Defining the Function

Internal relations is the broad function of managing relationships with internal stakeholders strategically; using research, internal communication, negotiation and conflict resolution, organizational culture, defining mission, vision, and values, and training and incentive systems (often implemented by the Human Resources [HR]) to incorporate and reinforce internal stakeholders' values and priorities into daily operations that build and maintain relationships. Ideally, those relationships should result in some mutually beneficial gains to internal stakeholders and organizations alike.

Internal relations is a broad function, but as mentioned earlier, it is heavily reliant and conducted through internal *communication*. As an interdisciplinary management function that integrates the elements of communication, HR, and marketing, internal communication has been defined from different perspectives (Verčič, Verčič, and Sriramesh 2012). In public relations, internal relations has been termed as "internal communication" or "internal public relations," which emphasizes the management of relationships with internal stakeholders (i.e., employees). Adopting a stakeholder approach, Welch and Jackson (2007) defined internal communication as "the strategic management of interactions and relationships between stakeholders at all levels within organizations" (p. 183). In marketing, the concept of *internal marketing* has been developed to address organizational interactions with employees. Under this approach, employees are viewed as internal "customers"; satisfying the needs and wants of internal customers is deemed important beyond achieving the objectives of the organization (Berry 1981). A basic assumption underlying this notion is *the need for satisfied employees to obtain satisfied customers.*

Kalla (2005) recognized the multidisciplinary interest in internal communication and proposed the idea of "integrated internal communication" that incorporates four interrelated research domains: business communication (focused on communication skills of employees), management communication (focused on management capabilities and leadership communication), corporate communication (addressing corporate formal communication), and organizational communication (focused on more philosophical and theoretically oriented issues). It has also been broken down into four dimensions based on the stakeholder groups: line management communication, internal team peer communication, internal project peer communication, and internal corporate communication (Welch and Jackson 2007).

In a more recent dominant view, internal communication is perceived to include three fundamental building blocks, namely (1) hierarchical communication, (2) mass media communication, and (3) social networks (Whitworth 2011). Hierarchical communication is represented by top–down or bottom–up communication among the successive layers of executives, managers, supervisors, and non-management employees. Managers at different levels play an important role in pushing or cascading messages until they reach every employee, and they pass back employee concerns to the top management.

Research has consistently suggested that immediate supervisors are the preferred sources of information for employees and that they have more credibility with employees than senior executives (e.g., Larkin and Larkin 1994; Whitworth 2011). However, companies do not rely solely on managers and senior leaders to communicate with their workforce because managers vary in their communication abilities and skills and in their willingness to share information with their followers. A second major component of internal communication is the use of mass media, such as newspapers, newsletters, magazines, bulletin boards, intranet, TV, webcast, e-mail, and social media, targeted at employee audiences. Such communication programs often start from the communication department and provide control over message timing and wording.

A third major component of internal communication is informal networks. According to Berger (2008), a network represents the flow of information in an organization. In a formal communication network, messages travel through official channels (e.g., e-mail, newsletter, and others) that reflect the hierarchy of an organization (i.e., from higher-level management to employees). By contrast, messages in an informal communication network flow horizontally and often through interpersonal communication among employees (i.e., from employees to peers on a same or similar level in the organization). Employees give, take, share, and exchange the information they receive from managers and read in newsletters and other channels. Although such information may be inaccurate at times, employees often perceive it to be more authentic than formal communication (Berger 2008).

Despite these various approaches to defining the concept, and the differing components comprising it, researchers have come to understand that internal communication encompasses all kinds of formal and informal communication that takes place internally at all levels of an organization. Internal communication is a central process in the organization through which employees share information, meanings, and emotions. It helps to create relationships, construct the culture of the organization, participate in decision-making, and facilitates most other organizational activities. Communication is a process that combines philosophies, values, purposes, people, meanings, channels, and practices. In summary, internal communication plays an enabling role and serves as the foundation of modern organizations (D'Aprix 1996).

Evolution of Internal Communication: Historical Perspectives

Examining the historical context of internal communication is important to fully understand its function and practice. The following section traces the origins of internal communication from 1930–1940 and offers a sketch of the evolution of the practice in the last century. Five theoretical perspectives (i.e., scientific management, human relations, HR, systems, and culture) that shaped the development of present companies, businesses, and corporations (Berger 2008; Harris 1993) offer insights into the evolution of internal communication.

Early Origins: 1930–1940

In their 1965 book, *Business and Industrial Communications,* W. Charles Redding and George A. Sanborn traced the origins of internal communication to the famous "Hawthorne" studies. Elton Mayo and colleagues from the Harvard Graduate School of Business came up with the following conclusions, which represent the first serious addressing of employee communication problems:

1. "The attitudes of the employees were more important than the physical conditions as determinants of efficiency."
2. "Direct observations of shop departments yielded considerable information concerning the social organization of employees, their informal interactions, and horizontal communications in general."
3. "A massive interviewing program constituted a noteworthy pioneering effort in the area of industrial communications" (cited in Hay 1974, 8).

In 1938, in *The Functions of the Executive*, Chester I. Barnard emphasized the importance of managerial communication and noted that "The first function of the executives is to develop and maintain a system of communications." He recognized that the authority of the message sender alone would not yield acceptance. Instead, the communication must be understandable, consistent with the purpose of the organization, and compatible with personal interest. Alexander B. Heron was credited in 1942 for providing one of the earliest statements of goals and criteria for successful employee communication. He advocated the idea that communication with employees should not be a propagandistic or a persuasive campaign. Employee communication requires "two-way sharing of information" and "the freedom to ask question, get answers, and exchange ideas" (Hay 1974, 8). Communication is a joint process that requires efforts from both management and employees. The notions of two-way communication and participation are still a part of our research in public relations theory today.

The theory and practice of internal communication started during the 1930s and 1940s. Since then, the field has evolved for decades in parallel with the development of perspectives in understanding organizations. Previous scholars such as Bruce Berger and Thomas Harris summarized the following views in the evolution of internal communication. Built on their discussion and insights, the next section focuses on the influence of the evolution of organizational structure, behavior, and management philosophy on internal communication formats and characteristics.

Scientific Management Perspective

Scientific management is grounded in a classic approach to organizations, which emphasizes the structure, predictability, a high division of labor, and control of the organization through careful job design to increase efficiency and productivity. Three theorists in the 20th century contributed to the early management theoretical perspective and practice. Frederick Taylor (1911) highlighted the responsibility of managers in designing work setting, educating workers, and providing them with proper tools to complete the job. He argues that all workers can be top performers if they are scientifically assigned to the correct task. He also pointed out that the only real incentive for high performance is good and fair pay.

Henri Fayol (1949) is another representative scientific management theorist. Fayol advocated that maximum efficiency could be achieved through the most rational approach to management. Organizations should have a classical and hierarchical pyramid of command, where order is given from the top and cascaded down to the bottom. Strict specifications, accountability, and clear commands at each level are expected. Similar to military operations, it indicates a centralized and rigid organization structure where information flows from the top down. However, Fayol also recognized the need for managers to connect with one another to coordinate activities in times of emergencies or exceptional cases; this early notion of "horizontal communication" was known as "Fayol's bridge."

Eminent sociologist Weber (1947) contributed to the scientific management theory and practice by introducing *bureaucracy* to human organizations as a rational and effective system of management. Bureaucracy was originally a concept intended to introduce efficiency to an organization through a set hierarchy and standardization of procedures. Thus, the term, as originally used, has little resemblance to the term's use in modern parlance. Weber's bureaucracy was a structure and system where individuals are hired or rewarded based on their ability to do the work, specific rules, policies, processes, and regulations for a rational system, instead of caprice, habit, favoritism, tradition, or nepotism that had hindered organizations in the past. Weber (1930) also advocated the Protestant work ethic that pervades Western culture.

Scientific management provides essential processes for efficiency, productivity, and effective use of manpower. Organizations are treated as machines with individuals as interchangeable parts (Morgan 2006). In such a robust system, communication is dominated by a top–down and centralized way of information dissemination. Communication mainly provides clear task-oriented instructions, reduces misunderstanding, and conveys management directives and decisions to increase work efficiency and productivity, providing an advantage for organizing large systems of production. One-way communication that relies on traditional print media channels is the key feature of internal communication at that time. In this approach, communication is relatively one-way, based on a chain of command or hierarchy, controlled, formal, rational, and task-oriented.

Human Relations (Humanistic) Perspective

The human relations perspective resulted from the Hawthorne studies (Sonnenfeld 1985). The researchers believed that increased attention and employee attitude change increased productivity, regardless of better or worse working conditions. Thus, greater emphasis should be put on the human relations and social aspects of the work setting. Hawthorne's studies experimentally challenged the premises of the classic scientific management approach. "A day's pay for a day's work" is *not* all that is needed for effectiveness in the workplace. The motives, human needs, attitudes, and relationships of employees at work are equally, if not more, important than the job design, organizational structure, and rules in the workplace. Later research illustrated the complex interplay of these and many other factors, both humanistic and organizational, in creating effective workplaces.

A people-oriented management philosophy developed whereby managers were told to make employees feel valued and appreciated and to make them feel important in relation to their task objectives and organizational goals. A basic assumption underlying this thought is that improvement of employees' social aspects of work would make them feel content and happy, leading to higher productivity. Paradoxically, happy employees are not always the most productive (Harris 1993). Similar to the assumption that excessive control leads to stress and burnout, over emphasis on humanistic management can lower productivity when comfort overrides efficiency, or when an individual's needs supersede the organization's needs. Subsequent debates and attempts gradually provided evidence that scientific management and human relations are equally important variables.

Given the shift from task orientation to people orientation, communication adopting a human relations approach emphasizes building relationships and boosting employee satisfaction. Although top–down hierarchical communication remains dominant, managers pay more attention to upward communication, listening to employees, and feedback is gathered to gauge employee attitudes. To facilitate social interactions, face-to-face communication plays a vital role, in addition to the traditional kinds of communication, such as intranets or newsletters. Managerial communication at this stage becomes less formal and more open. Overall, *communication is relationship-oriented, people-oriented, and less formal, and it combines upward, downward, and horizontal communications.*

HR Management Perspective

Developed in the 1960s, the HR approach was built on the evolution of scientific management and human relations approaches. HR management recognized the need for both structured development and awareness of human needs in the organization. Theory X–Theory Y, developed by Douglas McGregor (1960) laid an important theoretical foundation for this approach. Theory X assumed that individuals who lack ambition and motivation are indifferent to organizational needs, resist change, and prefer to put forth as little effort as possible to receive strong rewards. Thus, Theory X managers tend to be more authoritarian and to rely more on control and coercion to achieve the desired organizational outputs. By contrast, Theory Y managers viewed employees as responsible and potentially motivated individuals. They believe that if employees are provided with proper opportunities for growth and development, they are likely to perform extremely well. With such trust, Theory Y managers show individual respect to employees and offer opportunities for their individual growth and personal development.

Another major contributor of the HR approach is Rensis Likert (1967), who also combined the scientific management and humanistic perspectives. He held that an employee-centered management style with clear task orientation would produce the best results. In Likert's explanation of his System 4 framework, the important role of supervisors or managers is emphasized as "linking pins" connecting followers from one level to the next level, all the way to the top or bottom of the organizational hierarchy. Supervisors and subordinates form groups, and communication happens not only top–down or bottom–up in the organization, but also from groups to individuals. System 4 delegates some power to employees and invites their participation in the decision-making process. Trust in employees is valued.

HR communication is multidimensional, horizontal, top–down, and bottom–up across different levels in the organization. Information is provided for employee growth and individual development. Two-way and open communication invites employee participation and boosts innovation in the organization. Feedback is gathered so that employees' perspectives are considered in the decision-making process. The importance of managerial communication and group communication is increasingly recognized. Trust, empowerment, and participation emerge as important issues.

Systems Theory Perspective

Sociologist Niklas Luhmann developed a comprehensive theory of organizations as systems known as the systems theory (1979, 1984). Theories in the 1970s adopted the systems perspective to understand the way organizations work. The systems theory argues that an organization is a system composed of interrelated parts (i.e., subsystems) that are interdependent with the internal and external environments (Bertalanffy 1934, 1968; Weick 1979). An organization does not operate in a vacuum. An organization relies on *inputs,* such as energy, materials, personnel, money, information, and other resources, to operate normally. *Throughput* describes what happens *inside* the organization in terms of the use of inputs to create goods, services, or strategic plans. An organization then delivers products, services, and information as *outputs* to the environment after processing and transformation. This perspective considers an organization as a living organism that cannot survive without exchanging materials and information with the environment in which it exists.[1]

---

[1] See also: Morgan (2006).

As the environment changes, the organization needs to adapt to maintain a steady state. This adaptation requires information gathered from the environment, which is called *feedback* (Bennett 1987). In an open system, an organization should constantly monitor or scan the environment to identify information useful for its decision-making process. In reality, organizations often rely on public relations professionals to act as *boundary spanners*. As boundary spanners, public relations professionals proactively collect information from the environment regarding the effectiveness of the current operations of the organization. They also identify opportunities and issues and analyze the environmental context for the future strategy formulation of the organization. One modern definition of public relations, which emphasizes the management of the interdependence and relationships between the organization and its strategic constituencies, is actually rooted in the systems theory (Grunig, Grunig, and Dozier 2002) and one we agree with.

For an organization, its internal environment is as important as the external environment. Internally, functional areas, departments, teams, dyadic groups, and executive committees act as *subsystems*. Employees at different levels are among the most important stakeholders of the organization, and the organization is interdependent with them. Rice (1963) argued that the primary task of leaders is to manage the relationship of the system with its environment. Communication is an essential tool that manages such interdependence (Grunig, Grunig, and Dozier 2002). From a systems perspective, *internal communication serves to cultivate relationships between the organization and its internal stakeholders.* Internal stakeholders are nested in the organization as individuals, dyadic groups, and teams. Thus, internal communication requires joint efforts from HR, public relations, and managers to build a cross-enterprise communication system (Men and Stacks 2014). Information flows two-way in such a multidimensional and multilevel communication system. Feedback is emphasized. A modern relationship-oriented, employee-centered, balanced, open, and transparent communication approach is encouraged; thus, participation and collaboration become more prevalent.

Organizational Culture Perspective

Culture emerged as an important perspective in understanding organizations beginning in the 1960s by Halpin and Croft (1963) and expanded to corporate culture by Harrison in 1972. It remains a top issue and has become the primary challenge faced by businesses around the world today. Culture is the collection of key values, symbols, meanings, beliefs, and assumptions shared by organization members (Sriramesh, Grunig, and Buffington 1992). It is often referred to as the "social glue holding the company together" (Baker 1980, 8). Culture emerges as a new company learns to adapt and survive over a period of time. It is simply the way things get done. Organizational culture is created, sustained, and lived by its members. There are two general views of culture. *Functionalists* view culture as something that an organization *has,* whereas *interpretionalists* perceive culture as something that an organization *is* (Bormann 1983). The former focuses on explicit, tangible, and superficial cultural manifestations. Functionalists assume that culture artifacts can be observed, altered, reinforced, or eliminated. The latter focuses on the interactions and processes that lead to shared meaning. Interpretionalists emphasize the deep, implicit, and unconscious source of culture.

The communication of vision, mission, core values, goals, strategy, stories, and shared meanings and experiences through formal and informal channels all combine to shape the organizational culture. To answer the question on how a strong corporate culture can be built, Kennedy (1983) pointed to effective communication. Bowen (2002, 2004a) found that organizational culture is a determining factor in how executives make decisions, playing a larger role than even individual belief systems.

According to Berger (2008), a reciprocal relationship exists between communication and culture. Culture also influences the characteristics of communication itself because the underlying assumptions, rules, and values determine the climate for communication in an organization—how open or closed decisions are, what is said, and how. For instance, an open culture, such as Google, may require two-way and transparent communication practices in place. A customer-oriented service culture such as Southwest Airlines nurtures friendly and dialogical communication. A participative culture that encourages employee empowerment and sharing of decision-making duties contributes to open symmetrical (give and take) communication (Grunig, Grunig, and Dozier 2002). The values and leadership communication of the founders of the company also help define and shape the organizational culture. A typical example was Steve Jobs of Apple Inc. and the innovative culture of the company.

Summary of Perspectives

In summary, internal relations use communication to create a strong, suitable, and positive organizational culture that contributes to the success of an organization. Internal communication communicates the mission, values, priorities, goals, and legends of the organization. These are co-created by the organization and its members; new members become a part of that process through socialization to the norms and values of the system. Internal communication is the function responsible for creating shared meanings through multidimensional and multimedia communication, such as interpersonal communication, managerial communication, corporate mass communication, and informal networks. A positive organizational culture will boost its communication climate, practices, and effectiveness.

The perspectives reviewed in the preceding sections demonstrated the growth and evolution of internal communication. It is not necessary to assume one particular approach is most useful. In fact, the elements of all these approaches are found in contemporary organizations and research. New perspectives continue to emerge, and a "contingency approach" may represent a widely adopted view of effective internal communication by strategically choosing strategies, tactics, channels, and messages based on situational factors, such as communication needs, purposes, and resources. Overall, *internal communication is a process co-created by the organization and its employees.*

Internal relations is the *strategic management of internal communication* in managing interdependence and building mutually beneficial relationships between the organization and its employees. To achieve this goal, factors of ethics, values, leadership, mission, information, job design, HR, industrial psychology, organizational culture, structure, size, industry, power, communication channels, and regulatory macro- and microenvironments should all be considered.

Current Trends and Issues

Perhaps "change" is the only thing that remains constant. The environment is constantly changing; therefore, the way organizations keep employees informed and engaged also evolves. Organizations today face new challenges: ones that require them to be proactive and adaptive, embrace trends, monitor changing and emerging issues, and innovate. Five imperative trends and current issues that are implicative for organizational internal communication practices are introduced and further examined in the remainder of the book.

Employee Engagement

Engagement in the workplace has emerged as a central issue since the 1990s and has recently become a buzzword in public relations literature and in the business community. In a survey by Corporate Communication International on U.S. chief corporate communicators, employee engagement is revealed as one of the top three trends that organizations encounter (Goodman et al. 2009). Engagement is defined as "the harnessing of organization members' selves to their work roles" (Kahn 1990, 694) and "a positive, fulfilling, work-related state of mind that is characterized by vigor, dedication, and absorption" (Schaufeli et al. 2002, 74). Engaged employees are attentive, dedicated, and absorbed in their work roles (Men 2011).

What can communicators do to engage employees? First, an open, transparent, and involved communication climate engages employees. Authenticity, consistency, and transparency boost trust, which in turn helps to build relationships and this enhances engagement (Bowen and Hung-Baesecke, 2013; Bowen, Hung-Baesecke, and Chen 2016; Men 2014c). Moreover, when managers talk "with" employees instead of talking "to" them, employees can participate in the conversation, freely express ideas, and feel respected. Internal communicators can also help create engagement by aligning organizational and management behavior with ethical values and missions and by ensuring consistency and authenticity, encouraging employee free opinion and participation in the decision-making process, building trusting relationships, heightening trust, and boosting employee engagement. Evolving digital technologies, such as social media, personify executive and corporate communication, build a vivid organizational character, and offer real-time and interactive tools for organizational engagement with employees. In essence, *effective internal communication is an indispensable component for successful employee engagement.*

Evolving Technology

The rapid growth of digital technology has made massive amounts of data available to create and refine new strategies. It has also changed the basic landscape of communication, including the internal communication of companies. Companies can specifically segment stakeholders based on data and then access various communication tools to reach and interact with them. These tools range from traditional print publications, news media, and face-to-face communication to new technology platforms, such as blogs, instant messengers, and social networking sites. Social media can help personify the organization, blur internal communication hierarchies, facilitate employee conversation with management, and most importantly, build communities.

Research as late as 2014 showed that social media are still the *least commonly* used channels for workplace employee communication because risk aversion, time constraints, fear of negative feedback, lack of a social media strategy, and the need to protect the disclosure of proprietary and confidential information barriers. There is also realistic concern in access to technology in non-networked organizational settings; however, the effective use of digital tools strongly engages employees (Men 2014a). The use of social media by an organization (i.e., internal social networking sites, employee or leader journals, blogs, wiki sites, instant messengers, and audio or video streaming), including the leader, positively affects employee engagement. Overall, employees feel more engaged when companies use interactive tools, such as social media, more often to connect with them.

Social media allow top corporate leaders (e.g., CEOs) to create approachable and personable reputations. This approach brings CEOs to life. Men's recent study on the use of effective communication channels by CEOs found that although CEOs show a moderate level of social media presence, employees, in general, hold a positive attitude toward those who use social media (Men 2015a), and CEOs with stronger social media presence are more approachable, responsive, and authentic—as well as better communicators.

Although no clear consensus exists on the most effective social medium (i.e., one that is effective for a company may not be effective for another), and although the overall cost-effectiveness of enterprise social media remains inconclusive, companies that aim for employee engagement cannot simply ignore these thriving digital platforms.

Ethics and Values Communication

Ethics and the creation and management of core values, as well as communication of these values inside the organization, have become increasingly important for communicators (Bowen 2008). As public relations professionals rise in their levels of responsibility, with age and experience, they also increase the time and attention that they devote to matters of ethics, core values, and counseling management on a course of action (Bowen 2006, 2009). Corporate social responsibility (CSR) communication driven by the ethical counsel role is becoming more common and more important within modern organizations. Corporation ethics codes are required by the 2002 Sarbanes-Oxley Act, but many go further to create an ethics statement, core values, a mission, and a vision that encompasses moral responsibility, and an internal relations system that reinforces these priorities. Many corporations publish CSR reports in addition to the annual reports.

Research shows that honesty, consistency, authenticity, respect, rectitude, and trust all build or enhance relationships with stakeholders, for both internal (employees) and external stakeholders (e.g., consumers, media, government regulators). Corporate *transparency* has emerged as an often-discussed concept, particularly because of the exposure of deceptive practices that take place behind closed doors; advances in technology have created a world where transparency is expected among key stakeholders. New tools, such as social media, provide organizations with an innovative means to share information openly. The basic premise of transparent communication is making all releasable information available to employees in a truthful, timely, and balanced manner (Rawlins 2009). Transparency, however, is not a panacea or a one-step approach to ethics. Ensuring information sufficiency is not enough, so ethicists (Bowen and Prescott 2015) argue that transparency does not go far enough. Organizations need to provide employees with the information they truly need and want. Thus, a strong ethical framework guiding listening to employees, two-way information flow, and employee participation is essential.

Corporate *authenticity* is another major concept in the midst of various communication trends driven by social media. To be authentic, an organization has to be truthful to itself and to its stakeholders (Arthur W. Page Society 2007). An organization should act genuinely and non-manipulatively with its employees. Most importantly, the conduct of an organization should be congruent with its values, mission, principles, and rhetoric. In other words, the practices of a company should match what it says. Authenticity requires ongoing efforts by an organization to recognize and evaluate its own intentions in communicating with public (Bowen 2010). A company cannot be truly authentic if it holds back essential information from its employees. These concerns are first and foremost ethical issues that demand thorough consideration before embarking on any communication initiative.

Leadership Communication

The communication of top management remains a critical component of internal communication (Men and Stacks 2013, 2014). Leadership communication has recently gained increasing attention from scholars and professionals, as an increasing number of leaders are brought to life by new media. Leaders are the trustworthiest source of information for employees. The leadership and communication styles, selection of communication channels, and communication capability and skills of leaders directly influence employee outcomes (Men 2014a, b, c, 2015b). Further, leadership, as a nested form of influence in the organization, creates a climate and sets the tone for internal communication. Executive leaders, particularly CEOs, influence organizational direction, strategies, and relations with key stakeholders. Executive leaders manage company culture and are also "chief engagement officers" who are expected to come out of their offices and directly engage with stakeholders (Men 2015a). This action is particularly relevant in the social media era when communication hierarchies have been blurred and power distance is reduced by the interactive, personal, democratic, and relational features of social media tools. Management can communicate with their employees in a friendly, authentic, and informal manner. Leadership communication is an ongoing issue that requires efforts from HR, public relations departments, and leaders themselves. With leadership communication performed effectively, organizations build strong and efficient cross-enterprise communication forces composed of leaders across different levels.

Measurement and Evaluation

The importance of measurement and evaluation in achieving the success of communication programs can never be emphasized enough (Stacks, Dodd, and Men 2011). Without proper internal communication outcome measurement, management is unlikely to evaluate strategies, tactics, loss, and gains and to make corresponding adjustments or improvements. Industry research has shown that companies with highly effective internal communication are three times more likely to measure results than those with less successful internal communication. They are also twice more likely to outperform other companies in the market (Towers Watson 2014).

Measuring internal communication is challenged to connect direct results to long-term outcomes, desired behavioral change, and return on investment (ROI). The most intuitive measure adopted is measuring *outputs*, such the number of internal publications, event attendees, or social media likes or shares. As such, these measures involve counting but fall short of demonstrating attitude or behavioral change. An increasing number of companies use employee annual surveys to gauge employee satisfaction and engagement issues, but a measurement standard is lacking. How do we measure engagement exactly? We need to ensure that the questions in the survey measures the things we want to measure and are generating candid responses. With big data analytics, more advanced metrics of internal communication can and should be developed to address these issues.

Certainly, this list is not exhaustive. Other trends and issues such as work–life balance, diversity and globalization, organizational learning, knowledge sharing, change management, employee alignment, and traditional issues such as trust, employee satisfaction, and organizational identification continue to evolve. Internal communication plays a critical role in resolving these issues. No one can offer a one-size-fits-all solution, but the research insights and examples presented in this book will provide a sound strategic framework, followed by real-world professional guidance for effectively managing internal relations.

Summary

Internal relations is the strategic management of communication in managing interdependence and building mutually beneficial relationships between the organization and its internal public. Internal communication informs, acculturates, and connects stakeholders and plays an essential role in building relationships, employee identification, and internal communities. This chapter traced the origins of internal communication from 1930–1940 and sketched its evolution and five perspectives (scientific management, human relations, HR, systems, and culture) that shaped the development of present companies, businesses, and corporations and influenced internal communication practices and research were reviewed.

The fast-evolving and increasingly competitive business environment requires organizations to be proactive and adaptive, embrace trends, monitor changing and emerging issues, and innovate. This chapter ended with five emerging trends and issues that shape the internal communication practices, including employee engagement, technological advancement, ethics and value communication, leadership communication, and measurement and evaluation.

CHAPTER 2

Understanding Your Internal Publics

Excellence in internal relations and communication management requires a thorough understanding of the working of an organization and the organization's understanding of internal publics. Internal relations can be used to help build a competitive advantage in the marketplace for the organization because a cohesive organizational culture can create highly motivated, efficient, and successful employees and lower the costs for the organization associated with employee turnover. Internal relations, then, is an important part of the overall organizational strategy to build good relationships with internal stakeholders and publics.

Although it is common to hear the terms used interchangeably, "stakeholders" can be differentiated from "publics." Stakeholders refer to groups or individuals who are affected by decisions, policies, and practices of an organization or whose decision-making can affect the success of an organization. Therefore, stakeholders are linked to or have a stake in the organization (Grunig and Repper 1992). Most people in the category of stakeholders are passive (i.e., customers, community, investors, and the government). Stakeholders become "publics"—a more active stance—when they become aware and active around an issue or problem. Grunig and Repper (1992) noted that publics often arise independently and choose an organization to give their attention (p. 128).

Employees are the organization's primary stakeholders and are naturally interdependent with the organization. They are mostly involved in organizational issues, problems, or events. However, not all employees are similar. Internal publics can also be further segmented on the basis of certain characteristics (e.g., demographic, physiographic, and behavioral) and common interests, similar to how external publics can be broken down into interest groups. Grunig and Repper defined segmentation as the process of dividing "a population, market, or audience into groups whose members are more like each other than members of other segments" (p. 129). Better segmentation facilitates better-targeted communication. This chapter examines and introduces several ways to segment internal publics, a foundation for effective employee communication and engagement.

Hierarchical Structure: Employees Across Levels

Top–down communication and bottom–up communication across different levels inside an organization are two of the most common forms of internal communication. The hierarchical segmentation of internal publics examines employees who have unique information needs and communication purposes at various positional levels in an organizational structure. Frontline workers, line managers, middle-level management, senior management, and executives are often recognized as internal publics with distinctive functions and communication needs.

Frontline Workers

Frontline workers include both service employees who are behind the counter, on the phone, online at Twitter and Facebook responding to customers, or walking the floor, and blue-collar workers who perform manual labor, such as manufacturing, mining, custodian work, construction, mechanical maintenance, and technical installation. Frontline service employees of various industries (i.e., retail, hospitality, manufacturing, energy, and health care) represent the main segment of their company's workforce. They have the most direct contact with customers, and thus can shape the company's reputation and influence customer relationships. Moreover, they are the best sources of observatory research because they can obtain firsthand information and feedback from customers and the field. For example, waiters know the most frequently asked food items or unfinished food items. Sales personnel in retail stores know where people go first or what frustrates them the most. Customer service representatives know what the most complaints or compliments are about. Blue-collar workers play an equally, if not more, important role in influencing many organizations' and the industry development. In the United States, professionals and managers account for only 40 percent of the workforce and the remaining 60 percent belongs to blue-collar occupations, such as technicians, repair workers, laborers, operators, and so on (Vnmanpower.com 2016). Blue-collar workers' engagement can be easily tied to their work efficiency, productivity, cost of operations, and performance.

Frontline workers have a great impact on the organization's success, but they are often the least considered group and most difficult to reach in reality. One reason for this situation is that the frontline workers are often geographically dispersed and operate within their own ecosystems and cultures. Therefore, corporate communication does not easily penetrate management and communication processes (Raywood 2015). Careful planning and communication efforts are greatly needed to build an engaged frontline workforce that directly contributes to customer service, branding, and productivity. Edelman's recent employee engagement report (Raywood 2015) lays out six steps to successfully connect with frontline workforce: (1) get to know frontline workers and fully understand their needs and work environment, (2) design a select and limited set of channels, particularly tailored for frontline workers needs and routines (e.g., Capital One Bank in Nottingham uses dressed up "messengers" who carry messages around the building instead of using traditional e-mails and newsletters, and other companies use mobile apps to push information and gather feedback), (3) limit the volume of information to deliver more focused, actionable, and relevant messages, (4) integrate new technology to foster dialogs, gather feedback, increase engagement, and build a community, (5) involve frontline managers, provide them with communication training, and prepare them with messages and toolkits, and (6) have patience and take the time and effort to make frontline workers live easily. Frontline workers want to be engaged in the overall organization strategy and activities. Organizations should be ethical, authentic, and transparent in their communication and gather feedback from frontline workers on a regular basis. Keeping them informed, listened to, connected, and engaged is a rewarding process for both the organization and its employees.

Line Managers

Line managers (or frontline managers) can be employees' most trusted and reliable source of information about the organization (Men 2014c). Line managers are positioned in the middle of a hierarchy and are important channels for the organization to distribute information to lower-level employees. They are also information suppliers for senior and top management. Therefore, excellent communication skills to actively listen and interpret messages from frontline employees and those cascaded from top management are necessary for line managers and supervisors. Line managers can facilitate effective internal communication by translating corporate messages into a local context to make them relevant and understandable for the staff and by selecting useful feedback from frontline employees to include in corporate strategic decision-making. On the flip side of the coin, there is a phenomenon known as the "Concrete Middle" (Burton 2016). It simply holds that at some point in the chain of management, information will not pass down or above. The Concrete Middle exists because managers at the level at which it operates are threatened by change, want to hold onto information as "power," fear shared control, or do not know how to effectively communicate for shared gain.

Line managers interact with employees on a daily basis. A significant amount of research shows that line managers' treatment of their employees directly affects employees' satisfaction and the overall attitude toward the organization (Men and Stacks 2014; MacLeod and Brady 2008). Line manager relationships represent employees' work environment to some extent. Good relationships with supervisors provide a supportive working condition for employees, whereas poor relationships only distance and disengage employees. According to Buckingham and Coffman (1999), "people join companies, they leave managers." Employees view line managers as those who personify and represent the organization. Therefore, line managers' supervisory communication remains an indispensable component of an organization's internal communication system.

Organizations should provide appropriate training to line managers to equip them with effective communication strategies, skills, tools, and messages for these managers to fully enact supervisory communication roles. Line managers should completely understand the goals and expectations of the organization before interpreting them to frontline employees.

Companies may prepare briefing kits or newsletters to make the information easily digestible for line managers. Best practices and effective line manager communicators as role models should be shared and celebrated within the organization. Moreover, line managers should be empowered to communicate in a two-way, interactive, and engaging manner to foster employee participation and discussion and proactively gather feedback.

Middle-Level Management

Middle-level managers are important connection points among internal teams and members. Their access to top management and knowledge of operations place them at a unique position in the organization (Beringer, Jonas, and Gemünden 2012). Senior executives depend on middle-level managers to execute company vision and strategies. Therefore, middle-level managers are a critical driving force needed to achieve the organization's strategic goals. Moreover, middle-level managers cascade information from the top to frontline managers and are responsible for explaining the rationale of the rules and policies and making them concrete and specific enough for employees to digest and interpret. Therefore, middle-level managers are mediators between business strategy and daily operations.

Frontline mangers' roles focus more on managing followers and work units, whereas middle-level managers often deal with peer relationships and communicate horizontally with other middle-level managers. For instance, an organizational initiative may involve efforts from the marketing, legal, information technology (IT), human resources (HR), and public relations departments. Middle-level managers who work together on a task may experience tension and resentment because of competition for resources, specialized perspectives, and loyalty to their own departments or self-interest (McKinney, McMahon, and Walsh 2013). Brownell (1991) offered some constructive suggestions for managers to smoothen horizontal communication and build relationships with peers: (1) The behavior or problem should be discussed instead of making judgmental statements toward peers. (2) Finding solutions should be the focus instead of placing blame. (3) Open-mindedness and tolerance should be practiced instead of insisting one's own positions or opinions. (4) Concern and respect for others' position and point of view should be shown

(p. 59). Organizations should also build a collaborative culture and atmosphere and foster openness and trust. Middle-level managers should spend less time protecting their own territory and reputation, develop a holistic view of the organization, and visualize the big picture with the same vision and direction to obtain a supportive working environment. They generally report to senior management: those who have been in the organization long enough to earn a position among the ranks of management trusted with much responsibility across operational areas of a function, or even responsible for the entire functional area. At this high level, reporting lines and titles begin to blur somewhat. Beyond senior management is the highest echelon of executive management.

Top Management and Board of Directors

Top managers, executive-level management, and board of directors act as the key decision-makers within the organization. They determine the organization's direction and strategies, influence organizational relations with key stakeholders, and embody the organizational image for internal and external publics (Men 2015a; Resick et al. 2009). Top managers are often regarded as visible leaders and role models for other managers and employees. They establish a collective purpose, communicate a vision, help define and communicate core values, and manage culture (Bowen 2006). The heads of an organization's functional areas (such as production, finance, R&D) or component parts are normally top executives, holding influence and authority. They often hold a tile "Chief of _____" and in laymen's terms, this group is often referred to as "the C suite." The top communicator is often the chief communication officer, or CCO, who oversees all communication functions—including internal.

Internally, top managers are also expected to be the role models and motivate employees to move toward the same direction. Pincus, Rayfield, and Cozzens (1991) found that employees desire a more open and closer relationship with top managers. The perceptions of employees on top management are "closely linked to their overall perceptions of the organization as a place to work and the general state of the morale" (Pincus, Rayfield, and Cozzens 1991, 9). Externally, top management, especially the chief executive officer (CEO), is perceived as the external face and spokesperson for the organization. The character, credibility, and reputation of top management can affect the public's confidence in the company.

Moreover, top management sets the tone for internal communication, helps establish the organization's communication philosophy, and allocates resources and provides support for the communication function. Smith and Mounter (2008) noted that "the scope for the dedicated team is far in excess of what it would otherwise be" when the CEO truly believes in internal communication. "It is not just about money or budget: if the CEO is behind it, the standard is set for other leaders to follow," Smith and Mounter added (p. 27). Therefore, internal communication managers should become think-tanks and business strategists for top management; gain a seat at the decision-making table; equip CEOs and other executives with strategic communication mindsets, strategies, and tools; establish the system; and help CEOs enact their "chief engagement officer" roles.

Internal publics can include other interest groups (i.e., volunteers and trustees for nonprofit organizations) depending on their nature. Some organizations contract out or outsource certain activities. These groups are considered "shadow employees" who can have a dramatic effect on employees' attitudes and behavior (Burton 2016). For instance, airline companies often use contract workers for their onsite agents at the airport. These contract workers may also pledge their first loyalty to the subcontracted company instead of to the organization for which they provide service (Smith and Mounter 2008). Moreover, these publics may not share the background and culture of the organization with other regular employees. Therefore, communication messages and styles have to be tailored to the particular needs of these special audiences through segmentation of those publics.

Segmentation of Stakeholders, Publics, and Audiences

The specialized tailoring of messages for targeted groups is based on research that segments stakeholders, publics, and audiences based on their attitudes, behaviors, inclinations, or on descriptive variables (age, gender, etc.). An industry of research firms specialized in providing data fills the need for segmenting stakeholders and publics along numerous lines of analysis, from aggregate trends provided by big data to specially targeted tiny stakeholders groups interested in a single issue.

Research should be conducted in order to fully understand and segment stakeholders and publics, both internal and external. Much more detail on the research component of that process can be found in Stacks and Michaelson (2010) and on the segmentation of stakeholders and publics in Bowen, Rawlins, and Martin (2010). Most CCOs hire a research firm to conduct surveys that can offer statistics (quantitative research) and make inferences to understand (qualitative research) certain groups of people, including how to reach them, what information they need, and what keeps them interested in the message. Research firms can offer specialized analyses on targeted questions, or data about differing segments of an audience. In general, quantitative (statistical) and qualitative (in-depth) research are both conducted in order to gain a full understanding of a topic and the stakeholders, publics, and audiences surrounding it.

Budget limitations often require research on a smaller, internal scale to be handled by the lead communicator through less-expensive internal channels. Either way, the segmentation of stakeholders and publics is a key component to understanding the working and communication flow of an organization as well as what information is needed by each public, so that it can be specifically tailored to meet their communication needs. Ways to segment those groups or for internal stakeholder mapping include examining behaviors, active or passive communication style, demographics, psychographics or attitudinal variables, and the use of aggregate data, all for communicating with internal publics.

Behaviors

Employees can be segmented on the basis of behavioral variables (Goyat 2011), such as general media consumption habits, involvement and engagement levels, organizational citizenship behaviors, and adoption stages of new initiatives or changes. The traits of employees who prefer certain attributes of media can be a foundation for media mix—meaning which channels are used to reach someone and how often—and content strategies in internal communication. Heo and Cho (2009) segmented audiences into three clusters based on their media usage: print-oriented information users, mediocre passive users, and sensual video–audio fun seekers. The communicator can mix specific media types (i.e., newsletters, magazines, online news, and blogs) to keep the print-oriented information publics updated and informed. Interactive media (i.e., social networking sites, TV, and mobile applications) with entertaining, fun, and gaming elements can be more effective to engage sensual video–audio fun seekers.

The Situational Theory of Publics

One theory that is specific to public relations and uses the behaviors of publics to segment them into active information seekers or passive information recipients is the situational theory of publics. The situational theory of publics (Grunig 1978) is a theory that allows the segmentation of groups depending on how active versus passive their communication behavior appears to be. Research can then segment these publics based on how much information they demand, need, or want from the organization, and how likely they are to take a more active communication stance on certain issues. For example, the information needs of factory foremen will be substantially different from those of engineers in the R&D function, and those needs will differ from the information desired by administrative staff. The situational theory of publics allows the communicator to understand and segment those publics by not only job title, but by variables underlying their communication behavior. Surveys are used to determine how active or passive a public's communication behavior is, and a predictive analysis allows the communicator to prioritize and focus on those publics most in need of information.

The situational theory of publics measures these specific variables: *level of involvement, problem recognition, and constraint recognition* (Grunig 1983). The *level of involvement* asks a person to rate how personally involved they are with an issue or concern related to the organization. For an employee, this type of question may relate most highly to their job function and how much they will or will not be impacted by impending changes or policies. A highly involved stakeholder will require much information because their behavior is active—they are often information-seekers.

The *problem recognition* measure asks a person the extent to which he or she recognizes an issue as a problem. Those with high problem recognition are likely to become active. It is crucial to understand that the level of involvement and problem recognition are variables that operate separately from one another: one stakeholder may be highly involved with an issue, yet not recognize it as a problem. Another person may believe a problem exists, but may have no personal involvement with it, and therefore will remain passive on the issue even if the problem becomes quite large. These two variables do not operate in tandem, but can and do operate in concert in many instances.

The third variable, *constraint recognition*, measures the extent to which someone wants to get involved with an issue, believing that he or she can make a difference. It also implies that the person knows how to get involved—how to locate a senator's office phone number, address, and e-mail address, for example. Thus, a low level of constraint recognition often implies a higher degree of self-actualization, education, and affluence. A high level of constraint recognition shows constrained behavior—it means that one feels powerless to affect change, that one does not believe personal efforts will matter, or that one does not know how to go about seeking the change. Thus, this variable operates in an "inverse" manner to the first two. For example, a person with high level of involvement and high problem recognition but also holding high constraint recognition has every reason to get involved in an issue, but likely will not unless constraints or barriers are lowered. This very reason is why you see petition drives where the letter is already written to the appropriate recipient, all that is needed is a signature.

Publics who are not involved and do not recognize any problems with an organization are nonpublics, not really a likely or useful public for segmentation in internal relations. Publics who are involved with an organization but do not recognize problems are latent publics. As anyone who has seen a political campaign can attest, latent publics are often targeted in communication campaigns with efforts to convert them into active publics by increasing their problem recognition. If the problem recognition of a latent public grows, they may become active depending on how enabled versus constrained they feel. Internal stakeholders who have high or growing levels of involvement and problem recognition are likely to become involved in an issue, as aware publics, and later, as the level of involvement grows, active publics. These publics most likely need information from the organization and efforts at symmetrical or two-way communication in order to understand their issues. Publics with low constraint recognition who have high levels of involvement and high levels of problem recognition are the most active and potentially dangerous type of public: an active public. They are likely to organize and form an opposition group or activist public in which they act or lobby together on behalf of their issues or concerns. Activism "limits the effectiveness" (Grunig 1992, 503) of organizations because activists divert resources to responses that are not a part of strategic planning, and the resulting media coverage can often cause reputational damage.

Using the situational theory of publics with internal publics can offer insight into what stakeholders and publics exist in an organization and who is likely to become active if their needs are not met. The wise internal communicator can use this theory to predict and resolve the problems created by activist publics, such as a labor union strike, protest, or walkout. Often, diligent efforts at segmenting these publics offer satisfying instances in which management can meet the communication needs of publics almost magically, before such needs are uttered. Such forward thinking prioritization of internal publics shows them that their views and needs are valued and prioritized rather than being an afterthought.

Allowing the differing needs of publics to drive the communication with them often results in more effective communication efforts overall and a higher ROI for the internal relations dollar. Knowing the needs and specificity of detail that certain publics demand allows communication to be tailored to meet those needs and even exceed expectations in many cases. Using the situational theory of publics to segment internal groups also allows problems to be identified and addressed before they grow to the level of activism, lawsuits, walk-outs, or other costly employee actions. It also helps the organization create a good, enduring relationship with internal publics of all kinds, and is worth the initial research investment over the years of relationships built, employee satisfaction created, and problems averted.

Demographic or Geographic Factors

Communication inside the organization can also target employees segmented by observed variables such as *age, gender, education, qualifications, ethnicity, income, work tenure, job classification, physical location,* and *employment status.* Millennial, baby-boomers, generation X, and generation Y may prioritize different aspects of their jobs. Full-time, part-time, or contract-based employees may have different information needs regarding their job and the organization. Communication with new employees may require different approaches and messages compared with that of the older workforce, which has spent most of their lives with the organization. Different types of jobs, such as technical (e.g., engineer), client facing (e.g., customer service and sales), central or support service (e.g., HR, accounting or finance, marketing), or blue-collar (e.g., maintenance, production line, packaging) workers, require different aspects of communication training (Moroko and Uncles 2009). Moreover, other researchers have found that employees with different demographic characteristics engage in different degrees within the organization (Robinson, Perryman, and Hayday 2004; Men 2011; Jiang and Men 2015). Ethnic minority employees, younger employees, high-income employees, and managers are more engaged than their counterparts (Jiang and Men 2015).

Psychographic Factors and Attitudinal Variables

Demographic factors remain the important criteria and bases for targeting and segmentation, and they cannot be ignored. Conversely, psychographic variables provide better research outcomes and broader information for communicators than demographic factors (Lin 2002). Psychographic factors include *personalities, lifestyles, values, attitudes, political views, social needs, culture interests, desires,* and *entertainment preferences.* Employees can be segmented on the basis of their personal values, social needs, work styles, career focus, and desired career benefits. Moroko and Uncles (2009) segmented employees' career focus into three general categories: industry (i.e., the desire to apply their specialization in a particular industry), vocation (i.e., the desire to pursue specialization in any industry), and company (i.e., the desire to pursue opportunities associated with the employing company). Some employees look for security, stability, and predictability in terms of career benefits. Others look for change, growth, opportunities, and professional development, and others are more concerned about remuneration and economic rewards. Moreover, employees can be segmented on the basis of their attitudes toward or attachment to the organization (i.e., satisfied or somewhat satisfied or unsatisfied employees or loyal or somewhat loyal or disloyal employees). These factors are mostly internal and are not readily observable as demographics. Therefore, the factors need to be gauged through a formal measurement (e.g., survey).

These demographic or geographic, psychographic, and behavioral factors provide an alternative horizontal approach to categorize internal publics into homogeneous groups with distinct needs, characteristics, and interests aside from segmenting them by position level. However, "no rules" or solid lines for segmentation have been found. Each criterion can be used alone or combined in reality. As Goyat (2011) pointed out in his critical review of the market segmentation literature, "Each successful segmentation process is different, unique, and unrepeatable" (p. 51). Practitioners need to strategically select segmentation tools that are identifiable, substantial, accessible, and actionable (Wedel and Kamakura 1999) to closely examine their target publics.

Characteristics of Today's Workforce

With the economic, social, and technological development, today's workforce is unlike that of anytime before. A quick summary of its characteristics marks its uniqueness and provides employers with important implications to better understand, engage, and more effectively communicate with their primary stakeholders.

Multi-Generation

Multi-generation is an unprecedented phenomenon in which four generations (i.e., silent generation, baby-boomers, generation X, and millennials) come together in the workplace today (Harrison 2015). Members of each generation have their own distinct styles, values, attitudes, and behaviors. They come to work with different expectations, assumptions, priorities, and work and communication approaches. Such diversity can contribute to innovation and multiperspective problem-solving. However, these differences can become sources of conflict if ignored. PricewaterCooper's (PwC's) recent global survey shows that millennials will form 50 percent of the global workforce by 2020. Millennials entering into employment will reshape the world of work. Some of the characteristics or qualities identified for millennial workers in previous research include: (1) less loyalty to employers (e.g., "who you work for does not shape who you are"); (2) emphasis on development and work–life balance over financial reward; (3) value of workplace diversity; (4) preference for electronic communication than traditional face-to-face communication; (5) career progression as top priority; (6) emphasis on employer's brand, values, and corporate social responsibility efforts; and (7) strong appetite for overseas work (PwC 2011). These unique characteristics of millennial workers require employers to have a new strategic approach that attracts, retains talent, and effectively communicates with such workers.

Diversity

Diversity is another core value that a growing number of companies embrace today because of an increasingly diverse and globalized marketplace. According to the State of Diversity report issued by the Center for American Progress, people of color make up 36 percent of the labor force in the United States as of June 2012. However, diversity does not only encompass race, gender, age, generational differences, but also varieties in background, education, cultures, and personalities. Many benefits come with workplace diversity, including increased adaptability, attraction of talent, broader service range with a wider collection of skills and experiences (e.g., cultural understanding and languages), variety of perspectives and ideas, and innovation and creativity (Greenberg 2004). However, diversity poses some challenges such as cultural and language barriers, prejudice, discrimination, and stereotyping (Green et al. 2012). Communication is the key to overcoming these challenges and effectively engaging a diverse workforce. Solutions may include cultivating a culture of openness and inclusiveness, providing diversity and communication training, and fostering mutual understanding, respect, and collaboration.

Globalization

The workforce as a product of the economic, political, social, and technological forces has become more global (The Economist Intelligence Unit Limited 2014). A recent industry report "What's Next: Future Global Trends Affecting Your Organization" by the Economist Intelligence Unit Limited listed several characteristics of the globalized workforce: (1) older, more gender and ethnically diverse workforce with increased interconnectivity; (2) country of origin and ethnicity is no longer dictating a worker's geographical scope; (3) easy communication and collaboration across national borders and time zones; and (4) increased global connectivity and work flexibility. Therefore, the importance of internal communication becomes more preeminent in the globalized workplace. The satisfaction of employers and employees, especially remote workers, is hardly achieved without effective communication that is culturally sensitive, caters to employees' preferred language, methods of communication, and connectivity.

Powered by Technology

The workforce today has become more tech-savvy. The millennial generation grew up in an ever-changing digital world by learning and using technologies. Therefore, this generation is more receptive to enterprise social media and other digital tools. PwC's recent survey shows that 41 percent of the millennial respondents would rather communicate electronically than face-to-face or over the phone. Therefore, enterprise social media have been increasingly adopted for internal communication among workers in recent years. These tools have the potential to support more transparent and open communication among workers, foster greater knowledge sharing in the workplace, facilitate distant communication, and build a strong corporate identity across boarders (Treem et al. 2015). Companies and managers must embrace the trend, understand employees' technology competence and needs, and incorporate emerging digital tools in day-to-day employee communication to fully connect and engage with today's digital-savvy employees.

Work–Life Balance

The workforce today places higher emphasis on work–life balance, personal development, and learning (Munn 2013). Such demand for work–life balance started from working mothers. However, the pressure is now from all employees, including employees caring for aged parents, single parents, fathers, mothers, and employees who simply want more flexibility and time committed for personal activities and well-being. Millennial generation workers place a high value on work–life balance even over financial returns (PwC 2011). Millennials are comfortable working remotely because they grew up in the digital age. Moreover, they actively seek employers who offer flexible options. Therefore, companies should recognize and understand employees' work–life balance and actively promote and communicate work–life initiatives to build employee relationships and drive engagement.

Understanding internal stakeholders and publics is an essential step toward building quality relationships. Organizations need to carefully interact with and observe employees to understand and effectively communicate with internal publics to build an engaged workforce.

Summary

Excellence in internal relations and communication management requires the organization's thorough understanding of internal publics (i.e., employees). Not all employees are similar. Segmentation of internal publics based on certain characteristics and common interests betters targeted employee communication. This chapter reviewed various approaches in segmenting internal publics, including segmentation on the basis of the organization's structure and internal publics' demographic, psychographic, and behavioral variables. In particular, segmentation based on the hierarchical structure of the organization groups employees into categories of frontline workers, line managers, middle-level management, senior management, and executives, who are positioned at different levels of the organization and have unique information needs and communication purposes. Segmentation based on demographic variables analyze and group employees based on observed data such as age, gender, education, qualifications, ethnicity, income, work tenure, job type, physical location, and employment status. Segmentation based on psychographic factors looks at employees' personalities, values, attitudes, social needs, culture interests, desires, work styles, career focuses or desired career benefits, and entertainment preferences. Employees can also be segmented on the basis of behavioral variables, such as general media consumption habits, involvement and engagement levels, organizational citizenship behaviors, and adoption stages of new initiatives or changes. Grunig's situational theory of publics and its implications for internal public segmentation were also discussed. Additionally, the chapter summarized the characteristics of today's workforce, which include multigeneration, diversity, globalization, powered by technology, and an emphasis on work–life balance.

CHAPTER 3

Building Ethical Internal Relations

A Principled, Organizational Approach

Two things fill the mind with ever-increasing wonder and awe, the more often and the more intensely the mind of thought is drawn to them: the starry heavens above me and the moral law within me.
—Immanuel Kant from Critique of Practical Reason (1799)

Building an ethical system of internal relations is perhaps the most important challenge facing any communication manager. Ethics helps an organization build relationships, be effective, and stay out of trouble. We have already seen that an excellent internal relations system requires a solid knowledge of the organization, the issues it faces, the industry, and a thorough understanding of stakeholders and publics—these are foundational elements. Add to that already complex list a working knowledge of moral philosophy and applied ethics, as well as the ever-present potential for product failure, natural disasters, scandal, and corruption; it is clear why the area of ethics presents a challenge.

Still, in creating an ethical internal culture through the use of internal relations, communication about ethics, training programs, and ongoing ethical decision-making is arguably the most important aspect of any type of organizational communication. Before diving into ethics, a look at why it is so vital will be useful.

The Ethical Mandate

Ethics is not an optional concern for modern business (De George 2010). Rising criticism via readily available social media channels (Li 2015), growing public demands for accountability and social responsibility, coupled with infamous corporate scandals, such as the Enron collapse, have created widespread cynicism about business, a distrust of corporations, and a dislike for their leaders. Several decades ago, economist Milton Friedman (2002) argued that the only business social responsibility was to increase its profits. Although insightful in its economic theory, Friedman did not foresee the unethical activities, scandals, and resulting new spate of government regulations that would occur over the next four and a half decades. Those activities, scandals, and new government regulations and regulatory agencies mean that trust is a scarce and valuable commodity, and ethics cannot be ignored.

Public trust in both business and government is at an all-time low on a global level (Edelman Trust Barometer 2015). According to that study, the credibility of NGOs, media, CEOs, and spokespeople has continued to decline year after year, and building credibility is becoming harder and more complex. The 2015 Edelman report contended that employees are the key to building credibility, writing that across industries "a company's in-house technical experts are, on average, 22 percent more credible than the CEO" (np).

In order to create long-term relationships with stakeholders, both internal and external, organizations simply must pay attention to ethics. As a valuable asset of an organization, employees must have a sense that they are being treated fairly and can trust the organization to do their best work. Based upon research and experience, satisfied employees are those who feel secure in their employment, having some sense of trust in the fairness and continuity of their employer.

Employees are exceptionally important to an organization. It has been argued that employees are even *the* most important asset of an organization, giving a competitive advantage when other factors are equal, and even acting as ambassadors during times of organizational need. But in order to offer both of those advantages, employees must have a sense of trust instilled by ethics that includes fairness and integrity, and that the organization will treat them with good intent. Ethics builds trust: attention to ethics builds ethical awareness and creates ethical behavior, and in turn ethical behavior enhances trust.

Research from many disciplines shows that ethics is a vital part of strategic management and organizational decision making. Some perspectives talk about character, others' integrity, and others about honesty and moral principle. Some perspectives talk about the greater good or public welfare and social justice. Other perspectives talk about corporate social responsibility (CSR). It has recently become part of this dialog to talk about a "social license to operate," holding organizations to do good works in the societies of which they are a part.

Many thinkers have argued that a business exists by permission of society, and thus the argument for a social license to operate is inferred. At any rate, one simply needs to look at the examples of activist groups who have stopped organizations from operating when they find their consequences unacceptable. Whether one takes the perspective that ethics is driven from a social obligation, part of corporate responsibility, or an obligation imposed by others, such as governments and activists, we simply must attend to matters of ethics. When organizations do not attend to creating their own set of ethical values, someone else's values will be imposed upon them.[1] To maintain autonomy and independent decision-making responsibility seems to be the most morally aware, strategic, and efficient means of creating an ethical framework.

What is Ethics?

Ethics is how we determine good from bad behavior, norms for society, personal beliefs, and norms for acting within an organization (Sims 1994). In short, ethics guides behavior both in the *normative* sense of what we should do in an ideal setting, and also in the *positive* sense of what we can do in our specific situation. At its best, *ethics is an analytical*

---

[1] We see this happening all the time as government in hindsight has limited and restricted corporate activity through legislation such as Sarbanes–Oxley Act of 2002 that originated as an aftermath of the Enron scandal.

way of thinking that allows rigorous consideration of multiple perspectives, resulting in thorough analyses and defensible conclusions.

Ethics stems from *moral philosophy* as the rigorous, analytical, reasoned study of what makes actions right or wrong. Moral philosophy consists of *metaethics* or how we know morals and ethics exist; normative ethics or seeking ideal ethical frameworks to guide decisions; and applied ethics that studies the application of moral frameworks to real-world situations. Normative ethical frameworks guide applied ethical solutions, so you will see both forms in the public relations literature often seen as corporate conscience, character, dialog, symmetrical relationships, transparency, authenticity, trust, and many other similar terms.

In ethics, studying the normative or ideal solution to complex problems determines the underlying moral principle that is the basis for an ethical decision. Studying that normative ideal helps to determine what actions we can take in the positive sense, in a specific situation that may offer limited options. Though moral philosophy and ethics are highly theoretical and often normative; studying those approaches can help to identify, analyze, and resolve ethical problems in an everyday, applied setting.

Ethics is not for solving easy issues or simple matters. Ethics excels at allowing the examination of complex problems, and creating well-considered, thorough analyses of difficult decisions with multiple implications and dueling priorities. Simple yes or no questions rarely need a full ethical analysis to determine the best course of action. The questions with multiple competing right answers, or a limited range of any good answers, are those best suited to conducting an ethical analysis, as discussed later in this chapter.

What Function is Responsible?

Considering which organizational function should be responsible for ethics: ideally, where should that function be located? And, who is responsible for ethical decision-making? The difficulty in answers to these questions shows the pervasive nature of ethics throughout organizations and throughout the human condition. Many people argue that the ethics of an organization falls to everyone, the legal department, or to the CEO alone. A closer look at the research reveals a more complicated and rather circular answer.

Bowen (2004a) addressed the question of if business ethics originates in individuals or organizational culture, sometimes called "the chicken or the egg problem" of which comes first. In summary, the answer is *both work in conjunction*. Every individual person is responsible for being an ethics officer, or doing the right thing. But the organizational culture was the *most* important and pervasive factor in determining ethical behavior, values, and the importance of ethics in the workplace. Where that culture originates is a combination of many factors, including communication, leadership, values, and internal relations.

In 2005b, Bowen showed that in the best organizations, ethics can also be centralized in the public relations function because communication understands the views of multiple stakeholders both inside and outside the organization, rather than taking a narrower view. In that manner, public relations can serve to enhance and protect the reputation of the organization, building relationships with stakeholders that are based on ethical responsibility. In the internal relations function, helping to foster an ethical vision, mission, and organizational culture, as well as counseling other executives on ethics and reputational impact, are part of daily activity.

A worldwide study found that public relations professionals say they counsel the CEO and management team about ethics, and that they believe public relations is the right organization function to conduct ethical analyses (Bowen 2006). Likewise, professional communicators indicated that as their careers advanced, their need for ethical understanding and counsel to senior management was in high demand (Bowen 2006, 2008). In one of those studies (Bowen 2008), some public relations professionals admitted that they knew little about ethics and did not feel comfortable counseling an organization on the right thing to do. However, studying ethics clearly pays off. High-level public relations executives indicated that counseling on ethics helped to catapult their careers, giving them avenues to the CEO and management team policy and strategic decision-making not previously available (Bowen 2009). Further, studying ethical reasoning has been found to offer a more complex ability to engage in strategic thinking than those who study only codes of ethics without their basis in philosophy (Bowen and Erzikova 2013).

Corporate Conscience: Does it Exist?

Can an organization have a conscience? Or, is an ethical conscience up to individuals, governments, or even situations? Scholars describe the debate between individual ethics and corporate ethics as factious, and responsible for much criticism of business. Seeger (1997) explained: "Viewing the individual as the only moral agent tends to release the organization from an ethical obligation" (p. 8). He noted that courts, laws, and CEOs often acknowledge a social responsibility and obligation, and De George (2010) offered that regulatory actions will impose accountability where it does not exist; therefore, the argument is largely a straw man debate. However, regulatory action and legal compliance are not substitutes for ethical accountability but different considerations entirely, as argued by Sims (1994), Bowen (2004b; 2010), and Bowen and Heath (2005).

Organizations and people are best viewed as ethical points on a continuous loop rather than competing opposites. As De George (2007) explained: "Moral people are needed to create and sustain moral structures. The two reinforce each other" (p. 110). Further, scholars (De George 2010; Seeger 1997) argued that organizations must go beyond pure profit motives associated with individual ethical responsibility; they assert that the modern view holds organizations as collectives who are responsible for ethical behavior.

Although this debate may not be permanently resolved, organizations can be understood as having cultures that arise as greater constructs, in the *suis generis* sense, from the individual moral actors within them. Some (Goodpaster 2007; Seeger 1997; Sims 1994) argued that an organization can have a conscience and even a moral intention that can be studied and has been modeled (Goodpaster 2007, 76–83). Moral conscience is both an individual concept and one that can be applied collectively, as moral awareness and insight requiring "the coordination of self-interest alongside respect for others" (Goodpaster 2007, 53). In that sense, a corporate conscience exists independently of the organizational actors who comprise it. However, we must also realize that there is some ambiguity because organizations are comprised of individuals with their own moral values that sometimes compete or conflict with those of peer groups and the organization—sometimes for the better, as an activist for ethical behavior, and sometimes for the worse. In such cases, potential for negative outcomes increases through stifling of individual moral autonomy or myopic groupthink,[2] retribution, pressure, denial of responsibility, and so on. Many infamous cases of ethical breaches, such as the deception in emissions testing at Volkswagen, may result (Bowen, Stacks, and Wright, in press). Individuals with strong moral values and an organizational culture that considers ethics (Bowen 2004a; Sims 1994) both help creating a corporate conscience when public relations acts as the corporate ethical conscience (Ryan and Martinson 1983).

Trevino, Weaver, and Reynolds (2006) found that organizational culture, rewards and punishments, situational factors, and locus of control all exert more influence on ethics than individual standards. The researchers found that organizational ethics takes precedence over personal ethics as a form of insurance against self-interested or unethical behaviors. Sims (1994, 21) explained that compromising one's personal beliefs in the interests of an organization's ethical standards was *positively* related to managerial success. It is not enough that an enterprise be made up of ethical individuals and hold a strong organizational culture; it must be an organizational culture that values ethics and seeks to act with moral intention (Goodpaster 2007). In summary, internal relations can play an enormous role in creating and enhancing a corporate conscience that supports ethics.

The Role of Internal Communication

Internal communication is a conduit for creating an ethical organizational culture. Culture creation occurs in numerous ways that are more often implicit than explicit. *Institutionalization*, or the process of incorporating

---

[2] Irving Janis (1972) defined and operationalized this as an organizational behavior that resulted when a charismatic leader or senior group see their actions based on misperceptions of others, especially in negative or demeaning terms; specifically, groupthink occurs when a group makes faulty decisions because group pressures lead to a deterioration of "mental efficiency, reality testing, and moral judgment" (p. 9).

ethics and how the organization conducts its daily affairs, is an important part of building this culture. Institutionalization occurs when ethics is incorporated into the official operating system of an organization: on-boarding (hiring) procedures, training programs, incorporation in daily decision-making processes, evaluation systems, routine certification or competency programs, reward and punishment systems, award competitions, and so on. Internal relations should regularly communicate about the values and initiatives the organization has decided to institutionalize. Institutionalization can happen through any mediums and channels at the disposal of internal communication.

These communications help to build organizational culture by telling internal stakeholders what to focus on, organizational priorities, and values. Many organizations use initiatives to run campaigns for a specified time period focusing on specific issues; some have a constant attention and reinforcement of ethics, while others may institute an "ethics month" in addition to ongoing training.

Both routine discussions about ethics and special ethics initiatives appear to create the strongest institutionalization and most beneficial organizational cultures for employees (Bowen 2015; Goodpaster 2007). In other words, a one-time initiative such as an "ethics month" may backfire by giving the impression to employees that during the other months ethics is not as important. However, ongoing institutionalization can also become routine. As employees become accustomed to policies and procedures, they "assume" they are doing things correctly and no longer ask questions (Bowen 2002). Both approaches have flaws. Therefore, using institutionalization of ethics, combined with differing initiatives special activities, and so on keeps ethics at the forefront of internal decision-making.

For example, the Hilton Hotel Corporation has an institutionalized ethics program based on prioritized values and responsibilities. In addition to the institutionalized program, Hilton sponsors an annual worldwide competition for an "ethics champion." In that award, the nominated employees describe their solution to an on-the-job ethical dilemma. The winner gets a $10,000 prize, which, depending on the country of residence, can be life-altering. In this example, we can see that ethics is both institutionalized and incentivized; it is fresh and living in the minds of internal publics and in the decisions of management.

Excellent Symmetrical Systems of Internal Relations

The Excellence study (Grunig 1992) examined which factors help the public relations function contribute to organizational effectiveness at an optimal-level organization, leading to the Excellence theory. The Excellence theory is based on 10 generally applicable ("generic") principles of excellence, which have been published throughout countless studies and three books (Dozier, Grunig and Grunig 1995; Grunig 1992; Grunig, Grunig, and Dozier 2002). The first book in this series, Bowen, Rawlins, and Martin (2010), included an overview of that complex research in their chapter 12, but offered a concise summary of the excellence principles:

1. Involvement of public relations in strategic management
2. Empowerment of public relations in the dominant coalition or a direct reporting relationship to senior management
3. Integrated public relations function across the organization
4. Public relations as a management function, separate from other functions
5. Public relations unit headed by a manager rather than a technician
6. Two-way symmetrical (or mixed-motive) model of public relations
7. Department with the knowledge needed to practice the managerial role in symmetrical public relations
8. Symmetrical system of internal communication
9. Diversity embodied in all roles
10. Ethics and integrity. (Verčič, Grunig, and Grunig 1996, 37–40 and 58)

Each of these components adds to the ability of the public relations function to advise the CEO and engage in the strategic management process, incorporating the ideas, values, and priorities into organizational actions when possible. That participation increases organizational effectiveness because it builds relationships, trust, commitment, and satisfaction among publics over time (Bowen, Hung-Baesecke, and Chen 2016). For the purposes of this volume, please draw your attention to number eight, symmetrical systems of internal communication.

Symmetrical systems of internal communication was found to be a component of what makes organizations more effective. Incorporating means of feedback and input from employees increases their participation in the organization, gives them voice in executive strategic planning, and fosters better understanding of their views to help resolve conflict and foster teamwork. Symmetrical systems of internal communication should flow in a bottom–up fashion, and within peers, in addition to the traditional top–down flow. It includes a willingness to change on behalf of the organization and management due to the concerns, influence, or ideas of employees. This adds value to the management by including diverse ideas and perspectives into management, avoiding the myopia that causes many problems for an organization.

Symmetrical systems can take many forms. They can be routine communications with dialog-based components built in, such as question and answer sessions with leadership, comment boards, forums, and other forms of feedback loops. They may need to take on a component of anonymity to ensure the candor of internal publics in sensitive situations, such as toll-free phone lines, anonymous e-mails, and so on. However, *most employees say that they want follow up, even if their tip is handled anonymously* (Bowen 2015). They want to know someone cares and is acting on their concerns. Symmetrical systems of internal communication ensure that employees, contractors, labor unions, and other internal publics have a voice. That voice can be used in issues management to identify and solve problems before they become larger crises, to incorporate views of internal stakeholders into management, and to create a more committed workforce. They are an essential element to an ethical and supportive organizational culture.

Organizational Ethics Meets Moral Philosophy

Organizational ethics evolves in numerous ways. Sometimes, a strong mission from a founder guides an organization. In other organizations, a formal study of core values is undertaken, in which research helps to identify the core beliefs of internal stakeholders for solidification into a statement or policy. Although the ethical values of an organization can arise in a myriad of ways, the common thread is that ethics must be a part of day-to-day discussions, activities, and considerations. Ethics in an organization should be *institutionalized*, meaning that they are made part of the organization's culture, through its internal relations, on-boarding and training, routine decision-making, and used in its evaluation and reward system (Goodpaster 2007). Institutionalization means the ethics becomes a part of the organization, not an afterthought, addendum, or a dusty and long-forgotten policy manual.

Ethics in an organization arises from a complex myriad of factors, including the mission and vision of the organization, the industry, competitiveness, and the turbulence of an organizations' environment. It also includes organizational structure, activism, the power of the organization, its dedication to ethics internally, and the strength of industry or professional association ethical standards. One can examine how ethics is codified throughout the organization: what ethical language is used in ethics statements, on-boarding, ongoing ethics training, incentive programs, communication initiatives about ethics in the organization, and the leadership of the organization. A strong organizational culture will include ethics in strategic management decisions, working to incorporate the values of the stakeholders upon whom it depends into strategy, and activities of the organization.

Leadership is an exceptionally important variable in this complex confluence of factors. Leadership happens at various levels throughout the organization from supervisory positions to those in management and executive management. However, the ultimate leader of an organization is its CEO, the tone-setter for organizational ethics. Therefore, leadership and ethics must be discussed concurrently. Leadership and ethics are intimately conjoined and can be untwined for the purpose of scholarly study, but in the real world, *organizational ethics often depends on having an ethical leader.*

What does it mean to be an ethical leader? Scholars have long discussed this question. In fact, ethical leadership is a question so old that it dates back to the origin of democracy in ancient Greece with Socrates, Plato, and Aristotle. Modern-day scholars in business ethics, public relations, management and organizational behavior, and leadership studies also addressed this question. A good synopsis is offered by Northouse (2007) who surmised that ethical leadership is composed of five principles:

1. Respects others
2. Serves others

3. Shows justice
4. Manifests honesty
5. Builds community (adapted from p. 350)

These manifestation are highly based on a principled form of ethical reasoning called *deontology*. A closer look at deontology, or principle-based reasoning, provides a powerful means of ethical analysis.

Deontology: Ethical Analysis of Duty and Principle

Deontology was invented by the philosopher Immanuel Kant in the 18th century. No serious study of ethics would be credible without an examination of Kant, the most renowned of the enlightenment philosophers, specifically his treatise on ethics (1785 and 1964). For many years, Kant studied ethics, in addition to mathematics, logic, political philosophy, and geography. The resulting school of ethics is an enduring paradigm of analysis known as deontology or the study of duty. It has been applied extensively in normative and real-world public relations (Bowen 2004b, 2005b).

This form of ethics based on principles examines moral duties, obligations, and rights under a universal moral law that compels *all* rational beings to judge decisions without prejudice. This theory is said to be universal because it is based on equality: it obligates all rational beings equally—without preference to organizational hierarchy, social class, education, or demographic variables—to follow moral principle by virtue of reason alone.

Kant's deontology offers three tests to determine our ethical obligations in a decision, and also helping to rule out bias and pure self-interest. Kant called these decision tests categorical imperatives because they are not subjective or conditional but categorically apply to all rational beings, and imperatives because we are obligated universally to uphold them. A decision must pass all three forms of Kant's categorical imperative.

The three decision tests known as categorical imperatives are:

1. Am I upholding my *duty to a universal moral principle* that any rational person would also see and follow?

2. Am I maintaining the *dignity and respect* that are owed to others in this decision?

3. Am I acting out of good moral will or *good intention* to do the right thing?

Although this moral philosophy is far more nuanced and complex than these three decision-making tests can encapsulate, they lie at the very core of Kantian philosophy. Kant designed them to help illuminate a decision from numerous vantage points, instead of simply considering what is best for oneself (selfishness) or trying to predict future consequences of a decision (consequentialism). In that manner, he eliminated selfishness and the introduction of potential bias into the decision. Further, the decision is not based on predicted consequences or outcomes but on the ethics of the situation alone. That type of decision-making is based on moral principle rather than consequences, and it is thought to be the most rigorous test of moral philosophy.

Symmetrical systems of feedback for internal stakeholders, sometimes anonymously, are vital for the research needed to understand all sides of an issue in this type of analysis. Through incorporating the views of each rational perspective, deontology overcomes the "majority rule" problem that is inherent in ethics based on the greatest good for the greatest number, a utilitarian approach based on consequences. Instead of the majority always winning a decision, deontology resists reducing people to numbers and focuses on the moral principle that underlies a decision. It recognizes that a small minority or even one employee can have a really good point.

On which principle, value, or duty is the decision based upon? In examining the moral principle of a decision, the organization can determine a course of action in accordance with its values. These moral principles can be placed in an order of importance according to the issue under scrutiny. Once these factors are assessed for an issue, that which is the most important moral principle—called the *deciding factor*—guides the decision. For example, what is more important: the value of human life or a financial gain for the company? It would become obvious that recalling a potentially lethal faulty product from the market would be the correct decision over financial gain based on the deciding factor of valuing human life.

Another common deciding factor is *honesty*. Honesty is a moral principle that every rational person can agree upon as a basic good and necessity. If you could not assume a level of honesty existed, something as simple as paying bills from your online bank account would not be possible because you would not know if the bank truly sent the correct funds. Without honesty, society would break down into anarchy. Honesty is a moral principle that is often the deciding factor in public relations.

In internal relations, concealing information about employee layoffs might seem the kind thing to do momentarily, but is it ethically right? What is the deciding factor? In that example, honest disclosure would overrule kindness as the deciding factor. Disclosure could then pass the three tests of deontology: (1) universal duty to moral principle, (2) dignity and respect, and (3) good intention. Table 3.1 offers a step-by-step summary of these decision tests to facilitate implementing a deontological analysis.

Ethical decision making is never an easy pursuit. Philosophical analysis requires logic, research into the views and values of internal and

Table 3.1 A deontological ethical analysis*

CI	Decision test	Priority of duties
State the issue	What options are available to resolve the problem?	Which potential principles are involved in the issue?
Qualifier: Autonomy	Am I acting from the basis of reason alone, ruling out selfishness, fear, greed, and so on?	Rational; objective as possible; multifaceted view
1	What is my duty that any other rational person would also see and follow as a moral principle?	Universal principle underlying problem
2	Are dignity and respect provided to others?	Integrating research and alternate views
3	Am I acting from good intention alone?	Doing the right thing—because it is right
Pass all three tests?	Revise and integrate options for resolving; determine the best decision option to implement	Prioritize values to uphold as the deciding factor

*Table 3.1 shows how to implement the categorical imperative tests of deontology and determine a deciding factor of the most important principle to uphold.

external stakeholders, creating integrative options to resolve a problem, collaborative problem-solving, revising based on new data, innovation, extended analyses, and innovation. Personally, it takes tenacity, intelligence, moral imagination (e.g., empathy), and patience. Creating symmetrical systems for internal feedback, input, and ideas from employee stakeholders is key to having the full understanding of many sides of an issue or differing values necessary to implement a deontological analysis.

The results of conducting a deontological ethical analysis are worth the time and effort. Decisions created using that paradigm are rigorous and lasting. They are less likely than other types of decisions to create negative outcomes or unanticipated fallout, such as government regulatory penalties and fines, lawsuits, boycotts, union strikes, negative media coverage, loss of customers, and so on. This confidence in the decision is because those made from a deontological approach are understandable, defensible, logical, respectful, universal, and based on good intention.

In internal relations, using principle-based ethics creates a trusting environment in which employees are heard and respected, and some of their views are integrated into strategic management and problem-solving. These attributes create loyalty, efficiency through less demand to revise policies because of unforeseen problems, a consistency that internal stakeholders (as well as external ones) come to rely upon, a means of meeting demands for responsibility and accountability, and a reliable and knowable organizational culture, mission, and values. Using this type of ethical analysis has also been shown to offer potential inclusion in executive-level decision-making for communication professionals, as well as the opportunity to advise and counsel the CEO on ethical dilemmas (Bowen 2008; 2009).

Although the public relations function, and specifically the internal communication manager in this text, will be charged with spearheading ethical analyses, anyone in the organization can also use a deontological approach if it becomes a part of the organization's culture and training. Leaders, managers, and followers can use the principle-based reasoning of deontology to assist in creating an organization that places ethics first among its considerations.

Leadership's Role in Ethics

Organizational culture can be created by internal relations alone. The activities, policies, statements, and modeling behavior of organization leaders show employees which beliefs and values to emulate, both positive and negative. Leaders demonstrate what is acceptable, and sometimes demonstrate what is *not* acceptable, often before an ouster. They act as role models in the organization, helping to ethically train and socialize stakeholders in terms of the norms and expectations for their own behavior.

What type of leadership is best? Research has studied charismatic leaders who seem to lead by the magnetic strength of their personality, transactional leaders who were more distant and businesslike, and transformational leaders who offer change or enhancement. However, the two leadership styles that are often associated with ethics and high employee performance are servant leadership and authentic leadership style. A quick look at each style reveals the key characteristics of successful leadership.

Servant Leadership

The *Servant leadership style* views the CEO as serving the needs and interests of everyone else in the organization. Although the CEO is normally at the apex of organizational charts, servant leadership views the CEO at the bottom or foundation of an organization, there to serve the interests of many stakeholders both internally and externally. This leadership approach has been around since Robert Greenleaf studied it in the 1970s, but servant leadership has been gaining popularity in recent years and is currently in use by organizations such as the Home Depot (Bowen, Rawlins, and Martin 2010). Servant leaders score high on ethics, social responsibility, and empathy in nurturing their followers (Northouse 2007).

Servant leaders view their role as enriching others by their presence in leadership activities in the organization. As Northouse (2007) explained, "A servant leader focuses on the needs of followers and helps them to become more knowledgeable, more free, more autonomous, and more like servants themselves" (p. 349). Our perspective adds that a servant leader should also include a high level of respect and reflexivity in their decision-making processes in leadership. *Respect* is an ethical construct that requires consideration of stakeholders involved or affected by a decision. Respect does not mean acquiescence; in ethical terms, respect means logical and rational consideration of the values, priorities, needs, and perspectives of multiple publics. *Reflexivity* is an awareness of one's own role in the decision-making process that has been conceptualized in both principle-based and in consequence-based ethical decision-making (Bowen and Gallicano 2013). To be ethically reflexive, a servant leader would examine his or her intention in the decision-making process as well as the potential consequences on internal stakeholders. Only decisions made from good intention or a good moral will pass the high bar of ethical decision-making.

Authentic Leadership

Authentic leadership offers a genuineness in how the leader models ethical behavior and relates to others, including transparency, honesty, and following up talk with action. The genuineness emphasized in authentic leadership style conveys trustworthiness and is highly valued by internal stakeholders. Authentic leaders appear to be true to themselves, without pretense or barriers, and tend to display an amazing consistency across multiple types of situations.

Authentic leadership has been found to have positive effects on both job satisfaction and employees' attitudes (Azanza, Moriano, and Molero 2013). Further, in researching authentic leadership style, leader integrity was positively associated with follower engagement and successful performance (Vogelgesang, Leroy, and Avolio 2013). In essence, the leader's role is to instill ethics in the organizational culture through modeling ethical behavior, demonstrating authentic leadership, including genuineness, transparency, and integrity. Organization followers respond to genuineness from various leaders in the organization, not just the CEO alone. The role of followers is to also act as an ethical conscience, emphasizing those aspects of ethical deliberation that are demonstrated by leaders in the organization, and institutionalized throughout its culture. The leader's role is not only to talk about ethics, but to demonstrate it with action. Leaders should model ethical behavior by doing something about ethics, talking about ethical analyses, and then taking concrete action based on the result (Bowen 2015). Before moving to action, a quick word on followership is warranted.

Followership's Role in Ethics

The other side of the leadership coin—followership— is also an important consideration in how ethical decisions actually take shape through implementation and follow through in the organization. Every leader is, at certain times and in some places, also a follower. For example, a powerful CEO may be the leader of a corporation but may also be a follower in his or her local religious congregation or philanthropic club. The ability to switch between such roles means that the leader must also be an adept follower.

Additionally, most leaders did not become leaders overnight. The background of many CEOs includes working in many different environments. What that means for public relations is that chief communication officers (CCOs) will often work with someone who does not speak public relations, and does not have reputation and relationship management at the forefront of their minds. But it does mean that the CEO has time in the trenches and worked his or her way up the chain of command and successfully competed for an enviable position. Those traits instill leadership, but they require followership first. A follower is a team member at any level of an organization. Often a follower is not the ultimate decision-making authority, but may have certain levels of authority and control because followers occur at all levels of an organization; and, there are many leaders who report to the top leader.

What is followership? Leader–member engagement studies oftentimes focus on the leader, with an undefined role of what the member or follower actually does or should do. To understand the situation personally, ask yourself, what kind of team member am I? How does one become a good follower? The ethics of *altruism* applies in this case. Many times, the follower is dedicated to advancing the cause of an organization and its leader out of devotion, loyalty, and duty, all ethical terms. Being a good follower often means supporting the vision and mission of the leader, sometimes at the expense of personal goals in order to achieve a common team or organizational goal. For example, working late without extra pay to accomplish a common goal is a frequently used example of dedicated followership.

Followers institutionalize ethics but putting those concepts into the currency of daily use, and over time, those values becomes part of the organizational culture. By acting in the interest of the organization upon the ethical decisions outlined by the leader, an adept follower consistently returns to the ethics expected and works on behalf of values that the organizational team espouses. Good leaders notice these attributes and reward high-performing followers, holding them up as examples of effectiveness, dedication, altruism, ethical behavior, or of respecting team goals above personal achievement in their service to the organization.

The follower is often the most important part of the ethical framework. It is here that the "rubber hits the road" in the form of carrying out organization ethical decisions on a day-to-day basis. Living the ethical values that were once analyzed in the board room is often the only way some stakeholders see the ethical "face" of a company, when representatives interact with customers.

It is through the sustained, day-to-day incorporation of ethical analyses, values, and decisions that an organization becomes who it says it is—an authentic enterprise (Arthur W. Page Society 2007, 2012), and that depends on followers at all levels for modeling ethical behavior (Bowen 2015). All the ethical analyses in the world at the top level are useless if they are not put into action throughout the organization at various levels by followers. Followers live and model the ethical values of leaders on a large scale, often a visible one, putting lofty ideas and abstract theory into action. Followers make organizational ethics visible, concrete, demonstrable, and real.

Sustained Shared Ethical Values

Followers play an enormous role in sustaining organizational values into the future, past the level of institutionalization, to the level of essential input that drives culture and ethical values. Internal relations must work to instill symmetrical systems of internal communication in which stakeholder views are sought and encouraged, but over time, these paths become normal, expected, and so well-used that they begin to drive themselves. Values are shared throughout organizational levels at this point, and are influenced by followers as well as leaders in a two-way fashion. Ethics has become enculturated, or part of the shared fabric of an organization's culture (Bowen 2015). How ethics is talked about in the organization, on a routine basis, becomes part of the shared meaning of the organization's culture, taxonomy (or terms), and vision. Recent research (Bowen 2016a) offered a refined understanding of ethical terms based on moral philosophy for use in the public relations discipline. Please see Table 3.2 for the suggested terms for enculturated ethics.

A discussion of these terms and their frequent use in analyzing the ethics of the organization and in internal communication is highly recommended in institutionalizing ethics. Goodpaster (2007) offered three steps to institutionalizing ethics within an organization's culture: (1) orienting, (2) institutionalizing, and (3) sustaining shared ethical values. *Orienting* involves defining with clarity the values, beliefs, and activities that an organization wishes to emphasize. *Institutionalization*, as mentioned earlier, involves many forms of creating a discussion around those values, living the beliefs of the organization every day through activities. And, *sustaining shared ethical values* involves longer-term discussions,

Table 3.2 *Recommended ethical terms for public relations and media relations. Reprinted by permission of Elsevier, public relations review*

Common usage	Moral philosophy— "revised" recommended term	Philosophical underpinnings or synonyms
Character	Virtue	Life well-lived, human flourishing, reflexive, worthy
Transparency	Disclosure	Honest, contextual, as full as possible, respect, dignity
Authenticity	Frankness	Candor, moral courage, forthright, rational, autonomy
Values	Prioritized values	Multilayered values, societal norms, duty
Legalism	Ethics	Moral judgment, discernment, just or justice, fair, right

Source: Bowen (2016a).

integrations, and updates of shared values that drive the organization's culture over time—enculturation.

These activities create an organization that is responsive and enduring, with symmetrical means of internal communication that are sustained. These systems of ethical analyses and shared, sustained organizational culture offer a demonstrable advantage in the market to organizations who have incorporated principle and duty as first-order considerations. One could say that the organization has indeed developed a conscience.

Summary

This chapter reviewed current research and theory to illustrate an organizational approach based on principled decision-making should drive internal relations. Internal relations systems should be undertaken from a symmetrical communication approach that instills feedback, dialog, input, and shared decision-making. Organizations' ethical mandate rests on governance and regulation, including heightened demands for accountability. Ethics was defined in the terms of moral philosophy as how we can consistently and rationally differentiate right from wrong. Public relations is the function most suited to understand stakeholder values and priorities and incorporate these into organizational decisions and results in public relations acting as a corporate conscience. The vital role of organizational culture in ethics was discussed as well as how organizational ethics is supported by training and codification, or institutionalization.

Principle- and duty-based ethics, based on Kant's deontology, were reviewed as the most powerful form of ethical analysis available for helping to resolve dilemmas and guide internal relations. Incorporating recent research insights, this chapter offered a step-by-step approach and means of analysis that organizations can use to make principled decisions. That approach promotes honesty, candor, dialog, collaboration, respect, and good intention with stakeholder communities in their day-to-day practice. Deontology results in consistently rational ethical behavior that enhances the commitment, trust, and satisfaction of internal stakeholders. Leadership is discussed as a way to model that principled behavior, and followership is viewed as the valuable daily incorporation of ethical principles into operations that are the public face of an organization.

CHAPTER 4

Leadership Communication

Developing excellent communication skills is absolutely essential to effective leadership. The leader must be able to share knowledge and ideas to transmit a sense of urgency and enthusiasm to others. If a leader can't get a message across clearly and motivate others to act on it, then having a message doesn't even matter.

—Gilbert Amelio, Former President and CEO of National Semiconductor Corporation

Communication is central to leadership (Awamleh and Gardner 1999). Although traditional leadership theories on leaders' traits and styles; contingency theories on leadership; and theories on charismatic, visionary, and transformational leadership rarely consider the communication aspects of leadership (Johansson, Miller, and Hamrin 2014), many scholars and leaders have noted that effective communication is an essential element of leadership. For instance, Yukl (2006) recognized that leadership is implemented through communication. Motivating and inspiring employees are almost impossible without effective communication. Leaders are communication champions who unite and inspire people to work for the same purpose toward the same direction (Sriram 2014). Leadership communication represents an indispensable component of an organization's internal communication system. This chapter examines leadership with an emphasis on the relationship between leadership and communication, and presents a list of theory-informed and research-validated recommendations to help leaders effectively communicate in the increasingly competitive business world.

Definition of Leadership

Leadership has been defined from a variety of perspectives, such as the "traits, behaviors, influences, interaction patterns, role relationships, and occupation of an administrative position" (Yukl 2006, 2). For example, Burns (1978) noted that leadership is exercised when individuals "mobilize ... institutional, political, psychological and other resources so as to arouse, engage, and satisfy the motives of followers" (p. 18). Rauch and Behling (1984) defined leadership as "the process of influencing the activities of an organized group toward goal achievement" (p. 46). Richards and Engle (1986) asserted that leadership involves such behaviors as "articulating visions, embodying values, and creating the environment within which things can be accomplished" (p. 206).

Yukl and Van Fleet (1992) defined leadership as an *influence process*, which encompasses "influencing the task objectives and strategies of a group or organization, influencing people in the organization to implement the strategies and achieve the objectives, influencing group maintenance and identification, and influencing the culture of organization" (p. 149). House et al. (2004) defined it as "the ability of an individual to influence, motivate, and enable others to contribute toward the effectiveness and success of the organization of which they are members" (p. 15). According to Stogdill (1974), "there are as many definitions of leadership as there are persons who have attempted to define this concept" (p. 259). Consequently, researchers normally define it according to their individual perspective or the aspects of leadership they are interested in (Yukl 2006), but leadership is generally accepted as a nested form of influence prevalent in an organization. It influences not only the attitude and behavior of followers and group performance, but also organizational structure, climate, culture, and effectiveness (Yukl and Van Fleet 1992).

Leadership and Communication

Leadership and communication are intertwined in many ways. At the organizational level, top-management leadership plays an enabling role and sets the tone for internal communication. If senior management challenges the value of public relations or communication and provide limited support or resources, the purpose of communication is unlikely to be achieved. In their work on excellence in public relations and communication management, Dozier, Grunig, and Grunig (1995) concluded that a top communicator in an organization is a key to building and maintaining excellent communication and that excellent communication occurs in organizations where senior management understands and demands excellence, and encourages communication to achieve excellence. An eminent communication champion is Cisco's former CEO John Chambers. Chambers fundamentally believes that everything he does is driven by communication. "You've got to communicate, communicate, communicate," Chambers said. With the support of its CEO, Cisco established a strong communication system and has been a leader in adopting interactive technologies to strengthen internal communication (Groysberg and Slind 2011). According to Kelly Lang, the communication counselor of Chambers, "When you have a CEO in place who strongly drives business strategy using communication, you can't *not* have a culture of communications" (Groysberg and Slind 2011, 93).

Senior-leadership communication also plays a critical role in shaping an organization's image in the eyes of internal and external stakeholders. The symbolic leadership, power, and communication demonstrated by CEOs influence stakeholder trust in leadership, confidence in the organization, and performance (Men 2011, 2015a; Park and Berger 2004). Employees often desire an open and close relationship with top managers. The employees' perceptions of senior management are "closely linked to their overall perceptions of the organization as a place to work and the general state of the morale" (Pincus, Rayfield, and Cozzens 1991, 9). For example, Men (2012) found that employees who perceive their CEOs to be trustworthy and competent leaders tended to perceive a better reputation of the company and were more engaged in the organization. Moreover, senior corporate leaders often serve as catalysts to vision, value, and communication philosophy formation, which is fundamental to the management of both external and internal relations. They are expected not only to convey vision and values and to interpret them, but also to live out those principles and act as role models (Bowen 2015).

At the manager–employee level, effective supervisory leadership communication is associated with many positive outcomes, such as commitment to the organization, trust, role clarity, satisfaction toward the management, job satisfaction, engagement, empowerment, and advocacy on the part of the employees (Derue et al. 2011; Jablin 1979; Madlock 2008). At the team level, effective leadership communication contributes to work unit cohesion, team confidence, and effective internal group operations, which eventually lead to high levels of performance (Johansson, Miller, and Hamrin 2014).

CEO or Senior Leadership Communication

The external roles of top leaders as corporate spokespersons or public representatives have long been recognized (e.g., Graham 1997; Hutton et al. 2001; Park and Berger 2004). Internally, an organization's senior leaders, including CEOs, define the DNA of the company and shape the character and culture of the entire organization (Garbett 1988; Hutton et al. 2001). Senior leaders are expected to be adept, conceptual, and strategic thinkers. A very important element of senior-leadership communication is *strategic vision communication*. By painting a compelling vision of a dream for the future (e.g., where are we going and what we stand for), senior leaders build a strong sense of shared purpose among employees (Sriram 2014).

Vision Communication

Numerous studies have supported the critical role of senior leaders' strategic vision communication in attaining organizational success (e.g., Avery 2005; Kantabutra 2008). A clearly articulated and well-communicated strategic vision of an organization unites and motivates employees and improves their work lives (Mayfield, Mayfield, and Sharbrough III 2015). It also transmits key organizational values to enhance external stakeholder understanding (Porter 1996). According to Westley and Mintzberg (1989), senior-leader vision comprises three parts: a sought-after future state, mental imagery well-articulated through extensive communication, and a model containing processes that enable followers to achieve the vision. A good vision structure (or content) should exhibit the attributes of "brevity, clarity, abstractness, challenge, future orientation, stability, and desirability or ability to inspire" (Baum, Locke, and Kirkpatrick 1998, 44).

Mayfield, Mayfield, and Sharbrough III (2015) extended motivating language theory and provided more detailed suggestions on how top leaders can develop and communicate a strategic vision to improve organizational performance. Specifically, meaning-making language that expresses shared organizational values, cultural norms, mental models, and visions for positive changes can enhance senior leaders' strategic vision communication; an example of which is Facebook's vision "To make the world more open and connected" (Mayfield, Mayfield, and Sharbrough III 2015). Furthermore, direction-giving language that dispels ambiguity and explicates organizational goals and objectives can enhance the vision and mission communication of top leaders; an example of which is the vision of Cytokinetics, which is "… to discover and develop mechanism medicines to make a meaningful difference in the lives of patients suffering from dreadful diseases" (Mayfield, Mayfield, and Sharbrough III 2015). An empathetic language that manifests organizational sensitivity to both internal and external publics can also enhance senior leaders' vision communication: President Emeritus Colleen Barrett of Southwest Airlines Co. stated, "Our internal mission is to always practice the golden rule. Treat others the way you want to be treated. Going with that is a respect for people. You don't judge" (p. 111).

The strategic visions and values communicated by senior leaders need to be diffused throughout their respective organizations. In achieving this goal, both leaders and internal communication professionals play important roles. The best leaders know that they need to publicize, interpret, and discuss visions and values over and over in a consistent way (Sriram 2014) at every opportunity; to act as role models; and to reward those who remember, understand, and practice the principles they have communicated. Both leaders and communication professionals need to use rhetorical skills to tell inspiring stories that illustrate the mission, culture, and values of their respective organizations. They also need to reinforce the desired behavior by creating legends, repeating anecdotes, and rewarding employees who demonstrate the desired behavior.

Senior leadership must consider diverse stakeholder groups when addressing vision communication. Senior leaders often need to balance the needs of multiple constituents who bring competing perspectives and needs to the table (Sriram 2014). Successfully leading conversations and resolving conflicts are important communication qualities of senior leaders.

Senior-Leader Communication Styles

Leaders may use different styles to effectively communicate with different people on different topics and at different times. Communication style (i.e., socio-communicative style) refers to the different skills individuals use in initiating, adapting to, and responding to interpersonal communication situations (Thomas, Richmond, and McCroskey 1994). Communication styles are divided into two broad categories: assertive and responsive (Thomas, Richmond, and McCroskey 1994). *Assertive leadership communication* focuses on the task dimension of relationships. Leaders act assertively to speak up for themselves, whether to make a request or express a feeling. Words that are commonly used to describe an assertive communicator include *dominant, forceful, aggressive,* and *competitive.* These assertive characteristics are often considered masculine qualities. Conversely, *responsive leadership communication* focuses on the relational dimension of relationships. A responsive leader is a good listener and someone who is responsive, empathetic, compassionate, understanding, friendly, warm, sincere, and interested. These qualities are often considered feminine (Porter, Wrench, and Hoskinson 2007). Senior leaders (i.e., CEOs) who demonstrate responsive communication characteristics are more likely to be perceived as better communicators (Men 2015a). Both the responsive and assertive communication qualities of senior leaders enhance the employee–organization relationship; however, the responsive senior-leader communication style plays a more important role in generating employees' trust, satisfaction, commitment, and feeling of shared control than the assertive senior-leader communication style (Men 2015a). In other words, CEOs' task-oriented, aggressive, forceful, and dominant communication may position them as a strong leader, being agreeable, responsive, and sensitive to the needs of employees, and recognizing the voice and contributions of employees lead to positive employee attitudinal and relational outcomes.

Senior-Leader Communication Channels

Traditionally, senior leaders communicate with employees most frequently through interpersonal channels, such as "management by walking around" and one-on-one meetings, followed by internal publications, group meetings, speeches, memos, and phone calls (Pincus, Rayfield, and Cozzens 1991). The communication landscape of organizations has considerably evolved over the past decades. Although traditional face-to-face channels and print media are still commonly used, recent studies have shown that electronic platforms, such as streaming media (videos/audios), blogs, and social networking sites, have become popular among CEOs (Men 2015a; Weber Shandwick Inc., 2014).

Face-to-face channels. The media richness theory (Daft and Lengel 1984, 1986) suggests that different media options vary along a media richness continuum based on four characteristics: immediacy of feedback or interactivity, the use of verbal and nonverbal cues, natural language (i.e., conversational style), and personal focus (i.e., direct messages to specific individual's ability). Face-to-face communication is the richest type of medium that can communicate complex information; it facilitates instant feedback, uses nonverbal cues, and directs messages to specific receivers.

Senior leaders can use formal and informal channels to communicate with employees. The informal "open-door" policy and management by walking around are practiced by many CEOs. Informal gatherings, such as Google's TGIF (Thank God It's Friday) and Cisco's Birthday Chat, are also welcomed by employees. CEO Chambers led the Birthday Chat every other month. The event, designed for employees' birthdays in the relevant two-month period, aside from its entertainment merit, it was actually an informal Q&A session, intended to stimulate candid discussions and help management understand what employees were thinking. Cisco's Birthday Chat proved a great success. Originally developed as a small gathering of dozens of attendants, the event is now conducted on video via satellite with hundreds of employees from around the world participating (Groysberg and Slind 2011). Nevertheless, face-to-face communication does not always work, often due to geographical limitations. This is when other electronic and digital forms of communication come into play.

Videos. Videos are game changers in internal communication. Senior leaders can use video technologies in many ways: delivering a speech or discussing the company's vision, mission, values, and strategies through the corporate TV or on-demand videos; hosting videoconferences with remote workers; making an announcement; celebrating milestones or employee achievements through streaming videos; and incorporating personalized video messages on social media platforms, such as blog sites and social networking sites. "Being able to see makes all the difference" (Groysberg and Slind 2011, 97). Visuals add a human element to an otherwise detached and bureaucratic exchange of information. Videos put a face on a leadership title, and thus personalize senior-leadership communication.

Social media. Social media platforms have increasingly become an indispensable component of corporate communication, prompting a growing number of CEOs to embrace it and incorporate platforms, such as Facebook, Twitter, LinkedIn, YouTube, and blogs, into their communication efforts to engage stakeholders. CEOs who maintain strong social media presence are more likely to be perceived as responsive communicators by employees. Social CEOs are perceived as better communicators. Internal stakeholders also create positive associations between the CEO's social media competence and the organization (Men 2015a). In 2014, the Edelman *Trust Barometer* initially used the term "Chief Engagement Officer" to highlight CEOs' communication role in the social media era. Particularly, the interactive, empowering, and relational features of social media can bring CEOs to life, narrow the gap between senior leaders and stakeholders, and blur communication hierarchies. The decentralized form of communication and communal orientation allow CEOs to be "one of the crowd" and foster dialogs and two-way information flow between senior management and stakeholders. For instance, on blog or social networking sites, senior leaders can personify themselves and talk in a friendly, authentic, and informal manner. This social media feature, *user-generated content,* encourages internal stakeholders to articulate opinions and concerns and voice alternative views, engaging in direct conversations with the senior management.

Many CEOs and senior managers are regarded as leaders not only in their companies, but also in their respective industries; thus, CEO or executive bloggers can also influence the opinions, attitudes, and actions of internal and external stakeholders through leveraging their social capital (Vidgen, Sims, and Powell 2013). Early in 2004, Sun Microsystems CEO, Jonathan Schwartz, began writing a blog that was visible not only to Sun employees, but also to the external stakeholders; he explained his rationale as, "It's basically an online journal—a whitespace … into which I can offer perspectives, opinions, and insights, and I can link to others and their views, and so on. Others can link to me and send me feedback, creating a massively connected community and open dialog …" (Barker 2008, 6).

Blogging has become a common practice among CEOs to build thought leadership and to stay connected with stakeholders. Many add pictures, videos, and all types of messages to their blog posts. For instance, Cisco's Chambers maintained a video blog entitled "On My Mind." The two to five minute video message was sent via an e-mail link. The blog included a comment function, where Chambers said, "I've told you what's on my mind. Now you tell me what's on your mind." He also encouraged employees to interact with his video posts by posting their own videos.

Using visual storytelling, CEOs can demonstrate genuineness. Employees consider visual storytelling not as corporate speak or a ghost-written message, but as an authentic message from the CEO. Instances of CEOs using social networking sites abound. According to the recent study by Weber Shandwick, Inc. (2014), 80 percent of the CEOs from the world's Fortune 50 companies are social. The number has surged by 122 percent since 2010. CEOs use a variety of social platforms, such as LinkedIn, Twitter, Google+, and Facebook, to engage employees and external stakeholders.

In a nutshell, today's senior management needs to recognize that their job is not only to develop strategies, but also to talk about such strategies through effective communication channels that reach their internal stakeholders. Senior leaders must ensure that everyone in the company understands what is going on, where they are going, why they are going there, and how they are going to get there. Senior leaders need to be open-minded and forward-thinking. They should embrace new trends and technologies, directly engage with stakeholders by talking "with" instead of talking "to" them, thus building long-lasting relationships.

Supervisory Leadership Communication

In management communication, a considerable number of studies have been devoted to exploring supervisory leadership communication and the relationship between leaders and followers. Supervisors interact and communicate with employees on a daily basis; thus, supervisor communication competence, style, channels, and effectiveness influence employees' attitudes, emotions, behaviors, and performances. For instance, at the individual (micro) level, supervisors' use of a motivating language directly influences employee self-efficacy and performance (Mayfield and Mayfield 2012). Specifically, Mayfield and Mayfield (2012) showed that, with an increased use of a motivating language by a leader, employee self-efficacy was 34 percent higher and employee performance increased by 20 percent. Madlock (2008) found strong positive associations between supervisors' communication competence and employees' communication and job satisfaction; more specifically, supervisors' communication competence accounted for 68 percent of the change in employees' communication satisfaction and 18 percent of the change in job satisfaction. Likewise, Vogelgesang, Leroy, and Avolio (2013) study revealed that supervisors' transparent communication led to employees' perception of the supervisors' behavioral integrity, which in turn improved employees' work engagement. The communication effectiveness of supervisors is a strong predictor of leader performance and also acts as a mediator of leadership behavior on performance (Neufeld, Wan, and Fang 2010).

At the organizational (macro) level, supervisors' leadership behavior and communication are parts of an organization's internal communication system and provide a context for the interaction between employees and the organization. Specifically, Men (2014a, 2014b, 2014c, 2015b) showed that leadership style and leader communication channels influenced employees' relationship with the organization, perception of internal reputation, and engagement.

Leadership Styles

Among various leadership styles, transformational, authentic, servant, and ethical leadership help organizations nurture a two-way symmetrical (balanced) and transparent communication climate, which in turn leads to various positive employee outcomes.

Transformational leadership. Transformational leadership is different from the influence exerted by bureaucratic authorities or influence emphasizing legitimate power, rules, and standards. Transformational leaders seek to motivate followers by appealing to their high-level needs, ideals, and moral values—such as justice, equality, peace, liberty, and humanitarianism (Burns 1978). Through visionary communication, transformational leaders improve followers' awareness of the importance and value of accomplishing tasks and achieving shared objectives, and consequently encourage their followers to transcend self-interests for the greater good of the organization or the group (Bass 1985; Men 2014a).

Transformational leaders lead by being role models and exhibiting a genuine interest in the well-being of their stakeholders, show individual consideration, and foster a climate of trust. To that end, transformational leaders often engage in close interactions with them to listen and understand their needs. Such leadership also integrates elements of empathy, compassion, sensitivity, and relationship building to create an emotional attachment between the leader and follower (Jin 2010). To motivate them to step up to higher ground, transformational leaders often have high expectations for their followers, stimulate their followers to think outside the box, and encourage their followers challenge old ways in their work. Additionally, transformational leaders delegate powers to their followers, provide their followers sufficient decision-making authority, and empower their followers in their work. In summary, transformational leadership communication is relationship-oriented, interactive, visionary, passionate, caring, and empowering (Hackman and Johnson 2004; Men and Stacks 2013).

Authentic leadership. The concept of authentic leadership can be traced to the recent upswing in highly publicized corporate scandals and management malfeasance (Walumbwa et al. 2008). As a new type of genuine and value-based leadership, authentic leadership aims to develop leaders who proactively foster positive environments and conduct business in an ethical and socially responsible manner (Cooper, Scandura, and Schriesheim 2005). Authentic leaders are deeply aware of their values and beliefs and demonstrate a passion for purpose. They know who they are, what they believe, and stay true to themselves. Guided by internalized moral values, such as honesty, altruism, kindness, fairness, accountability, and optimism (Yukl 2006), authentic leaders act according to the dictates of their conscience instead of group, organizational, and societal pressures to please others (Ilies, Morgeson, and Nahrgang 2005; Walumbwa et al. 2008). They practice these values with consistency. Authentic leaders also advocate transparent communication in their relationships with followers. They openly share actual thoughts, feelings, and genuinely present themselves. Moreover, authentic leaders listen to different views, including those which may challenge their deeply held positions to maintain a balanced and democratic decision-making process. Authentic leadership communication is, thus, characterized by values of integrity, genuineness, consistency, transparency, and relationship orientation.

Ethical leadership. Although both transformational leadership and authentic leadership include some ethical elements, none of these leadership styles by themselves constitutes ethical leadership (Brown, Treviño, and Harrison 2005; Men 2015b). Kalshoven, Den Hartog, and De Hoogh (2011) defined seven ethical leadership dimensions, namely fair treatment, power sharing, role clarification, people orientation, integrity, ethical guidance, and concern for sustainability. Ethical leaders act with integrity and treat stakeholders fairly without favoritism. They involve employees in the decision-making process and engage in an open communication with them to clarify job expectations, requirements, and responsibilities.

Servant leadership is one ethical leadership approach in which leaders sees themselves as the facilitator of success for others—a servant of their interests and of organizational interests. Servant leaders see themselves as pillars of support at the base of organizational hierarchy, when, in fact, they may have lofty titles and great authority. It is an excellent way of furthering organizational success while facilitating open internal communication. Home Depot is one organization that uses a servant leadership style, visioning the CEO at the bottom of an inverted pyramid structure (Bowen, Rawlins, and Martin 2010, 146) (Figure 4.1).

Ethical leaders demonstrate a people orientation and genuinely care and support their followers to meet their needs, serving the success of others and their organizations. They communicate about ethics, explain ethical rules, and promote and reward ethical conduct among stakeholders. Ethical leadership also shows concern for sustainability. Ethical leaders consider the effects of their actions beyond their self-interest and the scope of the organization; they care about the environment and the welfare of the society at large. Overall, ethical leadership communication

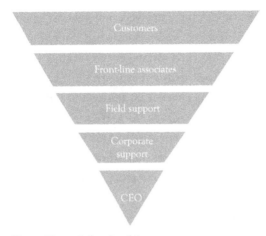

Figure 4.1 Home Depot's leadership structure

Source: Home Depot (2009), used with permission)

is fair, ethical, empowering, people-oriented, ethics-related, and environmentally conscious.

Leadership Styles and Internal Communication

Although transformational, authentic, and ethical leadership share some commonalities with respect to possessing high moral standards and people orientation, they emphasize different leadership behaviors. All these leadership styles are effective in developing a stakeholder-centered, two-way, empowering, symmetrical, and transparent organizational communication system (Men 2014a; Men and Stacks 2014). When employees are managed by visionary, empowering, and people-oriented transformational leaders; transparent, genuine, and consistent authentic leaders; or ethical leaders, they are more likely to perceive macro-level organizational communication as open, two-way, responsive, understanding, reciprocal, collaborative, and directed toward exhibiting genuine interest in their needs and concerns.

Different leadership styles are associated with different leadership *communication* styles. In the 1980s, leadership scholars (e.g., Penley and Hawkins 1985) concluded that human-oriented leadership corresponds more to communicative than task-oriented leadership: it emphasizes the relational aspect of treating employees and exhibits interpersonal consideration and warmth, whereas task-oriented leadership focuses on the content of information. Later, Awamleh and Gardner (1999) found that leaders' *delivery style* (particularly if expressive or enthusiastic) had more effect on perceptions of charismatic leadership and effectiveness than speech content. More recently, de Vries, Bakker-Pieper, and Oostenveld (2010) found that human-oriented leadership was strongly associated with the communication style of supportiveness. Transformational leaders have also been found to be communicative (Hackman and Johnson 2004); to better connect with followers, they often use information-rich channels—face-to-face channels or social media tools—to communicate with their followers (Men 2014b).

Indeed, *good leadership cannot be practiced without effective communication*. In other words, the act of leadership is intrinsically tied to the act of communication. Being a strong communicator may not make a person an effective leader; however, effective leaders are strong communicators.

Best Practices of Leadership Communication

Developing internal excellence and the best practices of leadership communication requires collaborative efforts between communication professionals and leaders. The following research-informed principles help organizational leaders communicate more effectively and become better leaders.

Organizational and internal communication professionals should

1. Provide necessary trainings to leaders at various levels in the organization to develop effective transformational, authentic, and ethical leadership styles, as well as equip leaders with strong communication competence, skills, and technological competencies in using emerging communication tools.
2. Engage leaders across all levels in the organization's overall communication efforts and groom leaders to become internal ambassadors.
3. Recruit and promote leaders who can communicate well and build relationships.

4. Act as the strategic counselors to senior management and offer communication insights and strategic views about the thoughts and the expectations of stakeholders from their senior leaders; thus, internal communication professionals need to be organizational strategists with business acumen and communication specialists and experts. (Knowing the organization inside/out can improve the credibility of communication professionals in offering advice to the senior management.)

5. Educate CEOs on how to have a public relations mindset; assist CEOs in developing an effective communication style that matches their personality, character, and the organization's values; and help CEOs decide *what* (i.e., the content), *how* (i.e., the channels), and *when* (i.e., the timing) to communicate with stakeholders.

6. Demonstrate the value of internal communication through appropriate measures and matrices and help leaders understand the links of effective communication with business performance and with personal, departmental, and organizational objectives.

Senior leaders should

1. Develop an open, responsive, dialogic, transparent, authentic, and empowering communication mindset.

2. Identify core ethical values of the organization and align those with the corporate vision, mission, and social responsibility; use those core values in both organizational culture and ethical decision-making.

3. Communicate and interpret the organization's vision, act as role models, and align their words and actions, corporate strategies, policies, and business objectives with the company's culture and values.

4. Be good listeners demonstrating empathy, compassion, understanding, friendliness, warmth, and sincerity when communicating, and genuine interest in employees' thoughts, personal goals, and needs.

5. Be open-minded and flexible to changes and use information-rich channels (e.g., face-to-face meetings and management by walking around; videos; and social media platforms) to proactively initiate conversations with stakeholders and communicate in an authentic and personal manner to build relationships.

6. Create an inclusive culture and an open-communication climate, seek and value inputs and voices, and create opportunities for decision-making participation.
7. Be supportive of the communication functions, empower the public relations department, and provide resources and support for communication and employee relations.
8. Work to demonstrate ethical behavior, showing a servant leader approach that facilitates the success of others.
9. Act as ethical leaders and conduct ethical analyses based on moral principles.
10. Make communication competence important in senior management hiring and incorporate communication effectiveness and relationship building as important components of executive performance evaluation.

Supervisors should

1. Be good interpreters and messengers, accurately understanding information from the senior management (including corporate vision, mission, and values) for followers, and giving clear directions and expectations to followers.
2. Listen to followers with a genuine concern for their welfare and needs and value their input. When followers feel they are being heard, they feel valued and encouraged to contribute ideas and be more willing to accommodate the leader's position. Identify and develop a new feedback channel and systems that can be trusted by employees, without fear of reprisals or punishments in reporting issues or problems of managers (Burton 2016).
3. Vary communication tone and style to suit the occasion and the desired outcome. (For example, a responsive, sincere, friendly, empathetic, and understanding communication style should be demonstrated during relationship building, and an assertive, strong, dominant, and competitive style should be adopted when making decisions.)
4. Recognize and understand their own emotions, know their communication strengths and weaknesses, and undergo trainings to develop essential communication skills.

5. Use face-to-face interactions as a primary mode to communicate with followers, talk "with" instead of talk "to" them, and provide regular and timely feedback.

6. Utilize new technological tools, such as social messaging applications and social networking sites, to connect and engage with digitally savvy followers.

7. Be fair in treatment of followers and involve them in the decision-making process.

8. Show servant leadership through individual consideration, care, support, and respect to followers. Treat followers as a whole person instead of a worker; care about followers' individual development.

9. Act as role models, give ethical guidelines, and demonstrate social and ethical responsibility.

10. Be transparent in the decision-making and communication processes, be consistent in communications and actions, and be accountable for what is said and done.

Developing effective leadership communication skills and building quality relationships between leaders and employees require time and commitment. Given the relationships of leadership communication with internal stakeholder outcomes and organizational performance, any organization that wants to succeed and continue to succeed must strive for effective leadership communication (Whitworth 2011). Being intimate in spirit, interactive in style, and inclusive in structure (Groysberg and Slind 2011), effective leadership communication can be achieved with the support and collaboration of leaders and communication managers.

Summary

Leadership communication is a major component of the organization's internal communication system. As a nested form of influence prevalent in the organization, leadership is intertwined with communication in many ways. Senior leadership sets the tone for internal communication and shapes the organization's reputation in the eyes of internal and external stakeholders. Supervisors interact with employees on a day-to-day basis and influence how employees think or feel in the organization.

This chapter discussed two essential aspects of leadership communication, senior leadership communication and supervisory leadership communication. For senior leadership communication, an important aspect is visionary communication—painting a compelling vision or dream of the future and building a strong sense of shared purpose among employees. Senior leaders' communication style and channels matter for communication effectiveness. Responsive communication style leaders are perceived as better communicators. Senior leaders use of information-rich channels, such as face-to-face communication and social media platforms help foster conversations and dialogs, facilitates listening, and reduces the power-distance between senior management and employees. Use of videos in senior leadership communication shows the CEO's face and personalizes senior leaders' communication.

Supervisors' communication competence and effectiveness influence many aspects of employees' attitudes, affections, behavior, and performance. Supervisors' leadership style and leader communication channels influence employee relationships with the organization, their perception of internal reputation, and engagement. Supervisors' transformational, authentic, ethical, and servant leadership behaviors help organizations nurture a two-way symmetrical open and transparent communication climate, which leads to positive employee outcomes. This chapter summarized a list of research-informed principles that should help all levels of organizational leaders communicate more effectively and become better leaders.

CHAPTER 5

Reaching Your Internal Stakeholders

Traditional and New Media Channels

Messages must pass through certain channels to reach the target audience. Over the past decades, the landscape of organization's communication has significantly changed with the evolution of new technology. Companies today possess a wide range of communication channels to reach and engage their stakeholders, ranging from traditional face-to-face communication (e.g., employee meetings), print publications (e.g., newsletters, magazines, and posters), to electronic media (e.g., phone calls, e-mails, teleconference) and social tools (such as intranet, blogs, instant messengers, and social networking sites [SNSs]). These channels vary in richness, formality, sociability, cost of production, easiness of control, ability in carrying messages, and more (Clampitt 2001; Gillis 2006).

For instance, organizational newsletters, magazines, brochures, posters, broadcast video or audio programs, and websites are controlled or *formal media* where the content and distribution are dictated by the company. Blogs, discussion forums, microblogs, and SNSs are less controlled and *informal channels* as employees can contribute to the content and engage in conversations. Daft and Lengel (1984, 1986) suggested that channel options fall along a richness continuum based on four characteristics:

1. immediacy of feedback or interactivity,
2. the use of verbal and nonverbal cues,
3. natural language (i.e., the ability to communicate in a conversational style), and
4. personal focus (i.e., the ability to direct the message to a specific individual).

In this sense, face-to-face communication is the richest channel because it facilitates immediate feedback, the use of natural language and multiple cues, and personal focus. Internal publications such as annual reports and posters are "lean" and impersonal forms of media channels, whereas e-mails and phone calls fall somewhere in the middle (Daft and Lengel 1984; Men 2014b).

Choice of channel or medium is important. "The medium is the message" (McLuhan 1964). Each medium engages audiences in different ways, affects the scale and pace of communication, and serves various purposes. Although new technological tools, such as social media, have been increasingly embraced by more and more organizations and have been found effective in building internal communities and engaging employees, old channels do not die; instead, they evolve, exist in new forms, and find new niches in the organization. This chapter discusses the extant corporate communication channels in today's ever-changing business landscape regarding their characteristics and specific functions. It provides a list of criteria companies and leaders can utilize to effectively select the appropriate channel for the right messages and stakeholder to achieve communication objectives.

Face-to-Face Channels

Research has consistently shown that face-to-face communication is the most preferred and trusted communication channel by employee stake-holders (Burton 2016; Clampitt 2001; Men 2014). Individual, group, or town hall meetings with CEOs have two-way, interactive, and transparent merit, giving employees the opportunities to engage in conversations, ask questions for clarity, and personally evaluate the credibility and completeness of organizational messages (Gillis 2006). Further, face-to-face communication provides audiences a wide variety of cues, such as visual images, body language, vocal tone, office décor, and even smell. Access to such signals allows employees to "sense subtle distinctions necessary to understand complex issues" (Clampitt 2001, 109).

Likewise, from the managers' perspective, face-to-face communication is the most dynamic medium as it allows emotions and feelings through facial expressions, gestures, and eye contact. Thus, a manager can feel whether employees are satisfied, happy, angry, cooperative, or resistant to the message or decision (Trevino, Daft, and Lengel 1990). Few other channels allow sending and receiving cognitively complex messages of such an interpersonal nature (Clampitt 2001). Furthermore, the element of interactivity and being personal reinforces intimacy: organizational efforts to become closer to, listen to, and display trust in employees (Groysberg and Slind 2011). Gillis (2006) noted that unit meetings with managers and visits by executive management are the most trusted and preferred means for internal stakeholders to learn about their roles in the organization.

However, similar to other channels, face-to-face communication does not come without limitations. When large, geographically dispersed audiences are involved, face-to-face communication becomes challenging. It is also more time-consuming to conduct face-to-face meetings. While it has merit in conveying complex information, knowledge sharing, and relationship building, simple information dissemination may be better through other channels, such as print publications and electronic media.

Print Publications

Print publications, encompassing newsletters, magazines, brochures, policy documents, posters, and memos, have been the chief media of communication for companies over decades. These media give organizations full control over message content and are predominantly used as a formal way to keep employees informed. The print media flow of information is mainly one-way, that is "pushed" from organizations to employees. With a lack of immediacy and sociability, print publications are arguably best at delivering information that is static and not time-sensitive. Keith Burton, Principal of Grayson Emmett Partners, recognized several benefits of print publications for employee communication. First, employees as "brand ambassadors" want tangible communications they can hold and read at their leisure. Second, print publications come with a utility that can go beyond employees to other audiences like contract professionals, vendors, and community members. Third, one can simply not overlook the importance of having a publication or newsletter that can be shared with spouses and dependents to extend good feelings for the corporate brand among family members (Burton 2016).

Typical objectives of internal stakeholder publications include increasing employee understanding and support for the organization's goals, plans, strategies, and activities; recognizing employees' accomplishment, developing employee morale, and building a sense of identification and community; and educating employees about specific organizational or task operations (Gillis 2006). Concurrently, researchers have found that the most commonly published articles in employee publications include those on employee recognition, company awards, personnel changes or promotions, benefit programs, department recognition, company policies, and the organization's community involvement. Other content includes companies' social functions, company-sponsored sports activities, future plans, safety, promoting goodwill between management and employees, financial results, and questions and answers (Clampitt 2001).

Internal publications such as employee handbook, policy documents, and orientation materials are *formal* channels. These materials are often designed to be read, saved as archives and references, or used as supplemental for face-to-face communication. Constructing them in a user-friendly manner is a key consideration because information overload is a major complaint in these formal publications. Magazines and newsletters are more dynamic than policy documents. Other than focusing on company policies and business news, newsletters and magazines could include more human-interest and authentic stories from employees (Gillis 2006). As these channels go digital, opportunities increase to construct two-way internal newsletters and magazines (e.g., inserting an employee poll or survey in a newsletter) to solicit feedback from and encourage employee participation and involvement.

Electronic Media

Broadcast and audiovisual media can be used to provide informational and educational materials to internal stakeholders. For instance, some organizations have live and recorded broadcast of presentations by executives or teleconferences. A message delivered through video channels is more expressive, empathy-driven, and impactful than those conveyed through traditional print media or e-mail. Visual storytelling, thus, has become a more and more central capability for organization's internal and external communication (Groysberg and Slind 2011). *Video conferencing* also has the ability to overcome geographical barriers and bring physically dispersed employees together, even though the technology has not been developed sufficiently to make it an entirely credible alternative for face-to-face communication.

Despite a wide range of channel options, *e-mail* has been found to be among the most preferred mediums by employees to receive information from the organization regarding new decisions, policies, events, or changes and to communicate with leaders and peers (Men 2014). On the one hand, e-mail can reach a widely spread target audience simultaneously in an easy and quick way. On the other hand, the reviewability of e-mails allows each participant in the conversation to have a record of others' comments and its revisability provides an option for message senders to double-check and correct a message before sending, which is unavailable with verbal communication (Lipiäinen, Karjaluoto, and Nevalainen 2014). However, despite these merits of e-mails, some argue that the ability to distribute messages quickly and easily may lead to information overload and an over-reliance on such channels at the expense of face-to-face communications (Hewitt 2006). In addition, as a relatively "lean" type of medium with the absence of visual cues, facial expressions, and body languages, e-mail may not be ideal for communicating emotional-loaded or complex information. However, with e-mail as an indispensable tool in employees' daily communication in today's workplace, organizations should consider how to harness it to get intended messages across to internal stakeholders in an efficient manner without flooding employees' inboxes. Technology such as artificial intelligence may change these channels, as we discuss in Chapter 10.

New Media Channels

The advent of social media has greatly changed the dynamic of internal communication. In a sense, social media allows internal stakeholders to engage in conversations across hierarchical levels, functional units, and geographical locations. On the one hand, the two-way nature of social media tools, such as blogs and SNSs, could facilitate upward and horizontal communication among them. Meanwhile, the libertine spirit of social media with its user-generated content encourages employees to articulate their opinions and concerns; share alternative views; and foster a culture of learning, participation, and collaboration (Men and Hung-Baesecke 2015). The concepts of "conversation," "interactions," and "dialogs," which are essential for successful internal communication, are made possible in the social media era. In addition, because of its feature of being a personal medium, social media allows executives to be perceived as real persons and build human bond and deep connections with lower-level stakeholders, yielding a reduced power distance that helps empower and democratize the workplace (Men and Tsai 2014). To date, numerous studies have demonstrated the value of new technological tools, such as intranet, blogs, SNSs, and instant messengers, for effective internal communications, community building, and engagement. While many organizations may only selectively adopt certain aspects of the tools and features available, the growing incorporation of social media in organizations has greatly reshaped the communication landscape of organizations today (Huang, Baptista, and Galliers 2012).

Intranet

An internal network, or intranet, should be built as a place where internal stakeholders can experience the organization at any given point. As a way of formal online communication, it is often used for strategic purposes such as to reinforce key corporate values, policies, strategies, and culture. In its initial manifestation, most intranets are designed as a repository of data, including internal documents, corporate news, newsletters, and annual reports. To compete for employees' time and attention, organizations often use tactics such as including not only "corporate" content, but also fun, entertaining, relevant, and engaging stories on the site; using a blend of articles, photos, and video features; and incorporating the latest business, technology, industry, and world news to capture employee interest (Groysberg and Slind 2011). Many organizations' intranet sites evolve into an internal news service. Some companies try to design features that let employees directly engage with the content. For instance, an option can be added on an intranet news article that users can comment on, share it via e-mail or social media, express opinions, or rate it on a scale of greater or less appeal or interest. With this rating scheme, stakeholders can see "highly rated," "five-star," "most viewed," or "most commented" stories. Companies can also display live intranet tweets by connecting a social media site to "the hub." Overall, intranet serves as an important portal and home base for employees and others to obtain information and communicate with one another. Although it is fundamentally a one-way medium, if designed properly with some interactive features paired with relevant, important, and interesting updates that meet employees' information need, the intranet plays a crucial role for the organization's successful internal communication (Lipiäinen, Karjaluoto, and Nevalainen 2014).

Push and Pull Social Media

Equipped with social thinking, many companies today use interactive tool, such as blogs, instant messengers, and social networking services (SNSs), to replace the traditionally pure "push" communication with a dialogical mode of communication with the "push-and-pull" dynamics. With its commenting feature, blogs allow employees to directly engage in the conversation with management and peers; ask questions, share ideas, thoughts, and experiences; broadcast their knowledge and expertise; and nurture a sense of community. In fact, Friedl and Verčič (2011) found that blogs were among the most preferred social channels by employees for internal communication. Given that knowledge published on an internal blog stays there, it allows the creation of a searchable, permanent archive of expertise, which fosters corporate "social" learning. Additionally, blogs that CEOs and senior managers maintain allow leaders to establish internal thought leadership, and in the meantime, give stakeholders the opportunities to gain a level of familiarity with executives, which fuels relationships and trust. Employees generally value leaders' authentic voice conveyed through the leadership blogs. Richard Edelman, President and CEO of Edelman public relations, has done a remarkable job maintaining his blog, *6 a.m.* (http://www.edelman.com/conversations/6-a-m/). John Swanson, as CEO of Computer Associates, made it his personal mission to blog after every town hall meeting and location tour, as he traveled throughout the world during an aggressive change effort (Burton 2016). As pointed out by Groysberg and Slind (2011), blog platforms engage employees at a more creative and introspective level; and blogs help promote open discussion and collaboration when they are made two-way and more transparent. A sense of community and engagement can be nurtured over time.

Social Networking Sites

The core purpose of deploying social tools for many organizations is to "come as close as you can to a person-to-person experience" (Groysberg and Slind 2011, 78). In the past years, internal SNSs, such as Yammer or Chatter, perhaps the most interactive, personal, participatory, and engaging digital tools, have been increasingly used by corporations to communicate with internal stakeholders, facilitate two-way conversations, gather ideas and feedback, build internal communities, and foster engagement. Recent research shows that the more organizations use SNSs in internal communication; the more likely they are perceived as being transparent and authentic, the more likely an engaged workforce will be built (Men and Hung 2015). Employees in general agree on the many benefits of the organizations' internal use of SNSs, such as allowing them to make connections easily with peers across units, seek for job- or corporate-related information, manage personal identity, instill a sense of empowerment and community, make their work more entertaining and enjoyable, and generate social capital (Men and Hung 2015). Simply, when employees are encouraged to participate in the company's SNS communication, the communal environment empowers employees to join the conversation, provide feedback and comments, and voluntarily share information. The democratic and interpersonal atmosphere formulated on SNSs is conducive for meaningful engagement and relationship-building among internal stakeholders over time.

It is generally agreed that the visibility and persistence of communication afforded by internal SNS use provide new and enhanced opportunities for social learning within organizations (Leonardi, Huysman, and Steinfield 2013). Take GE's internal social network—Support Central—as an example. Support Central allows employees across global business units to connect, chat, share information, and document business processes. The network has over 100,000 internal experts answering questions from over 50,000 communities created. The company also devised "Pinholes" on the network, where specific areas of the communities are open to customers, vendors, suppliers, and business partners to collaborate on specific projects (Naslund 2010). Such collaborative efforts create an ever-growing knowledge base and provide important opportunities for internal training and orientation programs, continuing education initiatives, and inspirations for employees to do their job more creatively, thoroughly, and effectively. Naslund notes, "giving employees opportunities to gather around common interest online and outside the bounds of physical locations can unlock great human potential" (p. 37). Small ideas may stimulate groundbreaking innovations. An innovative and learning organization can be formed through fostering open discussion, sharing and building on ideas in a collaborative format, identifying thought leadership and talents in the "backyard," and promoting people-to-people connections, enhanced and enabled by technology.

Beyond all the aforementioned benefits, internal SNSs can also be used by senior management to deepen their connections with employees. Holding a senior leader position, CEOs are often perceived as being intimidating and distant from employees. SNS tools with two-way, interactive, communal, personal, and relational features allow senior leaders to listen, respond in a timely manner, communicate in a genuine and personal fashion, and facilitate employee-upward communication. In this way, the communication hierarchy within the organization can be blurred, the power distance can be shortened, and senior management is brought into employees' everyday life.

According to a recent survey conducted by Weber Shandwick (2013), a CEOs' social media presence can provide a company with a human face or personality, demonstrate innovation, and provide a direct opportunity to interact with the CEO. Moreover, CEO sociability can instill positive employee feelings, such as feeling inspired, technologically advanced, and proud. Likewise, through a survey of 545 employees working in medium- and large-sized corporations in the United States (Men 2015a), it has been found that a CEO's social media presence is strongly related to employee perception of CEO communication quality and employee relational outcomes. Specifically, CEOs who maintain a stronger social media presence are more likely to be perceived as responsive communicators who are sincere, friendly, agreeable, compassionate, understanding, and willing to listen. Social CEOs are also perceived as better communicators, and such positive perception can be transferred to positive employee attitudes toward the organization (Men 2015a).

Social Messengers

Most recently, mobile technologies, especially social messaging apps, have bloomed. According to a recent study released by *Business Insider*, as of March 2015, the top four messaging apps combined (i.e., WeChat, WhatsApp, Facebook Messenger, Viber) have the same number of users as the top four social networks (i.e., Facebook, Twitter, LinkedIn, and Instagram)—2.125 billion. With the advancement of Internet connections and popularity of smartphones worldwide, social messaging is likely to surpass SNSs and become the new face of social media in near future.

Social messaging is a mobile-based instant messaging (IM) client that is built around social networking platforms and allows for features such as text or audio chat, group chat, video calls, message notification, status update, and media sharing (Wu 2014). Examples include WeChat (China), WhatsApp, Line (Japan), Viber, Facebook Messenger, and KaKao Talk (Korea). Social messaging is different from traditional IM as it does not require a computer and runs on iOS and Android smartphone devices (Lien and Cao 2014). Social messaging is also different from SNSs, such as Facebook and Twitter, in that it is primarily one-to-one (or few) communication where content is intended to be private or directed toward a specific group, whereas SNSs consist of "many-to-many" connections (IPG Media Lab 2014). Because of the intimacy and privacy that social messaging offers (Wu 2014), content shared on social messaging apps tends to be perceived as more credible and trustworthy. It, thus, offers an unparalleled tool for companies to personalize their targeted communication and build close and strong one-on-one connection with internal stakeholders. Especially for companies dominated by millennial workers, social messaging is a must-have as they are its mainstream users, leading the growth of social messaging apps (IPG Media Lab 2014).

Similar to traditional computer-based IM in the workplace, social messengers, such as Slack, are less intrusive than phone and face-to-face conversations, more immediate than e-mail. Moreover, many social messaging tools incorporate the entertaining and "social" features of SNSs (such as multimedia, tagging, and emojis—☺, ☹, ✍) and are often fun to use. The ability to communicate quickly, privately, and in real time in an informal, casual manner makes it an advantageous tool for employees to connect with one another in the workplace.

Undoubtedly, social media have become a pervasive tool for today's organizations to communicate with and engage the digital-savvy stakeholders. Despite the potential risks of internal use of social media, such as encroachment of privacy, legal issues, disrupting work, or distraction from work-related communication (Leonardi, Huysman, and Steinfield, 2013) and realistic concerns of the absence of technology in non-networked organizational settings (Burton 2016), the benefits of enterprise social media makes it an unparalleled platform for the organization's internal communication efforts: knowledge sharing; establishing connectivity, community, and relationship; creating social capital; and fostering an innovative, open, and transparent culture. Organizations should strategically evaluate their social needs and harness the power of digital networks for engaging today's digital-savvy workforce.

Effectively using social media tools *internally* requires strategic thinking and careful planning. Simply, "the emergence of social media technology doesn't change the fundamentals, which are about involving people in a conversation that leads to action. Where you have the software without thinking, you just get old wine in new bottles" (Groysberg and Slind 2012, 78). Huy and Shipilov (2012) made three vital suggestions when addressing the key to social media success within the organization. First and foremost, to be successful, internal social media initiatives must *focus on developing emotional capital*, a sense of goodwill toward the organization and the way it operates. Second, social media should be used to *build positive feeling of authenticity, pride, attachment, and fun* among employees. To that end, organizations need to identify authentic and trusted leaders within the company and provide them necessary training on social media strategies, tactics, and skills. Third, policies and rules should be in place to create a secured and positive internal "social" communication environment and management system, which eventually contributes to communication success and organizational success, as described in Chapter 7.

Selecting Appropriate Channels

With the bewildering range of medium options, many are tempted to just spin the wheel and select a channel. Indeed, there exists no "one-size-for-all" approach; however, companies can strategically use some criteria to optimize the selection of communication channels to achieve their respective communication goals. Gillis (2006) suggested three basic considerations for organizational planning for the use of internal communication media: (1) audience needs and preferences (social presence), (2) resources available, and (3) speed of delivery. No communication will be successful without considering who the *stakeholders are and determining what their needs and preferences are*. For example, a geographically dispersed workforce may prefer digital communications, such as e-mail, video conferencing, and social media, to print publications or face-to-face meetings. In times of changes, such as during acquisitions or layoffs where there are higher levels of uncertainty and insecurity, employees may prefer face-to-face communication to other channels, as it allows for interpretation of nonverbal cues, instant feedback, and clarification. Some consulting firms use communication audits to assess the effectiveness of the communication channels and gather employee feedback on which channels work, which are viewed as ineffective, and where gaps exist (Burton 2016). *Availability of resources* such as funds, talents, and time are realistic concerns for organizations when considering channel adoption. For instance, does the company have a tech support team for the digital tools? Do they have digital-savvy communicators who understand the tools well and could draft appropriate messages and produce related content? *Speed of delivery* is concerned with the urgency of the situation. The annual report provides an overview of the organization's yearly progress and financial review. Monthly or weekly unit meetings allow employees to discuss organizational or departmental issues, encourage creative problem-solving, and team building. E-mails are used to make daily announcements and keep people in the loop in an efficient and non-intrusive way. In general, the use of synchronous channels such as face-to-face communication or phones conveys a higher sense of urgency than the use of asynchronous tools such as e-mail or text messaging (Stephens, Barrett, and Mahometa 2013).

Clampitt (2001) summarized four categories of factors that organizations should consider in making appropriate channel selections, including (1) sender objectives, (2) message attributes, (3) channel attributes, and (4) receiver characteristics.

Sender Objectives

Internal communication serves various purposes, such as informing, educating, motivating, persuading, and soliciting ideas or opinions. Communicators need to recognize that every channel has its limitation that may filter out parts of the message. Organizations need to ensure that the intentions of their communication are congruent with the dynamics of the channel. For instance, although print publications may be effective in keeping stakeholders informed and updated, it may not be an ideal way to solicit ideas and opinions from employees. When a CEO wants to instill passion and emotions to conveying corporate mission, vision, and values, videoconferencing or face-to-face meeting would be channels of choice.

Message Attributes

Messages can vary along many dimensions such as the complexity, formality, length, tone, personal warmth, and degree of ambiguity. Clampitt (2001) differentiated the "what" channels and "who" channels. "*What*" channels, such as e-mail, web pages, and teleconferencing, tend to emphasize the information and messages being shared, while *"who"* says it fades into the background. By contrast, "who" channels, such as face-to-face meetings and formal presentations clarify ambiguities with the aid of visual cues and underscore the relational elements of the communicative events and activities. "What" channels may work well for communicating formal, simple, and less ambiguous messages, whereas "who" channels would be more effective in communicating personal, complex, and more ambiguous messages.

Channel Attributes

Different channels require different skills. Although effective e-mail and memo writing requires brevity and clarity, holding successful meetings requires knowing how to carry on a good conversation, what to focus on, what to ignore, how to encourage discussion, build consensus, and stick to an agenda (Clampitt 2001). Channel choice also affects power relationships. For example, the use of SNSs to build internal communities empowers employees and democratizes the workplace in a sense that leaders do not control the flow of information. In general, written communication through formal channels signifies authority, legitimacy, and responsibility. Face-to-face communication signals "a desire for team work, to build trust, goodwill, or to convey informality" (Trevino, Daft, and Lengel 1990, 86).

Receiver Characteristics

Effective internal communicators need to craft the message and select the channels in a way that is compatible with stakeholder characteristics. Various demographic, psychographic, netgraphic, or behavioral characteristics of internal audiences should be considered such as age, gender, race, education level, occupation, religious orientation, beliefs, values, personality profile, and channel access. For example, voicemail or e-mail may be particularly instrumental for communicating across time zones. Internal social media may best serve younger and digital-savvy stakeholders who are adept in using new technological tools. A key question to consider is, "what does the internal audience *need*?" Starting from understanding target audiences' needs for communication will help resolve essential issues stakeholders have in a more credible way (Burton 2016).

In sum, there is no one best communication channel that works across circumstances and through various contexts. To select the most appropriate channels, internal communication requires a complete and holistic understanding of various communication tools and the entire communication process (Clampitt 2001). Indeed, "the medium is the message," but it is not the entire message. The wide array of communication channels affords organizations opportunities to effectively reach and engage their internal stakeholders. However, all technologies and tools as "hard" assets require the support of "soft" assets, such as the communication worldview and culture, before it can yield value. Instilled with human spirit and guided by two-way, dialogical, transparent, and authentic communication philosophies, all available communication channels can be utilized to their most effective best.

Summary

Organizational internal communication landscapes have significantly changed with the evolution of new technology. This chapter discussed the characteristics and functions of various communication channels that organizations can utilize to communicate and connect with internal stakeholders. For instance, face-to-face communication is the most preferred communication channel, as it is instant, interactive, personal, and allows conveying and interpretation of emotions or feelings through nonverbal cues. Print publications are a formal way to keep stakeholders informed and are effective in delivering information that is static and not time-sensitive. Videoconferencing has the ability to overcome geographical barriers and bring the physically dispersed together. E-mail has the advantage of reaching a widely spread target audience simultaneously in an easy and quick way. Social media tools, which are interactive, empowering, relational, and communal, and foster sharing, collaboration, dialogs and conversations in the organization. Intranet is a way of formal online communication and is often used for strategic purposes, such as to reinforce key corporate values, strategies, and culture. Blogs can build thought leadership and promote open discussion and collaboration. SNSs allow employees to make connections and build relationships with peers and managers and engage in internal communities. Social messengers enable companies to personalize their targeted communication and build close and strong one-on-one connections.

This chapter also suggested the criteria that companies and leaders should use to select the appropriate channel for the right messages and audiences and to achieve communication objectives. These criteria included audience needs and preferences (social presence), resources available, delivery speed, sender objectives, message attributes, channel attributes, and characteristics of receivers.

CHAPTER 6

Organizational Structure, Culture, and Climate

Our focus now turns to understanding the context in which internal relations are managed in terms of organizations themselves, including environment, organizational structure, culture, and communication climate. Each of these factors has immeasurable impact on internal communication. This chapter continues the discussion of organizational culture that began in Chapter 3 (ethics) and continues the discussion of the valuable role of leadership in an organization. Yet, here we offer more explanation of how internal factors, such as organizational structure, can effect communication flow as well as understanding external factors that can also shape internal communication.

Socioeconomic Context

Organizations exist within a larger environmental context. The socioeconomic system in which they operate, the regulatory environment, the competitive landscape, size of industry, scope of trade, supply and distribution factors, as well as social concerns all have an impact on the organization, as well as the way in which it communicates internally (Giddens 1991). An organization that exists within a heavily controlled environment is likely to have more routine, bureaucratic, and authority-based communication and approval protocols. Conversely, an organization that exists within a more autonomous environment is likely to create more flexible systems of authority and communication that are more agile and less bureaucratic.

Socioeconomic context offers a macro-level view of how organizations communicate. In a communistic system, there is little or no private ownership of business, organizations at some level are all part of the government. Government control imparted by a communistic system offers little decision-making autonomy; thus, it is heavily reliant on authority and routine protocols or standardized procedures. For example, in perhaps the most heavily controlled socioeconomic system in the world, North Korea, private ownership does not exist and government control and authority are absolute.

In a socialistic system, there is a combined private ownership of property with heavy government regulation and taxation. Socialistic systems offer heavily regulated organizational behaviors and limited decision-making control over communication, which is regulated, required, and routinized by government. For example, extensive environmental requirements in the Norwegian oil and gas industry include mandated forms of communication and disclosure required by the government. The level of control in a socialistic system is heavily dependent on governmental functions and regulations, although a communistic system imposes almost total to complete control of organizations and communications (Giddens 1991).

Liberal democratic socioeconomic systems of government offer wide-ranging views of business and organizational communication. These forms of government—from democracies to representative republics—place the behest of decision-making responsibility more in the hands of individuals (Friedman 1962 and 2002), though some level of government regulation and required disclosure still exists to facilitate fairness, anticorruption, or competitive trade. In a capitalistic economy, based on merit and competition, good internal and external communication can be used to create a competitive advantage in the marketplace. The initiative for individual decision-making and communication is in the hands of the individual, offering the opportunity for innovation and high participation in decision-making (Bowen, Rawlins, and Martin 2010), rather than a reliance on authority or bureaucracy. These types of social systems facilitate organizational agility, rapid innovation, and flexible systems of communication, both internally and externally. For example, Ireland is one of the most deregulated economies for business in the world, and it is therefore an attractive system to organizations that focus on innovation and competition.

Understanding the socioeconomic environment, or environments, in which your organization operates can be key to a macro-level view of responsibilities to government, society, and for the role of communication.

Different socioeconomic environments require different communication standards, a challenge faced by global organizations. Even within smaller, more limited environments or regions, differing systems, social conflicts (Finet 2001), and varied responsibilities within different levels of government can pose communication challenges. An understanding of the socioeconomic environment can help an organization navigate both regulatory requirements and normative or aspirational ideals for operating effectively within that system.

The Communication Environment: Systems Theory

Systems theory, also known as general systems theory, was developed to explain all sorts of systems (Bertalanffy 1934, 1968; Holmstrom 2007), such as societies, economies, and so on, by German sociologist Niklas Luhmann. When applied to organizations, the systems theory (Luhmann 1984) offers a theoretical model in which we can view the interdependence of organizations with their environment. The organization exists within the broader socioeconomic environment, and that environment consists of many groups: regulatory agencies, media, consumer publics, advocacy groups, competitors, suppliers of raw materials, employees, labor unions, community members, and so on. The organization is conceptualized as *interdependent* with this environment as resources (such as raw materials) come and go across the boundary of the organization. For example, employees are members of community publics, and also cross the boundary of the organization to work within it.

Open and Closed Systems

In systems theory terms, organizations and other systems can be conceptualized along a continuum of how open versus closed their boundaries are. Open systems are those with permeable orders in which information, people, raw materials, and other components freely come and go. The more open an organization is, the more permeable is its boundary. Organizations that are more closed in nature offer less permeable boundaries and stricter control of information, people, and commodities that cross a boundary. For example, the Federal Bureau of Investigation (FBI) has a highly controlled boundary, but it is more permeable than the boundary of the Central Intelligence Agency (CIA). These organizations still have a moderately open system because human workforce members come and go across its permeable boundary, under a certain set of controls (identification procedures and so on). These organizations can be thought of as more closed than an organization with a very open system, such as a public relations agency.

Closed systems are rare in the real world. It is difficult for a truly closed system to exist because most organizations are interdependent with their environment in at least some components of their infrastructure, such as water or electricity. A prison system is a good example of a closed organization that still has some degree of interdependence with the environment. A religious commune that is totally self-sustaining is a good example of a truly closed system with very impermeable borders and little interaction with the environment. Closed systems are quite rare, and so, most organizations are conceptualized in systems theory terms based on their degree of being open, and the permeability of their boundaries.

Information in a System

Information can also be viewed as a commodity that crosses the boundary of the organization. When information comes into an organization, through formal research or informal means, it is known as *input;* when the organization analyzes and uses that information by incorporating it into strategy, it is known as *throughput.* When an organization then communicates that strategy to publics in the environment, it is known as *output.* Finally, *feedback* occurs when publics in the environment react to the information and communicate about it. That feedback can exist as multiway communication among many stakeholders, or can be thought again as input by the organization, forming a continual *loop* of communication.

Input can come into the organization both informally as opinion, feedback, information offered by industry associations, customer complaints and the like, or it can be formally sought by the organization. When information is sought by the organization, it normally takes the form of public opinion surveys, focus groups, or interviews. Basing an organization's strategic decision-making or throughput on research allows it to be strategic, rather than basing decisions on tradition, gut reaction, hunches, and so on. Further, research allows stakeholder segmentation, so that messages can be individually tailored as output to specific target audiences.

Environmental Scanning

When an organization seeks information from the environment, that process in systems theory terms is called *environmental scanning* (Stoffels 1994). Environmental scanning is the process of monitoring trends, issues, controversies, and problems external to the organization. Changes in the environment can be noted and monitored on a routine basis, subjected to formal research, such as public opinion polling and focus groups, as well as understood through informal research, discussions with colleagues and competitors, simple observation (i.e., participant observation), or information from industry associations and trade press.

Another way to conceptualize environmental scanning is as *strategic listening* for emerging trends, issues, potential problems, or threats. Industry changes can then be identified and studied as input, using that information as throughput to develop strategy, and output for active communication. Environmental scanning on a routine basis allows organizations to conduct effective issues management, and create communication that addresses the needs of internal and external stakeholders both. Environmental scanning is a proactive communication behavior that allows organizations to be agile, flexible, and quick to respond to threats and challenges.

Organizational Structure

Considering the shape and structure of an organization can help to understand how its management works, and thus how communication can and should flow within it. *Organizational structure* refers to the formal reporting chains or reporting relationships in an organization that result in its shape. Mintzberg's (1983) conceptualization of management emphasized control of the organization, and much of that control comes through organizational structure. In general, we can conceive of an organization

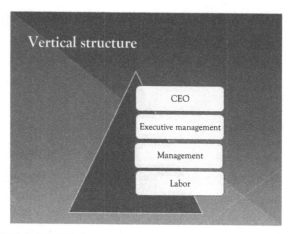

Figure 6.1 A simplified representation of vertical structure showing stratified layers of reporting hierarchy

as a triangle with the CEO at the top of the triangle, executive managers just below that, larger levels of midlevel managers in the center, and a large and wide workforce at the bottom layer of the triangle (Figure 6.1). This general conception allows us to see an abstract structural form and delineates reporting chains from the lowest level of production to the more high and narrower levels of executive management. This abstract triangle is customizable to different types of organizations: vertical and centralized or horizontal and decentralized.

Vertical, Centralized Organizational Structure

A vertical and centralized organizational structure can be conceptualized as a tall and rather narrow triangle. It is one that displays high degrees of command and control or decision-making authority in stratified layers (layers of reporting) throughout the organization. Defined job responsibilities, standard operating procedures, and well-reinforced levels of authority, very stratified organizational structures are in which one layer reports to the next layer, which reports to the next layer, and decision-making authority is centralized in the upper layers of management.

A vertical and centralized organizational structure means the most important strategic decisions are made at headquarters by management.

Relatively little decisional autonomy is experienced by stakeholders at the lower levels of the organization. Centralized authority means that a standard operating procedure is in place that recognizes the organizational behavior in the interest of efficiency. For example, requiring a request to be signed by multiple levels of authority before it is officially approved is one example of centralization. Centralized organizations offer a high degree of control over operations and are a natural choice for large-scale manufacturing or global service industries, such as fast food or hotel chains (i.e., "scientific management"). These types of organizational structures are vertical because of their steep levels of hierarchy, often seen as numerous layers of stratification throughout the organization. Figure 6.1 offered a simplified representation of a vertical organizational structure.

Communication flow in a vertical and centralized organization often implies *formalization* (Mintzberg 1983), meaning the existence of official channels of internal communication. Because of the vertical structure, communication often flows from top down in the organization, or horizontally among peers, but less often flows from the bottom of the organization upward. Up and down communication should be encouraged by the effective internal relations program, and may need channels in place to foster it in a vertical, centralized organizational structure, such as anonymous feedback lines, employee forums for questions to the CEO, and so on. A vertical and centralized organizational structure offers a number of advantages in efficiencies and economies of scale in organizing large and routine operations. However, a centralized organization's tight control of decision-making, strategy, and output from management offers less decisional freedom to lower-level stakeholders; a lack of autonomy or decisional freedom is often a source of frustration. Means to seek input from stakeholders are, therefore, an important part of a good internal relations program.

Horizontal, Decentralized Organizational Structure

A horizontal or less centralized organizational structure can be conceptualized as a low and flat triangle. Depending on the organization, the triangle may appear as an equilateral triangle, or become quite long and low at the bottom, with a very short distance to the top of the organization—due

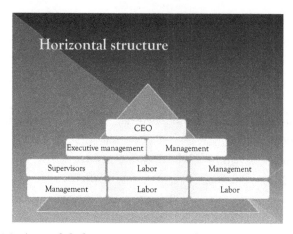

Figure 6.2 **A simplified representation of a horizontal structure**
showing decentralized reporting hierarchy. Decentralization could also
mean that multiple divisions, units, locations, factories, or operating
companies are organized similarly under one CEO at the apex

to lower levels of stratification (Figure 6.2). In this type of organizational structure, many people hold roughly the same amount of authority, or there are fewer standard operating procedures in place. In this type of organization, it is not unusual for work to be accomplished in two groups that cross functions of the organization or allow for innovation among specialties. A small consulting firm offers a good example of a horizontal and decentralized organizational structure.

Routine procedures of approval may be lacking or may be created on a case-by-case basis, flexible manner. Many employees have the decision-making autonomy and the ability to offer insight and innovation into strategic management. Mintzberg (1983) found that a decentralized organizational structure increased vertical communication, in a process that he called mutual adjustment and direct supervision. In horizontal and decentralized organizations, each employee has more routine decision-making autonomy and freedom, even though some stratification of employee levels still exists. Job roles may be often changing or independently created as needed, thus allowing a high degree of specialty among employees.

A decentralized organizational structure is very good in small- and medium-size organizations in which employee participation is sought. It encourages problem-solving, innovation, flexibility, as well as quick and agile organizational operations. However, there can be some confusion about role responsibilities, overlap of duties, or lack of role clarity due to the hazily defined job responsibilities. These types of systems can, therefore, be less efficient than those with a vertical structure, but can excel at solving complex problems and developing new product innovations.

Many implications exist for communication, in general, and internal relations specifically from less-centralized organizational structure. A decentralized organizational structure is accompanied by an overall increase in communication (Jablin 1987), including increased autonomy (Yammarino and Naughton 1988), perceived quality of communication, and increased time spent communicating (Weick 1987). A decentralized organizational structure can also lead to an increase in perceived communicative influence and more productive leader–follower relationships (McPhee and Poole 2001).

Communication flow in a horizontal and less centralized organizational structure normally takes place in both up and down directions, as well as horizontally between peers and diagonally across functional levels. Because some stratification exists, but is often changing based on the team structure or workgroup, communication flow is often non-formalized. In designing internal communications programs, it is important to realize that top–down or bottom–up conceptualizations alone will not be sufficient to capture the complex interplay that happens within a horizontal and decentralized organizational structure.

A decentralized organizational structure can be conceptualized as a flattened triangle or a few flattened triangles linked together at the top. In the latter case, each triangle represents a functional area of an organization that would be highly autonomous and responsible for its own area, only overseen at the highest level with the relative lack of coordination across operations. Decentralized organizations operate relatively independently of one another and are usually coordinated by a parent company in their overall operations. This is often seen in large enterprises with a number of subsidiaries reporting to an umbrella-like holding company.[1] A lack of centralization can pose the benefit of flexibility or the weakness of redundancies and lack of efficiency, which should be safeguarded against through strong systems of internal communication.

Organizational structure can be described in terms of both vertical or horizontal structure and central or decentralized authority systems. These dimensions of an organization can be studied independently, but for our purposes, it is enough to envision basic concepts because these components normally correlate together as described earlier. Each organization is different, and these general dimensions of organizational structure offer a basic guideline or understanding of how an organization works and how communication flows within it.

Organizational Culture

Organizational culture can be thought of as an organization's "personality." The organizational enterprise is comprised of numerous functions, subfunctions, and units. Those factors combined with its environment, policies, and human aspects, including communication and the meaning that is created by it, combine together in a *suis generis* sense to create organizational culture—organizational culture exists holistically, as a whole that is greater than the sum of its parts, as part symbolism and part performance (Eisenberg and Riley 2001). As such, an organizational culture is comprised of symbolism, psychological meanings and processes, representations, symbolism, and power (Smircic and Calas 1987).[2]

Organizational culture is nebulous, yet can be reliably described, felt, and measured (Eisenberg and Riley 2001). Further, organizational culture has a clear impact on performance, effectiveness, employee satisfaction,

---

[1] An example of this is often found in the energy sector, where a larger holding company manages several smaller operating companies, such as delivery subsidiaries by states operated in, pipeline companies that deliver oil and gas to the distribution companies. Each company will have its own organizational structure that works best for it.

[2] For an excellent discussion on the cultural organization, see Morgan (2006), *Images of organization*, chapter 4, pp. 115–48.

hiring, and retention. A purposeful and strong organizational culture can even offer a competitive advantage in the marketplace. Although organizational culture is made up of a complex interplay of factors, it can be theorized to exist as two opposite poles: authoritarian culture and participative culture. The reality of an organization would include some mix of factors that place it on the continuum along the spectrum between these two approaches, but they offer an extremely useful conceptualization of organizational culture.

Authoritarian Organizational Culture

Authoritarian organizational culture, as the name implies, is based on authority. This type of organizational culture is based on command and control systems of hierarchy and formalized structure, as well as standard operating procedures and codified policy. The authority of stakeholders is linked in an escalating chain of command and reporting lines (Goodpaster 2007). Authoritarian systems use an organized chain of command and some degree of reliance on bureaucracy and formalization (Jablin 1987). For example, if an employee's expense report must be approved by a supervisor, and submitted with both signatures to accounting, a formal approval process is in place creating a standardized workflow.

A number of strengths and weaknesses should be noted regarding authoritarian organizational cultures. They are excellent at organizing a large-scale enterprise and offering a standard, recognizable product or service. For example, the enormous fast-food chain McDonald's uses authoritarian culture to organize one of the world's largest new employee training programs in which routines and standard operating procedures are taught. The food is relatively standardized and recognizable at any McDonald's location throughout the world. Employees are organized with a standard and predictable economy of scale, with efficiency in mind. Labor is considered a relatively inexpensive and renewable resource, so that a frequent turnover rate does not hamper efficiency or product quality. Communications are routine and focused on role specificity, in order to help organize this large-scale enterprise. On-boarding is also standardized and a relatively high turnover rate of employees is expected (Jablin 2001).

Authoritarian organizational cultures are predictable and stable, but resistant to change and are slow to evolve. The status quo is valued because it reinforces authority systems. These cultures value stability rather than input and open communication, which is not encouraged or sought from most employees. Employees may feel undervalued or disconnected from the organization in an authoritarian culture, unless specific efforts are made through internal relations to communicate with them frequently and well. Further, input from employees is neither sought nor desired by management at higher levels of hierarchy. Employees are not viewed as a resource for ideas or innovation, so any upward communication is often stifled (Grunig 1992). Feedback on performance is often routine and may only be issued in negative cases because routinely acceptable performance is assumed (Jablin 2001). In an authoritarian culture, communication is often one-way or top–down based on specifics of job-related issues. Two-way symmetrical discussion is rare (Grunig 1992).

Because of the formal lines of hierarchy in authoritarian cultures, internal relations can be challenging. A good practice is to build lines of upward communication for employees, as well as to use the formal downward lines of communication that are in place. Communication can take place horizontally, across peer ranks, as well as in upward and downward fashion. Although two-way symmetrical communication is rare, generating stakeholder feedback and input into organizational processes may actually increase efficiency by gaining expertise from those on the front lines.

Authoritarian cultures should have stakeholder feedback loops built in to their communication programs, because when communication and input are not routinely sought, many problems can be suppressed or overlooked until they become crises. Anonymous channels for employees to communicate about the organization are essential. Because of the rigid hierarchy in place, employees may be afraid of retribution or simply "rocking the boat" and may be wary of doing so. Anonymous means of reporting problems or even asking questions generally encourage a higher degree of employee interaction with the organization, more commitment, and offer an early warning system for identification of potential issues or crises.

Although an authoritarian organizational culture may not be an ideal communication environment because it may lack collaboration and not offer opportunities for stakeholder input, it excels at organizing a large-scale undertaking and offering consistency of product or service. Efficiency and consistency can be valuable competitive advantages in the marketplace. As long as internal relations are attended effectively, an authoritarian organizational culture can offer a satisfactory work environment.

Participative Organizational Culture

A participative organizational culture, as the name implies, encourages participation across organizational levels by stakeholders. This type of organizational culture is able to encourage input, innovation, and collaboration. In a participative organizational culture, stakeholder input and participation in management and decision-making are commonly sought and encouraged (Goodpaster 2007). Rather than focusing on economies of scale and large-scale organization, a participative organizational culture focuses on innovation, input, collaboration, and team performance (Grunig 1992). Good ideas can come from any level within the organization, and thus seeks to be inclusive in seeking input and managerial decision-making. Whereas authoritarian cultures can be seen as top–down communication, participative cultures can be seen as bottom–up communication (Grunig 1992).

It is common to find a participative organizational culture in industries with highly skilled or highly educated workers, and in small- to medium-size enterprises. For example, a consultancy focused on finance and accounting may have a highly educated workforce in which hierarchies between reporting lines are minimized in a team-based structure that seeks input from all members. Some team members may be CPAs, while others may be tax attorneys, yet all have valuable input to contribute to the team.

Participative organizational cultures offer the main competitive advantages of innovation and flexibility. These types of organizational cultures generally foster stakeholder creative thinking and offer a fertile environment for problem-solving and building community (Eisenberg and Riley 2001). Information sharing and two-way symmetrical discussion can improve decision-making by offering inclusion for stakeholders at all levels of the organization. Participative organizational cultures have low turnover rates because they tend to instill commitment to organizational goals.

One should be mindful of the strengths and weaknesses of participative organizational cultures. Because of the high level and frequency of communication in a participative organizational culture, role ambiguity and confusion about responsibilities, or overlapping responsibilities, may be the norm. Some degree of inefficiency is introduced by this heavy reliance on communication and lack of role specificity. Further, participative organizational cultures function best when all are dedicated to the success of the enterprise and use their own initiative to enhance team performance and improve results. Stakeholders who lack motivation or personal initiative may become entirely disengaged from the participative process.

Participative organizational cultures are not as adept at organizing complex or routine enterprises as authoritarian cultures. However, these cultures offer speed and flexibility of problem-solving that make them responsive, agile, and highly competitive environments, such as the technology industry. In environments where innovation is a key component of success, you are likely to find varying degrees of participatory organizational cultures.

In a participative organizational culture, communication is both one-way and two-way. Symmetrical or dialog-based communication is used for more complex problem-solving and to generate stakeholder input. One-way communication is used as an organizational tool and may be more specific to job responsibilities. An interesting and valuable outcome of generating two-way symmetrical communication is that it enhances employee commitment to the organization. For example, asking stakeholders at all levels for ideas input and feedback about revising the organization's mission statement can lead to a greater "buy-in" or commitment to that mission from employees at all levels.

Participative cultures also need to have stakeholder feedback loops built in to their communication programs. Some employees, for instance, may feel that anonymous communication about the organization is safer for them, even in a participative environment. Generating input in such a manner is sometimes called creating *organic communication*, or organic leadership, that naturally grows from all varied levels of an organization. It is essentially two-way symmetrical communication seeking collaborative problem-solving and idea generation throughout the organization. Organizations with a participative culture generally tend to retain employees and have a lower turnover rate, requiring less reinvestment in recruiting, hiring, and training than authoritarian organizations. High employee retention also offers the competitive advantage of retaining more experienced employees who have more institutional knowledge of the organization itself (Goodpaster 2007). Internal relations within a participative organizational culture often tend to flow quickly, be less formalized, and be tailored to the workflow or needs of specific units within the organization.

Conclusions About Culture

In terms of internal relations, it is probably easier to motivate employees in a participative culture than those in an authoritarian one (Eisenberg and Riley 2001). However, the purposes of internal relations themselves may differ. Participative cultures tend to hold internal relations efforts that are focused on team building and innovation, whereas authoritarian cultures focus on individual contribution and efficiency. The scale of the enterprise, as well as its structure, can help to explain these different foci. Knowing which culture an organization predominately holds can help the internal relations program tailor communications that effectively meet stakeholder needs, while also helping an organization solve problems and avert crises.

Both participative and authoritarian organizational cultures have pros and cons. Envisioning them as two ends of an axis or two poles of a continuum allows the internal relations manager to understand the predominant culture and the complexities of differing priorities within specific organizations. Although most organizations fall somewhere toward the middle of the continuum, a predominant organizational culture can usually be identified and then can be used to address communication deficits, inspire performance, and motivate employees according to their needs in that culture.

Communication Climate Within Organizational Culture

A smaller, more specific concern is *communication climate*. Communication climate includes both organizational factors and external influences on communication outcomes (Falcione, Sussman, and Herden 1987). In other words, communication climate is organizational culture's impact on the communication process, combined with other individual variables such as psychological processes (Weick 1987). Communication climate is smaller than organizational culture because it can exist between as few as two people. However, communication audits can clearly identify the level of open versus closed communication climate in organizational units.[3]

Communication climate can vary between groups within the organization, and is a subjective construct that is regularly created through interaction within the organization. Communication climate can generally be thought of as open or closed, warm and supportive, or cool and detached. Researchers argue that *leadership style* is the most important factor in communication climate, but also note that it depends on a communication network, structure of the organization, autonomy, psychological factors, diversity, and reward or incentive systems (Northouse 2007). In other words, how free and forthcoming is communication? Is communication easily flowing, free, and open, or restrained by protocols, constraints, and procedures?

Fostering a communication climate that is more open and encourages symmetrical dialog is typically the job of internal relations (Grunig 1992). Dispelling fear of speaking out, valuing employee input, and lessening the likelihood of reprisals or negative reinforcement all can instill a more open communication climate. An open communication climate should be fostered within organizations because it can help identify issues, problems, inefficiencies, or areas in need of revision. Doing so can help the organization ultimately become more effective, inclusive, and supportive of stakeholder input. An open communication climate normally supports employee satisfaction, retention, productivity, and can enhance employee engagement.

---

[3] A communication audit is a major organizational undertaking that surveys all stakeholders, to include senior management, conducts numerous stakeholder focus groups and in-depth interviews across the enterprise, and includes active journaling, whereby selected stakeholders keep daily journals of their communications.

Management Style

The final dimension of an organization is *management style*. As introduced in Chapter 1 (p. 8), there are two basic dimensions of management style: Theory X and Theory Y management, as developed by McGregor (1960) who studied the human elements of enterprise. Knowing these two approaches to management style can help to refine one's own approach to management and help to conceptualize how management is conducted in the organization—as well as refining how it *should* be conducted. Many studies have been conducted on means to conceptualize management, as well as hybrid forms of these two approaches. Some modern approaches to management style are parts of proprietary programs that study dimensions of managerial behavior, team membership, personal attributes, and work style. However, the parsimonious approach offered through the Theory X or Theory Y management style offers a robust, yet accessible explanation of how managers approach the process of organizing, leading, controlling, and evaluating.

Theory X

The Theory X management style holds that internal stakeholders— employees—must be firmly controlled by management. Managers who operate under a Theory X paradigm assume that workers need to be controlled because they do not want to work, or not enjoy working, or both and must be forced to do so.

The Theory X management style is similar to an authoritarian organizational culture and they often go hand-in-hand. Rigid systems of authority and reporting chains are in place to help control employee behavior. Innovation, dissent, offering opinion, and individual autonomy are often not encouraged by the Theory X approach to management. Systems of codified authority and centralized power are in place. This approach sometimes puts management against labor and sees monetary motivation or penalty systems as the primary means of controlling employee behavior.

Employees who work for a Theory X manager normally experience relatively low levels of personal autonomy and decreased job satisfaction than workers who are more engaged by their management. Theory X management often results in high turnover and increased costs associated with that turnover, such as recruitment and training expenditures. Even in large-scale, complex organizations that use a highly stratified vertical organizational structure along with authoritarian culture, the Theory X management style is not necessarily productive or helpful. Other means of controlling stakeholder behavior are in place in the organizational structure and through hierarchical authority, so the Theory X management style becomes rather redundant and even can hamper the effectiveness of the organization.

Theory Y

The Theory Y management style holds that employees will accomplish more and better work when empowered to do so by the management. Managers who adopt a Theory Y style offer greater levels of decision-making freedom to their employees, encourage them to offer feedback and opinions, and incentivize problem-solving behavior. Theory Y style managers believe that employees are gratified by doing good work and strive to do so for recognition and commitment to a team or cause, in addition to material gains or avoiding penalties. Similar to two-way symmetrical communication (Grunig 1992), the Theory Y management style values dialog and open lines of input.

The Theory Y approach holds that motivated employees are more productive and successful than those who are unmotivated or disengaged. Even employees who prefer to work autonomously can still be motivated to accomplish the collective goals of an organization or contribute to a team effort by encouraging their input. Communication is used as both a means to empower employees and to understand their needs in the Theory Y management. Theory Y managers engage in team building and motivating others to strive for team goals. By encouraging input, they allow employees to buy into the mission of the organization and create a personal sense of belonging and gain when goals are accomplished.

The drawback to the Theory Y management style is that not everyone knows how to do it. Inexperienced managers—easily threatened by a loss of control or do not understand how to engage their employees—tend to fail at creating an engaged workforce because they naturally resort to more authoritarian Theory X management. Building symmetrical systems of feedback for employees, asking for input and ideas, recognizing good work, shared problem-solving, and creating team-oriented goals based on shared vision can overcome these problems and create a Theory Y management style. Although a common myth holds that the best managers are charismatic leaders, best practices in internal relations and research in the field both show that *authentic* managers are the best. Authentic managers seeking to create genuine communication and honest effort to motivate their employees are the most effective. Theory Y style based on authenticity can also be argued to create more ethically responsible management (Seeger 1997), more committed stakeholders (Sims 1994), and more conscientious organizations overall (Goodpaster 2007).

Theory Y style managers tend to be comfortable sharing control, listening to the ideas of others, and confident in their abilities to handle day-to-day challenges of managing. They also tend to have a high degree of vocational competence, on the individual, group, and organizational level (Jablin and Sais 2001). Sharing control does not threaten managers who use a Theory Y style, and they often ask for the input of others before making decisions. Often times, successful Theory Y managers display a sense of resilience, flexibility, a sense of humor, and humility.

Conclusions

Although this book seeks balance in describing the organizational variables and dimensions based on differences such as industry, competition, socioeconomic environment, and situation, it does not seek balance in this case. Both research and practice show that the Theory Y management style is clearly superior to the Theory X management style. Theory Y management excels in creating positive organizational outcomes and stakeholder experiences, such as higher rates of job satisfaction (Azanza, Moriano, and Molero 2013). Internal relations should be used to foster a Theory Y style of management among individual managers and throughout organizations to engage stakeholders, create satisfaction, input, dialog, and retention, and foster organizational excellence.

Communication	Structure	Culture	Management style
One-way predominates	Vertical/centralized	Authoritarian	Theory X
Two-way predominates	Horizontal/decentralized	Participative	Theory Y

Figure 6.3 Summary of communication by dimensions of an organization

Because of the complexity of studying organizational communication, the concepts represented here are simplifications of much more complex real-world constructs. However, they offer a readily accessible way to understand the organizational variables that can influence internal communication. Figure 6.3 summarizes the organizational dimensions discussed earlier, grouped along the lines of predominantly one-way communication (providing information) to predominantly two-way communication (persuasive communication or symmetrical dialog). Knowing the predominant communication style, structure, culture, and management style of an organization can help internal relations be optimized to fulfill the needs of employees and internal publics.

Organizational Dimensions

The flow of communication, as well as organizational structure, culture, and management style all influence the type of internal communications employed by an organization. Sometimes, two-way communication is undertaken to persuade, but at its best it is undertaken to create understanding through dialog (Grunig 1992). In that manner, symmetrical systems of internal communication contribute to overall organizational excellence through problem-solving and integrative or collaborative decision-making.

Focusing on two-way communication in which symmetrical systems of generating input and feedback are in place, the Theory Y management style can be used to create a positive communication climate within organizations relatively independently of structure and culture. In that manner, different sizes and types of industries are able to maximize the benefit of internal relations and create more engaged employees, resulting in retention and efficacy.

Summary

This chapter discussed the context of organizations in terms of their socio-economic environment and the responsibilities of management under different forms of governance, from totalitarian control to free-market competition. Organizational structure was discussed to illustrate how communication would differ, from vertical and centralized organizational structures to horizontal and decentralized organizational structures. Stratified hierarchy and reporting chains were discussed as affecting the degree of formalization of communication along the lines of standard operating procedures. Decentralized organizational structure offers a number of advantages for communication flow and efficacy, as well is higher degrees of employee autonomy and participation. A brief review of organizational culture offered two polarized approaches: authoritarian culture, which is highly controlled and based on hierarchy, and participative culture that involves input across all levels of an organization for integrative decision-making.

Two differing styles of management were discussed. Theory X management is a highly controlled and authoritarian management style that is based on dictates from management, and reward and punishment for employees. The Theory Y management style is an approach using shared control in which managers seek input and use team-building strategies to motivate employees based on commitment to the success of the enterprise. Theory Y management has been found to be superior to the Theory X management style.

It should be noted that organizational structure is resistant to change, but positive communication climates can be instilled in vertical and horizontal structures. Both participative organizational culture and Theory Y management style were said to hold parallels with two-way symmetrical communication involving dialog that is used to create organizational excellence. An internal communication approach based on the Theory Y style management should drive internal relations. Feedback for internal stakeholders and channels of input using internal relations systems should be undertaken to help foster dialog, input, and shared or collaborative decision-making.

CHAPTER 7

Employee Engagement

In the past decade, employee engagement has become one of the most popular topics and central issues among organizations, consultants, and management and communication scholars and professionals alike. In a survey by Corporate Communication International on chief corporate communicators in the United States, employee engagement is revealed as one of the top three trends that organizations encounter (Goodman et al. 2009). Such immense interest in the concept is not surprising, given the numerous claims and research evidence on the key role that employee engagement plays in organizational success and creating competitiveness (Saks and Gruman 2014). Specifically, studies have reported that employee engagement nurtures positive employee attitudes, such as job satisfaction and organizational commitment (Saks 2006); boosts employee task and job performance (Rich, LePine, and Crawford 2010) and organizational citizenship behavior (Saks 2006); and contributes to business unit outcomes, such as customer satisfaction, employee retention, productivity, profitability, and safety (Berger 2011; Harter, Schmidt, and Hayes 2002). A 2012 study conducted by Dalal et al. (2012) established that employee engagement is the best predictor of overall employee performance when compared with other factors, such as organizational commitment, job involvement, and perceived organizational support. The effect of employee engagement can also spill over beyond an organization. For example, when service or frontline employees are disengaged, their negative mindset can be contagious and affect how they perform, as well as how they treat and serve customers.

A dramatic difference in the bottom-line results has also been noted between companies with engaged employees and those without. For instance, in Gallup's 2012 meta-analysis using 263 research studies across 192 organizations in 49 industries and 34 countries, work units with high employee engagement outperformed units with low employee engagement by 10 percent on customer ratings, 22 percent in profitability, and 21 percent in productivity (Sorenson 2013). In another Gallup study, employee disengagement is estimated to cost $243–270 billion worldwide because of the disengaged group's low productivity; thus, importance of employee engagement has been supported and driving interest in it.

This chapter scrutinizes internal stockholder engagement from an employee engagement point of view by drawing from scholarly and professional research that address several key issues: (1) What exactly is employee engagement? What are engaged/disengaged employees like? (2) What are the drivers of employee engagement? (3) How does internal communication contribute to building an engaged workforce? Toward the end, an integrated normative model of employee engagement will be put forward to guide the engagement efforts of organizations and communication professionals.

What is Employee Engagement?

A general consensus or agreement on what engagement actually means is lacking. Numerous definitions of employee engagement exist today, but two influential ones have dominated: one is by Kahn (1990) and the other is by Schaufeli et al. (2002). According to Kahn (1990), engagement refers to "the harnessing of organization members' selves to their work roles; in engagement, people employ and express themselves physically, cognitively, and emotionally during role performances" (p. 694). Thus, engaged employees are fully and actively present, immersed, and bring all aspects of themselves to the performance of their work roles. By contrast, disengagement refers to "the uncoupling of selves from work roles; in disengagement, people withdraw and defend themselves physically, cognitively, or emotionally during role performances" (Kahn 1990, 694). Schaufeli et al. (2002) proposed another influential definition; they regard engagement as "a positive, fulfilling, work-related state of mind that is characterized by vigor, dedication, and absorption" (p. 74). Engaged employees demonstrate high levels of energy while working; feel strongly involved, absorbed, and engrossed in their work; exhibit passion, pride, and enthusiasm in what they do; and find meaning, inspiration, and purpose in their work. Subsequently, Macey and Schneider (2008) further defined engagement to include three levels: trait engagement (i.e., disposition and cognition), psychological state engagement (i.e., affection and emotions), and behavioral engagement (i.e., behaviors).

Therefore, engagement is not simply a trait or a one-time behavior. It describes employees' *enduring motivational and psychological states* in which they devote their hands, mind, and heart to their work; stay cognitively, physically, emotionally, and fully invested in their roles; and demonstrate energy, enthusiasm, involvement, efficacy, and deep-level connections (Christian, Garza, and Slaughter 2011). Thus, as numerous managers and professionals observe, engaged employees are willing to give extra time and effort for the organization. These employees genuinely care about their work and the organization. Instead of simply working for paychecks or promotion, engaged employees work for the goals and future of the organization.

Satisfaction, Commitment, and Involvement?

Employee engagement is a broader concept than job satisfaction, organizational commitment, and job involvement. Although all these ideas are closely related in the workplace, employee engagement can be distinguished from the three (Christian, Garza, and Slaughter 2011; Saks and Gruman 2014). *Job satisfaction* describes one's attitude toward the job or job situation. *Commitment* describes the emotional attachment of employees to the organization. *Job involvement* is concerned about the extent one's job is central to one's identity.

Christian, Garza, and Slaughter (2011) empirically differentiated these concepts. Employee engagement was found to be only moderately but positively correlated with job satisfaction ($r = 0.053$), organizational commitment ($r = 0.59$), and job involvement ($r = 0.052$).[1] Consistent with the findings of other researchers, Christian, Garza, and Slaughter (2011) found that employee engagement contributes more to employee

---

[1] The correlation is "a statistical test that examines the relationships between variables (may be either categorical or continuous); measures the degrees to which variables are [linearly] interrelated; see also: correlation coefficient, Pearson product moment coefficient, Spearman-rho, *r*" (Stacks and Bowen 2013, 7).

performance than job satisfaction, organizational commitment, and job involvement. As an enduring psychological and motivational state, engagement can actually be positioned between employee attitudes (e.g., satisfaction, commitment) toward the job or the organization and supportive and advocacy behavior. Engagement can be thought of as *antecedent* to job involvement, in that employees who are deeply engaged in their work become capable of identifying with their jobs. Although research has provided inclusive evidence regarding the *causal relationship* between job attitudes and employee engagement, some researchers argued that employee attitudes, such as job satisfaction and organizational commitment (e.g., Robinson, Perryman, and Hayday 2004; Saks 2006), are antecedents of employee engagement.[2] Others demonstrated that engagement contributes to positive employee attitudes. Both are equally likely. To date, research indicates a reciprocal relationship between employee engagement and attitudes, such as satisfaction, commitment, and trust.

Drivers of Employee Engagement

A central topic regarding employee engagement discussed among scholars and professionals alike concerns the question of "how," that is, *how to engage employees*. In other words, *what factors drive employee engagement?* Research suggests a long list of engagement drivers; drivers can be categorized roughly into "hard" organizational factors (e.g., work conditions, job characteristics, pay and compensation) and "soft" factors (e.g., leadership, communication, organizational culture). Additionally, employee individual factors, such as psychological capital (e.g., self-efficacy, optimism, resilience, and so forth), proactive personality, and conscientiousness, play important roles in engaging employees.

Work Environment

The job demands-resources (JD-R) model argues that the job demands and resources that employees experience at work affect their stress level

---

[2] Causation is the "relationship between variables in which a change in one variable forces, produces, or brings about a change in another variable" (Stacks and Bowen 2013, 4).

and other outcomes (Menguc et al. 2013). Research demonstrates that *job resources*, regardless of physical (e.g., work conditions, facilities) or social (e.g., coaching, supportive leaders and coworkers, development opportunities, work–life balance), are *positively* related to employee engagement (Bakker et al. 2007; Jiang and Men 2015; Saks and Gruman 2014). Availability and abundance of job resources are particularly critical in fostering employee engagement when job demands are high (Bakker et al. 2007). Similarly, job characteristics, such as *job complexity, task variety, autonomy,* and *significance,* positively influence employee engagement (Christian, Garza, and Slaughter 2011). Robinson, Perryman, and Hayday (2004) found that work group, work pattern, and work hour length affected the level of employee engagement to various extents. For instance, managers and professionals are generally more engaged than their colleagues in the supporting roles, and full-time employees are more engaged than part-time employees. The level of employee engagement declines as the length of service time increases. Other work environment factors, such as the amount of physical effort required by a job and health hazards, are also *negatively* related to employee engagement (Saks and Gruman 2014).

Although literature has not drawn a consistent conclusion regarding how job demands in the workplace affect employee engagement, job resources, including *rewards* and *recognition, opportunities for development, feedback, autonomy, job variety, positive workplace climate,* and *work-role fit,* have been concluded to significantly drive employee engagement (Crawford, LePine, and Rich 2010). For example, the current epidemic levels of "burn out" afflicting the German workforce have been attributed not to stress as originally speculated, but to a lack of recognition and rewards in the work environment (Turner 2016).

Organizational Leadership

Beyond work environment and condition factors, leadership as a form of nested influence in an organization has been identified as an important antecedent of employee engagement. Men (2011, 2015a) found that the leadership, credibility, and communication style of the CEO and the communication channels used influenced employees' perception of the organizational reputation, their trust and confidence in the organization, and their level of engagement. Midlevel supervisory leadership also plays an irreplaceable role in engaging employees. Simply, supervisors interact with employees on a day-to-day basis. They serve as role models, offer recognition, and act as the most trustworthy information sources within the organization. What supervisors say and do and how they treat their followers have everything to do with employee psychological well-being and their level of engagement. In the management arena, researchers have demonstrated that *transformational* leadership, which is visionary, empowering, relationship-oriented, and innovative, significantly engages employees (Christian, Garza, and Slaughter 2011). Likewise, *transactional* leadership, which is characterized by a contingent reward (i.e., leaders clarifying roles and task expectations and providing contingent rewards based on the fulfillment of job obligations), contributes to employee engagement (Breevaart et al. 2014). Recently, public relations scholars (e.g., Men 2015; Jiang and Men 2015) established the connection between organizational leadership and an organization's strategic communication system. In particular, when transformational, authentic, servant, and ethical leadership styles are prevalent in an organization, a two-way, empowering, employee-centered, and transparent communication climate can be nurtured, which in turn boosts employee engagement.

How leadership works in driving employee engagement can be explained through multiple theories, including the social exchange theory (SET) and JD-R theory. The central focus of SET is on *reciprocity and compensation between parties who are mutually dependent.* In this regard, social behavior is the result of an exchange. When leaders treat employees fairly, provide employees personal development opportunities, genuinely care for employees, and empower them in the decision-making process, they feel valued, appreciated, cared for, and involved. As a result, employees will reciprocate by fully immersing themselves in their work roles and expressing higher levels of commitment or "going the extra mile." The JR-D theory also explains the influence of leadership on employee engagement, in that leadership and supervisory support are critical job resources for employees. The guidance, influence, and information provided by leaders, as well as the quality of relationship (leader-member exchange [LMX]) built between leaders and followers shape the work environment of employees and largely affects the employees' growth, well-being, and engagement (Jiang and Men 2015).

Internal Communication

Among all the suggested drivers of employee engagement, internal communication plays a central role, if not "the" most important one. Communication can be found anywhere in an organization, from the macro-organizational-level corporate talk, the macro-level team or group communication, and to the micro-level dyadic interactions between supervisors and followers or peer communication among employees. Communication defines corporate culture and climate (Chapter 6) that influence various aspects of employee life in the workplace (e.g., work environment, employee's information satisfaction, psychological well-being, and so on), which can eventually boost the level of employee engagement (Jiang and Men 2015; Wayne et al. 2007).

The role of communication in driving employee engagement has long been recognized. However, empirical studies that attest to the relationship between internal communication factors and employee engagement have remained limited. Recently, through a survey of 200 Australian employees, Karanges et al. (2015) found that both corporate and supervisory communication had significant roles in driving and maintaining employee engagement. Specifically, corporate communication explained 23 percent of the variance in employee engagement, while supervisory communication explained 32 percent of the variance (Karanges et al. 2015). The positive effect of strategic communication strategies (e.g., symmetrical communication, transparent communication, and optimal use of communication channels) on employee engagement was revealed by Men and associates (Jiang and Men 2015; Men 2014a, 2014b; Men and Stacks 2014).

Crucially, these studies demonstrated that when an organization's communication system is symmetrical (i.e., it has a two-way information flow; it emphasizes listening, feedback, reciprocity, inclusion, and employee empowerment and participation; and it is employee-centered), internal stakeholders can develop a long-term, trusting, committed, and satisfied relationship with the organization, which further drives employee engagement. Relatedly, such open and symmetrical communication climates encourage ethical consideration and transparent communication practice (Chapter 3). Transparent organizational communication is evident when companies disseminate truthful and unbiased information in a complete, substantial, and timely manner is authentic and frank (Bowen

2016a); involve employees in identifying the information they need; and remains honest and accountable in what it says and does regarding employees. Furthermore, the company's and leaders' use of interactive communication channels, such as traditional face-to-face communication and social media tools to connect with employees, helps with employee engagement (Men 2014a).

Internal communication researchers find another interesting observation when considering both leadership and communication factors in the model of employee engagement. The influence of leadership on engagement often is largely mediated by organizational internal communication factors. For instance, Jiang and Men (2015) examined how authentic leadership, transparent communication, and work-life enrichment (i.e., employee work roles create an enrichment effect that spill over to their life roles) interplay to influence employee engagement. Their findings indicated that transparent communication and the resultant work-life enrichment fully mediated the influence of authentic leadership on employee engagement. Simply, *leadership is enacted through communication*. Broadly defined, everything that a leader says and does is a form of communication. As Jiang and Men (2015) found, authentic leadership reduces employees' frustration and uncertainty and fosters a positive work environment that contributes to employees' overall psychological well-being, as authentic leaders advocate open communication, welcome various perspectives, align their management behavior with beliefs, and objectively analyze all related information before coming to a decision. Such positive emotional state, self-fulfillment, and boosted confidence can go beyond the work domain and benefit employees' personal life experiences, thus driving employee engagement. Authentic leadership also promotes transparent organizational communication, which directly engages employees. Therefore, *communication at both leader and corporate levels is actually a determining factor of employee engagement*, even though in reality, all these factors, namely, work environment, leadership, communication, and culture, are intertwined.

Organizational Culture

In Chapter 6, we discussed how culture and internal communication interplay with each other to influence employee and organizational outcomes. When it comes to engaging internal stakeholders, culture (i.e., the fundamental values, beliefs, meanings, and assumptions rooted in the organization, lived by its members, and manifested in every way) cannot be separated from employee engagement. In fact, according to a recent study conducted by DU Press, culture and employee engagement issues have become the primary challenge in businesses around the world. In a 2015 blog article that Men wrote for the Institute for Public Relations' Organizational Communication Research Center, she summarized the 10 characteristics of organizational culture that drive employee engagement.

1. **Openness and transparency**: Employees feel free to voice their opinions, ideas, concerns, or even criticisms in the organization. Information is freely shared and exchanged in an accurate, substantially complete, timely, balanced, and unbiased manner in the company. Full and contextual disclosure is the norm.

2. **Integrity and trust**: Moral values, such as honesty, integrity, and truthfulness, are emphasized and implemented in the organization. The value of "no cheating, no lies" is stressed. Employers, managers, and employees are then able to trust one another.

3. **Participation and empowerment**: Employees are given opportunities to participate in the decision-making process, and they feel empowered to exert influence in the organization. Teamwork, dialogs, and collaboration are emphasized.

4. **Fairness**: Employees are treated fairly and without favoritism. They are also valued and appreciated for their unique abilities and contributions. They are provided opportunities for professional growth, praised, or given increased pay for enhanced achievement and performance.

5. **Supportiveness**: Employees are treated as individuals, cared for, and supported by the organization. Employees feel free to express individuality, as well as affection, tenderness, caring, and compassion for one another.

6. **Innovation**: Employees are encouraged to be open-minded, take risks, embrace changes, think outside of the box, and take innovative initiatives. Creativity, autonomy, and entrepreneurship are valued.

7. **Sharing and learning**: Employees openly share their knowledge, experience, and information within the corporate community. Sharing and continuous learning from one another is rewarded and encouraged. Input, opinions, and comments are encouraged.

8. **Diversity:** The organization embraces individuals for their uniqueness and diverse backgrounds regardless of their gender, race, religion, sexual orientation, and so on. Differences and various perspectives are respected and valued.

9. **Social responsibility**: The organization recognizes its association with the environment and the society at large, establishes an ultimate goal toward supporting a cause, and commits to solving community or social problems.

10. **Fun, joy, and happiness:** Fun, joy, and positive emotions are instilled in the workplace. Employees work in an easy, uplifting atmosphere, and a happy climate. Achievements are celebrated, appreciated, and rewarded.

Overall, organizational "hard" factors (e.g., job characteristics, work environment, pay and compensation), "soft" factors (e.g., leadership, communication, organizational culture), and the interplay between them play central roles in driving internal stakeholder engagement. These factors provide tangible and intangible resources for employees to deal with their day-to-day job demand. They also enhance their feeling of empowerment and identification with the organization (Karanika-Murray et al. 2015), build quality employee–organization relationships, and shape the internal reputation of the organization in their eyes, all of which lead to employee engagement (Men 2014c).

Individual Factors

Apart from the organizational "hard" and "soft" factors discussed earlier, employee individual factors make a difference with regard to engagement (Saks and Gruman 2014). Some pieces of evidence demonstrate that personality factors (e.g., core self-evaluations, conscientiousness, proactivity, and positive affect) positively influence employee engagement (Bledow et al. 2011; Christian, Garza, and Slaughter 2011; Saks and Gruman

2011, 2014). Employees' personal resources and psychological capital, such as optimism, resilience, self-efficacy, hope, and organization-based self-esteem, are also found to be important predictors of engagement. For instance, a recent study of Karatepe and Karadas (2014) revealed that employees' psychological capital was a critical personal job resource that boosts work engagement, which in turn leads to job, career, and life satisfaction.

An Integrated Normative Model of Employee Engagement

In a nutshell, research suggests that employee engagement matters not only for the organization's performance, bottom line, and success, but also for employee satisfaction, happiness, and overall well-being. An engaged workforce is a "win-win" outcome for both organizations and their number one stakeholder, employees. Engaging employees requires a thorough understanding of the internal audiences, including their needs and wants, as well as organizational "hard" resources (e.g., favorable work environment and conditions, fair pay and compensation, engaging job characteristics) and "soft" assets (e.g., effective leadership, strategic communication, and engaging culture values). Figure 7.1 sums up the aforementioned drivers of employee engagement along with its process and various organizational outcomes derived from literature.

On the basis of these findings, organizations and internal communication managers can lay out a blueprint to establish an engaged workforce over time; we put forward 10 concluding points that may help organizations shift from knowing to doing.

1. Establish a suitable, safe, positive, and supportive work environment with adequate physical resources, facilities, and conditions.
2. Provide coaching, offer employees personal growth and development opportunities and programs, and stress employees' work–life balance and enhancement needs in organizational initiatives and communications.
3. Place employees in job positions that fit their strength, capabilities, and skill sets and pay attention to the effect of job characteristics

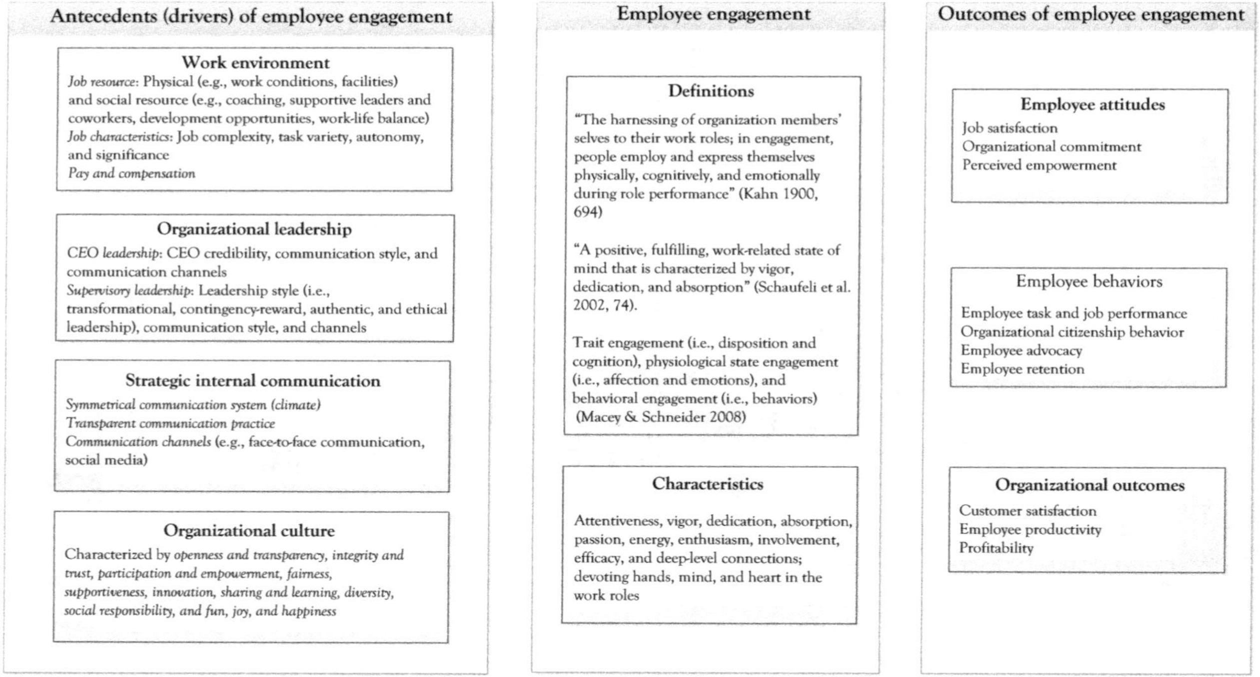

Antecedents (drivers) of employee engagement

Work environment

Job resource: Physical (e.g., work conditions, facilities) and social resource (e.g., coaching, supportive leaders and coworkers, development opportunities, work-life balance)
Job characteristics: Job complexity, task variety, autonomy, and significance
Pay and compensation

Organizational leadership

CEO leadership: CEO credibility, communication style, and communication channels
Supervisory leadership: Leadership style (i.e., transformational, contingency-reward, authentic, and ethical leadership), communication style, and channels

Strategic internal communication

Symmetrical communication system (climate)
Transparent communication practice
Communication channels (e.g., face-to-face communication, social media)

Organizational culture

Characterized by openness and transparency, integrity and trust, participation and empowerment, fairness, supportiveness, innovation, sharing and learning, diversity, social responsibility, and fun, joy, and happiness

Employee engagement

Definitions

"The harnessing of organization members' selves to their work roles; in engagement, people employ and express themselves physically, cognitively, and emotionally during role performance" (Kahn 1900, 694)

"A positive, fulfilling, work-related state of mind that is characterized by vigor, dedication, and absorption" (Schaufeli et al. 2002, 74).

Trait engagement (i.e., disposition and cognition), physiological state engagement (i.e., affection and emotions), and behavioral engagement (i.e., behaviors) (Macey & Schneider 2008)

Characteristics

Attentiveness, vigor, dedication, absorption, passion, energy, enthusiasm, involvement, efficacy, and deep-level connections; devoting hands, mind, and heart in the work roles

Outcomes of employee engagement

Employee attitudes

Job satisfaction
Organizational commitment
Perceived empowerment

Employee behaviors

Employee task and job performance
Organizational citizenship behavior
Employee advocacy
Employee retention

Organizational outcomes

Customer satisfaction
Employee productivity
Profitability

Figure 7.1 An integrated model of employee engagement

(e.g., complexity, variety, and significance) to minimize its negative consequences.

4. Establish a fair reward and compensation system to recognize achievements and outstanding performance.

5. Hire individuals with high psychological capital factors, such as optimism, resilience, self-efficacy, positivity, and hope.

6. Encourage organizational leaders, including executives, managers, and supervisors across levels, to implement transformational, transactional, authentic, and ethical leadership styles.

7. Provide communication training to senior management and develop an authentic and engaging communication style that is characterized by warmth, friendliness, empathy, responsiveness, and genuineness.

8. Use emerging technology and social media channels to build internal communities; foster conversations between leaders and employees, as well as employers and employees; promote openness, transparency, and dialogs; and incubate creativity.

9. Establish a two-way, empowering, participative, and stakeholder-centered symmetrical and transparent communication system; wholeheartedly listen to what employees have to say and make adjustments accordingly for their best interests.

10. Cultivate an engaging culture that values ethics, integrity, trust, employee participation, innovation, sharing and learning, fairness, diversity, social responsibility, equality, collaboration, and employee happiness.

Summary

Employee engagement is one of the critical issues that matter for organization's long-term success. This chapter delved into engagement by examining its definitions, drivers, and consequences. Employee engagement describes employees' enduring motivational and psychological states characterized by attention, absorption, dedication, vigor, energy, enthusiasm, involvement, efficacy, and deep-level connections. It nurtures positive employee attitudes, drives supportive employee behaviors, and contributes to business-unit outcomes, such as customer satisfaction, employee retention, productivity, and profitability.

Engagement is driven by various organizational factors that can be categorized into four groups: (1) work environment, such as abundant job resources, job characteristic, pay, and compensation; (2) organizational leadership, such as CEO credibility, top leaders' communication style and channels, and supervisory leadership style and communication; (3) organizational strategic internal communication, such as a symmetrical communication climate, transparent communication practices as well as corporate communication channels; and (4) organizational culture characterized by openness and ethics, transparency, integrity and trust, participation and empowerment, fairness, supportiveness, innovation, sharing and learning, diversity, social responsibility, and fun, joy, and happiness. The chapter concluded with 10 research insights that can help organizations shift from knowing to taking action on building a more engaged workforce.

CHAPTER 8

Change Management and Internal Communication

The only constant is change.

—Heraclitus

There is nothing more difficult to carry out, nor more doubtful of success, nor more dangerous to handle, than to initiate a new order of things.

—Machiavelli

An important prerequisite for modern organizations to grow and succeed in a dynamic and competitive global market is to scan and monitor its environment constantly, make necessary adjustments, and embrace change. In today's business world, technological advancement, increasingly keen market competition, and growing customer demands require organizations to seek various solutions to manage unstable and unpredictable situations rapidly and efficiently (Johansson and Heide 2008). Whether or not an organization is willing to evolve constantly, successful implementation of changes can be a major determinant of its long- or short-term success. However, research suggests that many organizational change initiatives fail, ranging from 30 percent to as high as 80 percent of attempted change projects (Appelbaum et al. 2012; Beer and Nohria 2000). One of the major reasons for the failure of change efforts identified, according to research, is *the lack of effective communication* (Barrett 2002; Elving 2005; Lewis 2000). For instance, over two decades ago, when Pharmacia and Upjohn merged, it required two additional years for the merger to complete and cost $400 million more in expenses than planned for two principal reasons: corporate cultural differences and a failure to communicate well during the consolidation period (Burton 2016).

Organizations, in general, seek change for many reasons, such as downsizing, mergers and acquisitions, disaster, adoption of new technology, expansion, and so on. Regardless of an organization's motivation to implement change, proper communication is always a critical need. Many factors contribute to the success of managing organizational change, such as strategic management, leadership, and communication. We do not dare offer a formula for effective change management in this chapter. Instead, we focus on the irreplaceable role of strategic internal communication for successful change initiatives.

Strategic Change

Strategic change is broadly defined as *a planned adaptive process that allows organizational systems and participants to adjust and behave differently to accommodate new contingencies, technologies, values, processes, and personnel* (Seeger et al. 2005). Beck, Brüderl, and Woywode (2008) described three general types of frequently occurring changes: (1) changes in the market niche (e.g., new product lines, acquisitions or mergers of other companies, brand changes, or mission changes), (2) changes in organizational leadership (e.g., reappointment or replacement of an organization's CEO), and (3) changes in formal organizational rules (e.g., change of organizational culture, reorganization). Likewise, Clampitt (2001) described change on a continuum from routine to non-routine, where routine changes occur on a regular basis and non-routine changes are more drastic, such as relocation, downsizing, and leadership change.

The Role of Communication in Strategic Organizational Change

Regardless of the type of change, unique change situations demand higher-level communication. During the change process, the normal reproduction of the organizational structures, routines, and rules is often interrupted to a greater or lesser extent, depending on the breadth and scope of the change. When the familiar processes, work routines, cooperation structures, and work environment of employees suddenly change, uncertainties and irritations occur, causing employees' attempts to seek information to reduce uncertainty.[1] Some may react with denial and display negative emotions, such as fear, stress, anxiety, and frustration (Luo and Jiang 2014). They also seek out and identify new landmarks that can anchor a new routine and new know-how. This re-orientation process takes place through continuous communication between employees and management and employees (Gergs and Trinczek 2008). Simply, *change management is impossible without proper communication* (Barrett 2002). As Kotter (1995) stated, "Transformation is impossible unless hundreds or thousands of people are willing to help, often to the point of making short-term sacrifices ... Without credible communication, and a lot of it, the hearts and minds of the troops are never captured."

Overall, research suggests multiple roles of effective communication in the strategic change process, which include reducing uncertainty, overcoming resistance to change, facilitating employee participation, and building shared understanding and mutual interpretation.

Reducing Uncertainty

When change occurs, employees often ask the question "why": "Why did this happen to me?" "Why is this happening at this time?" The feeling of uncertainty is typically about the aim, process, and expected outcomes of change and its implications for individual employees. Research demonstrated the relationship between communication and uncertainty. Difonzo and Bordia (1998) concluded that added and accurate information will reduce peoples' perception of uncertainty and proactively establish and maintain trust. Bordia et al. (2004) stated that systematic communication could lessen employee uncertainty and increase employees' sense of control and job satisfaction during changes. Often, gaps in expected communication and silence from the management side leave

---

[1] This follows Festinger's (1957, 1959, 1964; Festinger and Carlsmith 1959) influence model and cognitive dissonance reduction. As people are presented dissonant situations, they actively will seek information to reduce that dissonance and bring on a state of consonance.

a hole that employees will try to fill with their own fantasies and inter-pretations. Rumors, opinions, speculations, and moods could spin out of control (Gergs and Trinczek 2008). Based on three studies of inter-nal communication during mergers and acquisitions (M&A), Gerps and Trinczek concluded that formal or informal communication could help diminish employees' anxiety even if the communicated messages contain bad news. Withholding information during the phases of radical change is easily one of the worst mistakes in managing changes.

Overcoming Resistance To Change

Resistance to change is arguably one of the most challenging barriers for an organization to overcome (Bull and Brown 2012). Poorly managed change communication often results in resistance to change and exaggera-tion of the negative aspects of the change (Seeger et al. 2005). Meaningful communication informs and educates employees at all levels regarding the rationale, necessity, or urgency for change and motivates them to support the change. Open and transparent communication also nurtures the trust and positive attitudes of employees to change, which are vital for successful change programs (Kotter 1996). Effective communication on the change itself and its associated outcomes, particularly the benefits, could help employees understand and appreciate the proposed change and mitigate employee concerns. Communication also helps employees cope with negative emotions, such as anger and frustration, which facil-itates change. For instance, a caring two-way communication approach that allows employees to voice their concerns and express their feelings (while firmly emphasizing the need for change) would work better than simply cascading information to or ignoring the emotional reaction of employees.

Facilitating Employee Participation

Frahm and Brown (2007) examined how communication during orga-nizational change is linked to employee receptivity to change and found that including employees in the change process through frequent face-to-face meetings creates a trusting and open atmosphere. Often, employees feel frustrated with organizational change due to non-involvement in the change process. Conversely, if employees are involved in the change process from the beginning, they will feel more in control of the results. Appelbaum et al. (2012) noted that giving employees a small empowering opportunity could significantly affect their attitudes because it can provide them with some sense of control over the change process and help move the change effort along. In this sense, effective *upward* communication not only provides management an opportunity to listen, but also instills a sense of empowerment and involvement in employees, thereby leading to better participation and support for change. Research finds a positive relationship between participation and the successful implementation of strategic change (Lines 2007).

Building Shared Understanding and Mutual Interpretation

Organizational change often involves disrupting old roles, routines, and rules and establishing new ones. In fact, when a change initiative is implemented, it creates a new reality through communication. Employees facing the change initiative immediately try to make sense of it and understand its potential effects on them, particularly management-initiated changes (compared with grassroots—or employee-initiated changes). This sense-making accompanied with adequate information and communication from an organization could resolve uncertainties and ambiguities, and is thus fundamental for the outcome of a planned change (Johansson and Heide 2008). However, people in an organization have various backgrounds, roles, interests, experiences, positions, education, and so on. Thus, they may make sense of the same situation in multiple ways.

Research suggests that individual reaction and responses to change mutually interact and influence each other over time (Stensaker and Falkenberg 2007). Therefore, effective storytelling and communication are essential to building shared understanding and interpretation between management and employees, and employees with employees. For instance, organizations can create a vision of what the change is about, why it is needed, and how it will be achieved. Visionary communication carried out in a repeated and timely manner is critical to inform, create understanding, and modify attitudes and behaviors (Johansson and Heide 2008). Combining storytelling with the use of powerful visuals, such as learning maps that project the current and future state of an organization, is also helpful for companies undergoing change (Burton 2016).

Managing Strategic Change Communication

Ironically, although many organizations and managers recognize the importance of communication for effective change management, few of them develop strategic or systematical *communication plans*. Effective change communication requires a thorough understanding of the change process, context, audiences, as well as how communication works. From the management perspective, Kotter (1996) described eight steps to implement change and transform the organization, including:

1. establishing a sense of urgency about the need to change;
2. creating a guiding coalition of those with power, influence, credibility, and expertise in the organization to lead the change;
3. developing a vision and strategy regarding what the change is about and where the organization is going;
4. communicating the change vision by telling people in every possible way and whenever possible about the whys, whats, and hows of the changes;
5. empowering broad-based action and involving employees in the change efforts;
6. generating short-term wins, demonstrating that the changes are working, and recognizing the work being done by people toward achieving the change;
7. consolidating gains and creating momentum for change by building on successes in change and developing people as change agents; and
8. anchoring new approaches in the corporate culture to ensure long-term success and institutionalizing the changes.

Communication plays an essential role in most of these steps. Without communication, changes can be difficult to implement. In his book,

Communicating for Managerial Effectiveness, Clampitt (2001) outlined a strategic approach to plan and manage change communication efforts, namely, the Iceberg model. In the model, the author described contextual analysis as the base-level foundation, followed by audience analysis, changes communication strategies, and change communication tactics (i.e., channels, messages, spokespersons, timing, monitoring devices, and so on). Building upon Kotter and Clampitt's change management and communication models and incorporating recent research findings in this area, we present the following roadmap for strategic change communication and management.

Situational Analysis

Situational analysis is involved in almost any type of problem-solving. An organization will need to thoroughly analyze and understand the change context and the situation it faces before taking any measures.

Contextual Analysis

A contextual analysis could include examining the background of the organization, its historical communication patterns, whether internal stakeholders successfully assimilated changes in the past, whether changes are manageable and congruent with organizational culture, and whether the benefits of changes are readily observable. For example:

> The president of a small manufacturing company was concerned about the tough financial times the company would soon be experiencing. He felt that he had moral and ethical obligations to inform the employees about the situation. Thus, he called a company-wide employee meeting to discuss the difficulties and potential cost-saving measures that had to be implemented. Although he mentioned that the company had no plan for layoffs, ironically, a few days after the meeting, the entire plant was buzzing with rumors about closing the plant and wage reduction. (Clampitt 2001)

What went wrong in this situation? How could a well-intended message from the president be misinterpreted? Later, upon deeper analysis, it was determined that employees "legitimately, although incorrectly" reasoned that if the president called the meeting, there had to be something really bad and the president might not have told them all he knew because the company never held such a company-wide meeting before to discuss any issue. This illustrates the argument that *the context of the message could sometimes speak louder than the message itself* (Clampitt 2001). It is important for management to carefully consider the context of the employees who interpret the messages when instituting a change.

Audience Analysis

In addition to reading the context, analyzing who the organization is talking to during the change communication process is also important—how different groups of employees' work roles, routines, or relationships are affected by the change; how are they likely to interpret the change; what the employees' communication preferences are; who the key opinion leaders are; and so forth. Apparently, determining the key stakeholders will vary with the type of change. However, in general, all employees experience four stages of reactions to change: (1) discovery—realizing what is happening; (2) denial—showing initial emotional reaction to change often with comments like "it can't happen like that"; (3) resistance—a time of employee concern seeking why this is happening, how this is affecting them personally, and what would likely happen; and finally, (4) acceptance, a stage where employees are fully communicated with and reconciled to what is happening (La Framboise, Nelson, and Schmaltz 2002). Change communication efforts should be tailored to employees' information and communication needs at each stage. For instance, in the discovery and denial stages, managers should clearly and calmly communicate the particulars of the change by providing as much factual information as possible. Managers should be understanding and sensitive to employees' emotional reaction while emphasizing the need for change. In the resistance stage, organizations should continue communicating the rationale of the change, create a sense of urgency, and explain clearly and transparently what would be affected and how employees can be involved. Guttler and Ullrich (2008) proposed "magic five questions" regarding communicating change, namely,

1. "Why is change necessary?"
2. "What exactly is changing?"
3. "What is changing for me?"
4. "How can I support the change and what happens if I do not join in?"
5. "When and how will I find out the progress?"

To create a sense of urgency, research suggests multiple approaches. For instance, Clampitt (2001) noted that a diagnostic report by a consulting agency or the news media communicates a sense of urgency. Sharing data, statistics, research, and any hard evidence that demonstrates why the change has to be prioritized and done at this time helps employees understand the rationale and necessity of the change. The direct involvement of top leaders in initiating the change process also communicates the importance of the change. For instance, a CEO may travel to various branches of a corporation to discuss the need for change with local employees. Such communication efforts by the leader not only deliver the messages, but also symbolically magnify the importance and urgency of the issue. Additionally, the frequency of discussion regarding a change should create momentum, as it increases salience of the issue. Kotter (1995) noted that urgency is demonstrated when change is increasingly becoming a topic of conversation (whether negative or positive). Thus, internal stakeholders will feel change is occurring, and they need to rationalize and understand these events.

Finally, managers should also recognize that during the change process, different employees are affected in various ways to different extents depending on the type of change (e.g., acquisitions, mergers, reorganization, new product lines, or leadership change). Some employees may view the necessary changes as a welcome opportunity for personal gain or as an organization's efforts to tackle a problem carried over from the past. Employees' attitudes toward the change process can determine how much they will support or be involved in the change process. Research suggests that employees with a higher level of participation and engagement in dialogs respond more positively to a change. In summary, similar to other strategic communication efforts, strategic change communication requires a thorough understanding of the target audiences, as well as the change context, which is the soil for change.

Change Communication Strategies

As previously discussed, communication plays a critical and irreplaceable role in the successful implementation of changes. The communication strategies, tactics, and channels all matter in the strategic change management. As advised in other chapters of this book, honest, ethical communication is always the primary goal of internal communication, and that goal is even more pressing in times of change.

Transparency and Openness

Many authors agree that silence or information insufficiency breeds rumors. Gergs and Trinczek (2008) noted that "withholding information during phases of radical change is one of the worst mistakes in change management" (p. 152). Gaps in expected communication and management silence create a schism that employees will fill with their own information, including misinterpretations and rumors. Thus, the authors maintain that communicating incomplete information promptly and frequently is better than holding off information until some future situation when the complete and exact information can be communicated all at once. Constant communication sends out a signal to employees that the management is open and transparent, willing to share, and wants to keep them in the loop. In such radical situations, communication in any form, whether formal or informal, helps reduce anxiety about the change, instills confidence in management credibility, and protects trust, even if it causes bad news. Many assume that employees do not want a voice in every decision. However, they do want to understand management's goals, purposes, and intentions; what to expect during change; and fair warning on pending developments. Thus, an effective change communication system must provide orientation in an open, ethical, frank, transparent, and authentic way, which not only involves disseminating information but also listening and dialog (Gergs and Trinczek 2008).

Listening and Upward Communication

Clampitt (2001) noted that no matter how persuasively a change has been advocated, employees usually have some doubts, speculation, or dissent. Communicators need to eliminate dissent by proactively talking to them, soliciting their thoughts, and encouraging open and upward communication. Listening with patience, sensitivity, care, understanding, and compassion is critical because it conveys the message that "your anxieties are legitimate." Clampitt suggests some concrete measures for listening during change and fostering upward communication. For instance, managers could ask employees to voice their concerns and record them on a flip chart, which could be used by the organization to consequently legitimize and de-emotionalize the ideas and concerns of employees. This list can also be turned into a series of "questions and answers" that can be distributed to employees in a timely manner to clarify misunderstandings and show that their concerns are being handled. By doing this, management not only demonstrates confidence and accountability, but also solicits input from employees. This approach allows employees to understand they are included, empowered, and in control of the situation. Including their input into organizational decisions creates "buy-in," or a sense of ownership in the change in which they participate. Today, the prevalence and enterprise adoption of social media largely facilitate organizational real-time listening, employee upward communication, and voicing behavior even during the change process. By collecting feedback from informal social venues, such as blogs, social networking sites (SNSs), and messengers, and anonymous employee review sites such as Glassdoor, organizations can immediately gauge the employees' sentiments and concerns and address them real-time.

Leadership Involvement

Research consistently demonstrates that employees who are more satisfied with management communication during change saw more personal opportunities, have a positive state of mind on the organizational change, and thus respond more positively to the change implementation than those less satisfied (Bull and Brown 2012). They also feel more confident and comfortable in participating in the change process with effective leadership guidance and support. When changes occur, employees are often overwhelmed by feelings of uncertainty and danger, particularly for those whose work relationships or routines will be affected. The morale, employee confidence, and engagement level can suffer. As the top leader in an organization, the CEO needs to create a clear and sensible vision that unifies employees, guide them in the right direction, instill confidence in people, and portray a long-term shared purpose. Washington and Hacker (2005) study showed that managers who understand change efforts are more likely to be excited about the change and less likely to think that the change effort would fail. Additionally, supervisor communication is an indispensable part of the leadership communication efforts when change occurs. Employees expect to hear critical and officially sanctioned information from their immediate supervisors whom they interact with on a day-to-day basis and are perceived as the most credible information source (Seeger et al. 2005). Division heads and line managers are expected to have a better understanding of how the change initiatives will affect their units and are likely to offer practical and direct guidance for employees to become involved and proactively cope with changes. They are also well-positioned to observe and upwardly communicate the concerns, feedback, and reactions of their subordinates regarding the new initiatives.

Change Communication Channels and Tactics

Although using multiple channels is typically better (e.g., traditional and digital, one-way and two-way, mediated, and interpersonal communication channels) when communicating change because it increases the probability of employees hearing about change and reinforces the receptivity of messages (Clampitt 2001), the effectiveness of different channels may have various purposes. For instance, when introducing a change, providing sufficient information to address employees' queries is essential to reducing uncertainty, anxiety, and gaining acceptance to change. Although interpersonal communication, such as small informal discussions and general informational meetings, have been found to be the most effective, using mediated channels, such as television, videos, e-mail, and publications, has also been suggested to serve as best practices communication when introducing change (Lewis 1999). Overall, many have concluded that one-way communication still has a role in the change process, although information alone will not suffice. Two-way symmetrical, dialogical communication channels, such as face-to-face meetings or social media communication, are critical in fostering mutual understanding and shared interpretation on a new situation and building a new work consensus among those affected by change (Gergs and Trinczek 2008).

Face-To-Face Channels

Research consistently suggests the importance of face-to-face communication during change implementation. In fact, this channel becomes ever more crucial, as the changes become more complex. No other channel can be compared to face-to-face venues in terms of information richness and complexity. With two-way interactive features, town hall meetings, department meetings, workshops, site visits, or one-on-one-meetings not only allow management to get its messages across in a timely, accurate, and authentic manner, but also offer employees opportunities to voice their questions and concerns, observe, connect with one another or the management, and gain a better understanding and sense of control regarding the change. Instant feedback associated with face-to-face communication helps clarify misunderstandings and reduce uncertainty. Interpersonal approaches not only communicate verbal messages, but nonverbal messages of genuine care and emotions. The two-way give and take process often yields increased transparency and openness. This allows for direct employee involvement and participation in the change efforts and creates a sense of "we are all in for this."

Digital Channels

Digital tools, such as chat rooms, blogs, SNSs, and social messengers, are becoming popular internal communication avenues for organizations. Platforms such as Yammer, Chatter, Facebook at Work, Slack, and Spark are increasingly adopted by organizations. With the inherent features of being informal, relational, two-way, interactive, and communal, digital media could well supplement face-to-face communication, although it may not supplant the conventional interpersonal channels in change communication. According to a recent study by Weber Shandwick, partnered with KRC Research, 55 percent of the employees who experienced a change event at work stated that they wished their employer offered more digital and social engagement (Clayton 2015).

The social media component has become critical in any change plan. For example, Zappos CEO, Tony Hseih, announced that his company will lay off 8 percent of its workforce on Zappos' blog immediately after sending an internal e-mail to employees (Clayton 2015). Social media efforts demonstrated transparency that was appreciated by Zappos' employees. It also led to the increase in employees' Twitter engagement with leaders and among each other regarding the change. The open conversation generated on social media provided Zappos with important insights into how the sensitive situation should be handled and even helped some laid off employees find new employment opportunities (Clayton 2015). Internal social media can also help engage employees in shaping the future by soliciting innovative ideas that can be implemented to support the transformation. For instance, when Cisco's CEO Chuck Robbins took over, the company initiated a live thread asking employees, "What advice or suggestions do you have for Chuck Robbins as he transitions to CEO?" Over the course of four days, the post generated hundreds of comments. Crowdsourcing efforts not only empower employees by offering them an open channel to voice their opinions and ideas as well as involve them in the strategic change, but also provide management with an efficient means of listening to employees and gathering creative inputs. IBM also used social media to "jam" with its 400,000+ employees worldwide to gather information on mission change (Stacks, Wright, and Bowen 2014).

Source of Information

Who communicates the message is as important as, if not more significant than, what they say (Clampitt 2001). Larkin and Larkin (1994) argued that change is implemented most effectively by targeting supervisors as the spokesperson of change initiatives rather than having top management talk directly to frontline employees. As previously noted, supervisors are considered opinion leaders and are employees' most trusted source of information. Although messages that cascade from the senior level to employees through the line hierarchy often carry more significance, the lack of context may hinder employee understanding. Supervisors and line managers can put change initiatives into work unit context and interpret the information to employees with an emphasis on what this means for "me" and "us."

Messages

In terms of change messaging communication, many researchers agree that as a baseline, it is critical to provide sufficient information on why the change is happening, what the change is exactly about, and how the change affects the organization and employees. At a more tactical level, Clampitt (2001) suggests that organizations should always discuss the upside and downside of change, although management has a tendency to oversell the change by stressing the positives. Doing so could provide a realistic assessment of change and create a sense of trust by promoting objectivity and transparency. Messaging should also directly address the possible resistance points. Generic employee concerns during change include job security, job stability, inconveniences, loss of wages, and anxiety over the unknown. Organizations should anticipate these concerns and develop appropriate messages to address each. Additionally, reminding internal stakeholders that not everything is changing is important. It is not that "the entire world is upside down." Linking the change to the organization's mission, vision, fundamental values, and strategic imperative is a helpful step.

In conclusion, in an ever-evolving business world, organizations inevitably face and handle change. The more fundamental and complex the change is, the greater the extent of communication is needed to provide sufficient information, promote shared understanding and interpretation, and establish a new working consensus among organization members. Effective change communication cannot be achieved without the support and participation of all internal stakeholders, including top management, supervisors, line managers, as well as individual employees. With the wide adoption of new technologies, organizations should capitalize on the benefits of digital tools to maximize strategic change success. A strategic communication mindset with a thorough and deep understanding of the context, audiences, communications, and storytelling is essential to the successful implementation of change.

Summary

Organizations seek change for many reasons, such as downsizing, M&A, disaster, expansion, and adoption of a new technology. This chapter reviewed the roles of strategic internal communication for successful change initiatives and provided a roadmap for strategic change communication and management. Overall, multiple roles of effective communication in the strategic change process were suggested: reducing uncertainty, overcoming resistance to change, facilitating employee participation, and building shared understanding and mutual interpretation. Effective change communication requires a thorough understanding of the change process, its context, audiences, as well as how communication can facilitate the change process.

Strategic change communication should start with a contextual analysis, which examines the background of the organization, including its historical communication patterns, whether assimilated changes were successful in the past, whether changes are manageable and congruent with organizational culture, and whether the benefits of changes are readily observable. In addition to reading context, it is important to analyze target audiences, such as how different stakeholder work routines or relationships are affected by the change, how they are likely to interpret the change, and so forth, as different employees may be affected in various ways to different extents depending on the change type. Strategic communication that emphasizes ethics, transparency, openness, listening, and upward communication facilitates strategic change. Leadership involvement matters: CEOs and senior management need to create a clear and sensible vision that unifies stakeholders during change, with unit heads offering practical and direct guidance for employees to become involved and proactively cope with changes. Two-way communication channels, such as face-to-face meetings or social media communication, are critical in fostering mutual understanding and shared interpretation on a new situation and building a new work consensus among those affected by change.

CHAPTER 9

Measuring the Value of Internal Communication

The importance of measurement and evaluation can never be overemphasized in achieving successful communication efforts. Common adages are, "What gets measured gets done" or "No evaluation, no improvement." Measurement not only helps communication professionals to better understand communication problems, situations, issues, target audiences, and stakeholders, but also to determine the methods, tactics, tools, and messages that are effective and those that are not. More importantly, evaluative efforts provide hard data and evidence to document the success or value of communication programs and activities. Such data grants communication professionals negotiating power to obtain more resources and support from top management and allow them to eventually gain a seat at the strategic-level decision-making table.

Measuring internal communications is essential because these efforts are often tied to important employee outcomes, such as job attitudes, behavioral changes, and, more importantly, productivity, sales, and organizational performance (Berger 2008). However, for many internal communication managers, measurement and evaluation have been an important but challenging area. Melcrum's (2013) recent quantitative and qualitative data suggests that measuring, evaluating, and reporting on the effectiveness of internal communication strategies is one of the key challenges in the coming age of internal communication, along with the issues of workplace digitization and engagement. Communication leaders have identified a variety of barriers, such as insufficient resources (e.g., money and staff), difficulty in linking internal communication initiatives to business outcomes and return on investment (ROI), time constraints, lack of knowledge on quantitative or qualitative research and analytics, or absence of effective tools (Berger 2012; Rodgers 2006). In the international surveys conducted by Watson Wyatt, nearly 47 percent of the respondents reported that their companies had no formal assessment tool to evaluate the success of internal communication initiatives (Meng and Berger 2012).

Today, increasing competitiveness for budget allocations and pressure to develop ROI metrics for almost every communication expenditure have made internal communication measurement necessary for organizations. Although the adoption of new technologies, such as enterprise social media in internal communication, has complicated the matter of evaluation, it also provides built-in analytical tools and informal venues for organizations to gather employee data and solicit feedback. This chapter addresses the pressing needs for organizations to demonstrate the value of internal communication and delves into the important issues of measurement, such as what should be measured in employee communication programs (e.g., outputs, outtakes, and outcomes), how to measure them, and the alignment of communication outcomes and business objectives. The discussion in this chapter serves as a building block toward emerging standards for internal communication measurement that incorporates program-, organizational-, and business-level metrics.

A Review of Existing Measurement and Evaluation Models

Measurement and evaluation is a hot topic in public relations and communication management. Previous authors (Michaelson and Stacks 2010; Stacks 2010; Stacks and Michaelson 2010) have developed various measurement and evaluation models from different perspectives to guide evaluative practices. There are numerous award categories for campaign assessment, the *PR News* Measurement Hall of Fame, and an election-based membership organization dedicated to the topic named the Measurement Commission. There is also a *Dictionary of Public Relations Measurement and Research* (Stacks and Bowen 2013), now in its third edition, that is freely available online in eight languages (see www.instituteforpr.

org/dictionary-public-relations-measurement-research-third-edition/). Because initiatives, programs, and campaigns can differ in numerous respects, there is no one standard model for implementing the measurement of effectiveness. However, the industry disavows simple "counting impressions" metrics as well as ill-reputed AVEs (advertising-value equivalencies). Rather, there is an overall approach that is based on a "best practices" model—what should be done in an ideal scenario—with a goal in mind of measuring both attitudinal change and behavioral intention (Stacks and Bowen 2013). Stacks and Michaelson (2010) explained that, "Public relations best practices include (1) clear and well-defined research objectives, (2) rigorous research design, and (3) detailed supporting documentation" (p. 10).

A best-practice approach to measurement and evaluation also involves setting a *benchmark* by conducting research before any communication initiative (internal communication or otherwise) is undertaken. Sometimes, this phase of research is also called *formative research* because it happens at the formation or outset of a communication initiative. It may seem painstaking and burdensome to conduct research before actually doing anything else, but there is a good reason for that approach. The benchmark is the data that shows the attitudes and behavioral intention of your target stakeholders in an existent, unaltered state. This data will become the "before" benchmark to your campaign, as a comparison for your "after" data. It will allow the documentation of the amount of attitude and behavioral intention change among employees directly attributable to your internal communication activities.

Benchmark data is garnered by conducting research on the broad topic of your initiative with the strategic target stakeholders, normally through a *quantitative* survey followed up by qualitative data collection, such as focus groups or interviews. The survey normally covers a broad range of attitudinal variables (e.g., "To what extent do you agree with the statement 'X is an honest organization?'") and narrows to assess behavioral intention (e.g., "Please rate how likely you are to continue your employment at X"). When the survey is completed by as large of a sample of your population as is practical *at random*, statistical analyses and generalizations can be made.[1] There are specific guidelines that cover the level of competence and margin of error you can have with such data. However, a general rule is that the greater the number of people who complete the survey, the better your results. You can then make statements for later comparison such as, "40 percent of the employee sample agreed or strongly agreed that organization X is honest." Clearly, there is room for improvement in that example, and you would compare this before data with later data after your internal communication campaign and look for improvements in the measure of honesty.

A next step would be to gather *qualitative* data in which you ask participants for candid opinions about the areas of interest in your survey. For example, you may ask a focus group, "Can you offer any examples of when you believe the organization may have been less than honest with you?" or "What might have led you to feel that way?" Qualitative data can be used to add detail and in-depth understanding to your statistical results. Qualitative data is not generalizable, but excels in explaining why questions and offering insights into the data that are not possible to obtain from a quantitative sample.

Based on the analysis of these data, both qualitative and quantitative, an internal communication program (ongoing) or campaign (periodic) can be designed and implemented. Both ongoing and campaign programs would be assessed for their effectiveness. Program assessment would be conducted in order to measure effectiveness and retool elements of the program that were underperforming (i.e., research as feedback on the program), whereas campaign assessment would be conducted at the end of the campaign period.

Assessing the effectiveness of a program or campaign is conducted through using the *same* research measures that were used in the benchmarking phase of research. In this manner, assessment compares "apples

---

[1] The key term here, "at random" means that anyone in the target population can be chosen to participate in the research (Stacks 2011, 2017). Non-random or non-probability research can only say what was obtained and not generalize it to the larger group that may define the population; random selections allows for generalization within varying degrees of measurement and sampling error.

to apples" and be used to show the ROI to the organization through its internal communication initiative. The amount of change that is measured, with a new sample in the evaluation phase, is comparable to the data gathered in the benchmarking or formative research phase. For example, your analysis of program effectiveness could conclude:

Whereas only 40 percent of employees thought the organization was honest initially, after the internal communications ethics initiative, 56 percent of employees reported that the organization was honest. This data marks a 16 percent increase in perceptions of honesty among employees as a result of our ethics initiative.

Further, that data can be used to guide ongoing communication programs. For example, this report may conclude:

A 16 percent increase in employee perceptions of honesty was reported after a three-month ethics campaign, so we recommend that the campaign be extended for three more months with a target of another 15 percent increase in employee perceptions organizational honesty.

At that point, campaign effectiveness could be assessed again.

Although thinking of the best practices approach as taking a "before" and "after" snapshot of attitudes might be a bit of an oversimplification of the complex quantitative and qualitative research measures involved, yet it can be helpful in explaining the efficacy of our activities and justifying further expenditures on internal communication. Further, using this best-practices approach to measuring the effectiveness of our communication activities can help save money by budgeting for those initiatives that are achieving success and retooling initiatives that are not meeting goals or objectives. Measuring effectiveness helps the internal communications manager communicate with precision, targeted effectiveness, alacrity, and to effectively meet the needs of employees.

What Should Be Measured in Internal Communication?

No single *standard* is used to measure communication effectiveness. One coherent theme that emerged from the previously reviewed measurement models is that communication can be evaluated from different levels at different stages. This multistage or multilevel measurement approach is congruent with how human communication works. In the basic communication model, a message sender initiates the communication process by encoding the meaning into some sort of message. The message is then transmitted to the message recipients through certain channels, either interpersonal or mediated within a social or traditional (e.g., newspaper, television, radio) context. When the receivers receive the message, they decode its meaning to understand, interpret, and make sense of it. They then react with certain attitudes or behavior on the basis of their interpretation of the message. Therefore, following the communication "loop," as pointed out by Lindenmann (1993) and Broom and Dozier (1990), communication efforts can be evaluated as *outputs* (e.g., messages sent, paced, and distributed; channel effectiveness), *outtakes* (e.g., reach; impressions audience's reception, recall, and retention of messages; understanding), and *outcomes* (e.g., changes in audience awareness, knowledge, opinions, attitudes, and behaviors).

Repeated internal communication activities and programs influence employees' understanding of key messages and sense-making, which in turn affect their beliefs, attitudes, opinions, and changes in behavior over time. Eventually, positive employee behavioral changes, such as higher level of engagement, advocacy, and organizational citizenship behavior, cast a lasting impact on the tangible organizational outcomes of sales, productivity, and organizational performance. The three building blocks of internal communication—hierarchical (leadership) communication, corporate (mass) communication, and informal network (horizontal peer communication among employees)—should all be considered in the evaluation process. On the basis of recent professional and academic literature, the authors suggest a list of key performance indicators (KPIs) and evaluation criteria for each level of internal communication measurement.

Output Measures

Outputs are essentially the direct results of the tactics and channels used to implement internal communication strategies; in other words, an output refers to what is produced and distributed.

Message Products

This is the most straightforward measure to count the communication materials produced and distributed in the internal communication process, such as numbers of newsletters, magazines, CEO speeches produced, e-mails sent, events or meetings organized, and social media updates posted.

Channels

Beyond examining the message, the effectiveness of the channels should be continuously evaluated. Are the mediated or interpersonal channels working for your specific communication purpose (e.g., to inform, to listen, to acculturate, to connect)? Which channel is the most effective for which purpose—newsletters, magazines, intranet, e-mail briefings, conferences, "town hall" meetings, team meetings, one-on-one meetings, or social media tools? Is the channel appropriate for the content? Is the channel working for particular internal audiences? Are the channels chosen the ones used by audience members to gratify their information needs?

Outtake Measures

Outtakes are associated with how audiences receive, perceive, interpret, and react to the messages that are communicated to them.

Reach

The simple distribution of messages cannot guarantee the reach and reception of messages. For example, how many employees opened your e-mail? How many employees read your newsletter or watched your videos? How many unique visitors visit your website every day? What percentage of employees subscribed to the corporate blog, read your posts, or followed you on Facebook, Twitter, or LinkedIn?

Two-Way Engagement

The readership and viewership of messages indicate one-way message consumption. However, communication is a two-way, give and take, send and receive and re-send, dialogical process. Measures used in program evaluation should gauge stakeholder's level of engagement with the message(s). For instance, which blog or social media posts caught employees' attention and which one earned the most likes, shares, and comments? How many downloads and click-throughs were attained? How many pieces of content, such as blog posts and re-tweets, are contributed by employees?

Content

Messages can be evaluated from employees' perspective in terms of understandability or readability, relevance, clarity, and credibility. Questions can also be asked about the format or style of the messages: Is the message attention-grabbing? Is it memorable? Do the employees find the message interesting?

Message Recall or Retention

To examine whether key messages are successfully retained by employees, quick polls can be conducted to gather employee feedback on whether they could recall certain key messages, how much they could recall, and why they are able to recall it (e.g., was it because of the humor or emotional elements in the message?). Such measures offer feedback on the effectiveness of message appeals and types of content that stick with employees.

Information Satisfaction

This measure mainly evaluates whether the messages are meeting internal stakeholders' information needs. Is the information timely? Complete? Accurate? Consistent? Adequate? Sufficient? Added? Is it what the organization and leaders want to tell or what employees want to know? A difference exists between knowing what employees need to know and being in the know. Being always kept in the loop about happenings in the organization builds a sense of belonging, reduces uncertainty and rumors, and fosters employee advocacy (White, Vanc, and Stafford 2010).

Outcome Measures

In general, outcomes of communication can be measured at the cognitive, affective, and behavioral levels (Stacks 2002, 2011, 2017). In other words, the effect of communication can be gauged in terms of its influence on audiences' awareness, knowledge, understanding, opinions, attitudes, interests, and behavior (Broom and Dozier 1990; Lindenmann 1993).

Cognitive Level

Awareness/knowledge/understanding. Internal communication serves an important informational purpose. For instance, an organization's mission, vision, purposes, and core values must be continuously communicated, interpreted, and reinforced. Accordingly, measures should be undertaken to examine how much employees know about and understand the organization's identity, ethical values, and brand platform. As employees become more active corporate advocates and ambassadors in the increasingly connected and transparent social era, organizations need to invest more in educating and involving their employees symmetrically in their strategic initiatives, including defining who they are, what they believe, what they do, and why they exist. Additionally, during issues, crises, or change management processes, employees' full understanding of the situation can reduce uncertainty, prevent rumors, and instill confidence in management. Increasing employee awareness, knowledge, and understanding of what is communicated by the organization serves as a critical first step in changing employee attitudes or behavior. Michaelson and Stacks (2010, in press) talk about this in terms of the "communication life cycle" or the BASIC model (Figure 9.1). Understanding where stakeholders are in the life cycle through research provides a strategic starting advantage for any internal communication program, thus saving time and money.

Internal reputation. Defined as "employees' overall evaluation of the organization based on their direct experiences with the company and all forms of communication" (Men 2014a, 256), internal reputation is an

Communication objectives

● **BASIC** communication objectives for public relations efforts:

  ○ Build awareness

  ○ Advance knowledge

  ○ Sustain relevance

  ○ Initiate action

  ○ Create advocacy

Figure 9.1 BASIC communication objectives for public relations efforts

important performance indicator of an organization's internal communication efforts. Adopting the Harris–Fombrun Corporate Reputation Quotient (Fombrun, Gardberg, and Sever 2000), which is a valid, reliable, and robust tool to measure corporate reputation, we can examine internal reputation from the following six aspects from the perspective of employees: emotional appeal, product and services, vision and leadership, work environment, social and environmental responsibility, and financial performance. A sample measure is provided in Appendix A.

Perceived organizational ethics, core values, and transparency. Organizational ethics is the extent to which an organization acts on moral principles. They are how it defines, upholds, and enacts its core values—those values are key beliefs that govern the behavior of—and in—the organization (Bowen 2015, 2016a). The extent to which employees perceived organizational ethics can have a tremendous impact on how much trust they place in the organization (Bowen, Hung-Baesecke, and Chen 2016) as well as how they rate its transparency. Transparency can be evaluated as the openness and visibility of an organization's communication and reputation attributes (Rawlins 2009). From the employees' perspective, transparency can be measured in terms of whether the organization disseminates substantial, truthful, complete, accurate, and balanced information in a timely manner (information substantiality); whether the organization incorporates employees' voices to determine what information they really need, how much information they need, and how well the organization is fulfilling their information need (participation); whether leaders enact ethical behavior and follow words with actions (Bowen 2015); and whether the organization is accountable for their words, actions, and decisions and is open to criticism (Men and Stacks 2014; Rawlins 2009). A sample measure (Rawlins 2009) is provided in Appendix B.

Perceived organizational authenticity. Stakeholders, including employees, emphasize organizations' authenticity. Following the call to build an *authentic enterprise* by the Arthur Page Society in 2007, communicators have since endeavored to foster organizational authenticity characterized by truthfulness, genuineness, and consistency. Employees' perceived organizational authenticity can be measured by asking whether employees believe that the organization advocates truthfulness in its storytelling (Molleda 2010), whether the organization acts genuinely and does not manipulate employees, and whether the organization stays true to itself; in other words, the organization's conduct is congruent with its values, beliefs, mission, principles, and rhetoric (Men and Tsai 2014; Shen and Kim 2012). A sample measure (Shen and Kim 2012) is provided in Appendix C.

Affective Level

Employee–organization relationships (EORs). Organization–public relationships have been suggested as one of the major outcomes of public relations at the organizational level. Similarly, the effectiveness of internal relations can be measured by evaluating the quality of the relationships between employees and the organization. By definition, an EOR refers to the degree to which an organization and its employees trust one another (*trust*), agree on who has the rightful power to influence (*control mutuality*), experience satisfaction with one another (*satisfaction*), and commit themselves to the other (*commitment*) (Men 2014c). The EOR scale adapted from Hon and Grunig's (1999) measure of organization–public relationships is presented in Appendix D. This model has recently been adapted to also include ethics as a variable that must be present *before* any relationship can be built, as it is a facilitator of trust between an organization and publics or employees (Bowen, Hung-Baesecke, and Chen 2016).

Job satisfaction. Many believe that internal stakeholder's job satisfaction is the most focal employee attitude and is predictive of employees' job performance. Locke (1976) defined job satisfaction as "... a pleasurable or positive emotional state resulting from the appraisal of one's job or job experiences" (p. 1304). The two most extensively validated job satisfaction measures are the Job Descriptive Index (JDI) (Smith, Kendall, and Hulin 1969) and the Minnesota Satisfaction Questionnaire (MSQ) (Weiss et al. 1967). The JDI assesses satisfaction with five job areas: pay, promotion, coworkers, supervision, and the work itself. The MSQ has the advantage of versatility, providing both long and short forms of measures. Although internal communication is not the only factor that influences job satisfaction, it plays an important role in affecting employees' satisfaction with coworkers, supervisors, and the work environment.

Organizational identification. Internal communication builds shared understanding and interpretations, and thus nurtures a sense of belonging and organizational identification. Organizational identification is defined as "perception of oneness with or belongingness to an organization, where the individual defines him or herself in terms of the organization(s) in which he or she is a member" (Mael and Ashforth 1992, 104). A sample measure of organizational identification based on Mael and Ashforth (1992) is provided in Appendix E.

Employee empowerment. Defined as employees' feeling of competence and having decision-making autonomy and control in the organization (Men 2011), employee empowerment is regarded as an important mediator between leadership, communication factors, and employee outcomes. Open, transparent, and two-way organizational communication, sufficient information, and transformational leadership that emphasizes listening, participation, and care for employees instill a sense of empowerment. Thus, the effectiveness of internal corporate communication and leadership communication can be determined from the measurement of employees' feeling of empowerment in the organization. A sample measure of employee empowerment (Men 2011) is presented in Appendix F.

Employee engagement. Engagement is prevalently measured by organizations as a KPI of effective internal communication and management. Engaged employees are attentive, fully and actively present, immersed, and motivated to bring all aspects of themselves to the performance of their work roles. They also demonstrate high levels of energy, passion, and enthusiasm in what they do, and they find meaning, inspiration, and purpose in their work. Employee engagement describes employees' motivated state characterized by cognitive, physical, and emotional involvement. Organizations such as Gallup, Towers Watson, and IBM Kenexa administer annual and bi-annual engagement studies globally in the largest organizations. A sample measure derived from recent literature (Men 2015) is provided in Appendix G.

Behavioral Level

Behavioral change is the ultimate goal of communication. Organizations' internal communication efforts nurture employee attitudes, which eventually drive employee behavior and action toward a particular direction. The following list of outcome variables summarizes some key behavioral-level performance indicators of internal communication based on the literature.

Employee advocacy. The role of employees as organizations' informal spokespersons and advocates is more salient than ever before in this increasingly connected and transparent digital age. Successful internal communication nurtures positive employee attitudes, which turn employees into corporate ambassadors, who are considered to be more credible and trustworthy than CEOs or public relations managers as corporate spokespersons. Employee advocacy, defined as "the voluntary promotion or defense of a company, its products, or its brands by an employee externally" (Men 2014c, 262), is a major step forward in evolving employee–organization relationships. A sample measure of employee advocacy (Men 2014c) is presented in Appendix H.

Employee communication behavior. Employee communication behavior centers on the role of employees as information agents. Two types of employee communication behaviors are "megaphoning," which refers to employees' positive or negative external communication behaviors about the organization's accomplishments or problems, and "scouting," which refers to employees' voluntary efforts to search and obtain valuable organizational-related information and circulate and share such information with the organization (Kim and Rhee 2011). Such two-way voluntary information behavior can result from organizations' effective internal communication and quality employee–organization relationships. The measure of employee communication behavior developed by Kim and Rhee is included in Appendix I.

Organizational citizenship behavior (OCB). The concept of OCB denotes employees' organizationally beneficial behaviors and gestures that are neither enforced based on formal role obligations nor elicited by contractual compensation or reward systems. For example, if an employee voluntarily stays late to finish work when not asked to or goes out of his or her way to help a coworker who encounters a difficulty is considered an organizational citizen (Feather and Rauter 2004). Organizational citizenship behaviors are arguably predicted by individual dispositional factors, organizational characteristics (e.g., culture and communication), task characteristics, and leadership behaviors (Podsakoff et al. 2000). In addition, such behaviors are positive correlated with employee attitudes, such as job satisfaction, quality employee–organization relationships, and organizational identification (Feather and Rauter 2004), which are directly or indirectly affected by organizations' communication efforts. A sample measure of OCB as an indirect behavioral outcome of internal communication is presented in Appendix J.

Employee voice behavior. Voice behavior refers to employees' expression of constructive ideas, information, opinions, and insights about change in the organization (directed up, down, or horizontally) that are explicitly intended to benefit the group or the organization. Voice is a particular form of employee proactive or citizenship behavior (Botero and Dyne 2009), and it has been found to predict employees' job performance and creativity (Ng and Feldman 2011). Researchers have suggested a variety of voice behavior influencers, including leadership behavior (e.g., transformational leadership and authentic leadership), leader–member exchange (supervisor–follower relationship), and organizational culture (Botero and Dyne 2009), which are all intertwined with internal communication. Additionally, the availability of communication venues can influence employees' voice behavior. A sample measure of employee voice behavior (Botero and Dyne 2009) is included in Appendix K.

Employee alignment. Employee alignment refers to the degree to which employees understand, support, buy into, and are able to enact the organization's strategic initiatives (Gagnon and Michael 2003). Creating such alignment is vital for organizations because employees are those who will accomplish their objectives. Research has shown that internal stakeholders who hold positive attitudes toward the organization's strategic objectives are more likely to make decisions that are congruent and aligned with these objectives. Eventually, this alignment contributes to organizational performance. Van Riel, Berens, and Dijkstra (2005) found that management communication, communication about strategic initiatives, and communication climates affect alignment. Specifically, employees are more likely to hold supportive attitudes toward the company's strategy issues when they consider the flow, content, and climate of internal communication to be adequate. A sample item to measure employee alignment could be "Most members of my division take initiative to implement the [company] values in day-to-day work" (van Riel, Berens, and Dijkstra 2005, 18). The Institute for Public Relations' Commission on Organizational Communication (2016) released a white paper on organizational clarity that addressed employee alignment and provided specific measures. Access to the full report can be found here: www.instituteforpr.org/wp-content/uploads/Organizational-Clarity-White-Paper-05-06-16-Final-Online.pdf

In addition to the measures described earlier, other factors such as employees' satisfaction with the organization's overall communication, perceived leader credibility, and leader–member exchange are important intermediate measures that can be influenced by corporate internal communication or leadership communication efforts, which eventually affect the aforementioned cognitive-, affective-, and behavioral-level employee outcomes. Team- or group-level outcomes such as satisfaction, commitment, and performance can also be predicted by team or peer communication. The authors make no attempt to exhaust the list but summarize some key measures that can be applied to all levels of internal communication for the organization to start with.

Business Results or ROI

Similar to the evaluation of external public relations efforts, perhaps the most challenging but important step of measuring internal communication is to demonstrate its effect on the organization's bottom line, that is, to quantify how an employee communication program or day-to-day internal communication practices influence the company's business objectives or ROI. Such indicators include unit or organizational productivity, sales, revenue, employee retention, and customer satisfaction or retention. Broadly, the effect of internal communication practices on the organization's financial performance can be assessed by "money made" and "money saved." Whereas sales, revenue, and productivity are the *direct* measures of the business impact of internal communication, customer or employee retention and avoided crises or lawsuits because of effective internal communication save money for the organization, thus are *indirect* measures contributing to the company's bottom line. Indeed, multiple factors such as marketing, HR, and sales sometimes contribute to business results, and isolating the impact of internal communication practices may be difficult. Nevertheless, by using scientific methods, such measurement efforts can be achieved. For instance, a retail company can conduct an A/B test on two retail stores in the same city to showcase the effectiveness of their recently adopted internal communication technology and see how it affects employee morale, productivity, and sales. Faced with the rapidly changing and increasingly competitive business environment, communication managers today must make a direct and strong link between communication efforts and the organization's financial performance. Doing so not only helps communicators gain more management support, resources, and investment, but also contributes to the organization's long-term success and effectiveness. According to Meng and Berger (2012), high-effectiveness organizations are five times more likely to measure the business impact of internal communication than low-effectiveness organizations.

The list of internal communication KPIs may seem open-ended—for instance, employee communication practices also influence the organization's structural outcomes, such as organizational culture, innovation behavior, creativity, and organizational learning. Organizations and businesses may selectively use the measures introduced earlier depending on the needs, resources available to them, and purposes of communication. Knowing what to measure is a vital first step. The next big question facing communication managers then is "how," that is, how do we measure internal communication outputs, outtakes, outcomes, and business impact?

How to Measure the Effectiveness of Internal Communication

Measuring the results of internal communication requires a clear understanding of what the communication efforts try to achieve, for instance, to increase awareness or to change attitudes or behavior. Thus, setting up goals and SMART (i.e., specific, measurable, attainable, relevant, and time-bound) communication objectives that are output-, outtake-, or outcome-based is essential. Communication objectives should be developed on the basis of a thorough analysis of the situation (e.g., SWOT—strengths, weaknesses, opportunities, threats), the problem the organization is facing, resources available, and target audiences. Such objectives need to be aligned with business objectives. This requirement calls for communication managers who possess a strategic mindset, business acumen, knowledge of how the organization works, and the ability to step outside their department to work with senior management.

In addition to establishing communication objectives, communication managers must set up evaluation benchmarks, gauging the *status quo* with regard to what the communication practices aim to achieve (e.g., awareness, attitudes, or behavior) prior to any planned communication efforts. This aim can often be accomplished by secondary or primary research. Without something to gauge against as a baseline, communication initiatives can be hardly evaluated during or afterward with any degree of precision (Stacks, Dodd, and Men 2011). As noted by Stacks et al. (2011), communication research and measurement should be strategically planned like any other decision-making processes in the organization. With the baseline, benchmarks, and communication objectives in place, communication managers can ask relevant research questions or set research objectives for evaluative research, gather data through formal or informal research methods, analyze data, and draw inferences or recommendations for actions from the findings. As discussed earlier, a variety of data collection methods can be used by organizations to gather information on internal communication. These evaluative methods were broadly categorized as formal (quantitative) methods and informal (qualitative) methods.

Integration: Communication Audits

Formal methods are generally more expensive than informal ones, but neither approach alone is sufficient to provide a complete and comprehensive picture. Whereas quantitative approaches, such as surveys, can offer an objective view with representative data and may provide hard evidence with figures that showcase the effectiveness of an employee communication campaign, qualitative methods such as interviews could probe into details and help understand the rationale and behind-the-scenes stories regarding why such campaign was or was not effective. Successful companies seek to use a systematic and formal integrated evaluation approach such as a *communication audit*. The most complete format of a communication audit involves one-on-one interviews with top executives and opinion leader employees, focus group discussions, a well-conceived survey questionnaire, and a critical analysis of the strategic communication plan (Smith 1991). Such integrative methods not only provide both quantitative and qualitative data, but also incorporate the standpoints of the management and employees. The direct involvement of the management and employees in the evaluation process can help them develop a holistic view of how communication works in the organization and why it matters beyond the purposes of tracking communication performance and detecting deficiencies.

"Big Data" Predictive Modeling: Going Beyond Descriptive Analyses

Without thorough and sophisticated data analysis, information gathered can hardly be transformed into insights that inform management's decision-making. Traditionally, the lack of data analytical skills is a key challenge in measuring communication efforts. Using descriptions, such as frequencies, percentages, or means, may provide simple and straightforward information about what the status quo is like, such as to what extent employees are satisfied or engaged. However, without correlational or predictive analysis, we cannot easily gauge which factors contribute to the increase or decrease of employee satisfaction and engagement. Similarly, if communication managers seek to establish the linkage between internal communication factors and employee behavior or business success indicators, using correlational or predictive analysis is necessary.

Especially in today's digital era, a large volume of unstructured data from various sources are made available to organizations in real time. In fact, internal data are the primary source of big data within an organization (Melcrum 2013). Such data includes not only unstructured online data, such as information from online forums, web feeds, browsing habits, social media comments, and textual documents, but also internal structured data, such as HR records, web profiles, and employee data gathered from other formal methods. The proliferation of information, although unorganized, provides organizations with an invaluable opportunity to understand internal stakeholders at a deeper level. Companies can align their processes, culture, and operations to embrace and exploit big data to gain timely and differentiated insights about employees and make accurate predictions about employee attitudes and behaviors using new analytical tools. For example, Yammer partnered with a sentiment analysis startup, Kanjova, and incorporated big data analytics in the measurement of employee engagement. Yammer provides analysis on employee attitudes and perceptions on the basis of their conversations within the Yammer network. Instead of tracking or profiling individuals, the software aggregates and compares groups of conversations and produces a word cloud that depicts the company's trending conversations. It can also help showcase the most "liked" individuals in the office and locate the star employees and opinion leaders in different departments (Melcrum 2013). These new "big data" analytical tools unlock the value of the enormous amount of real-time employee-related information and allow companies to capitalize on it for competitive advantage.

Summary

Measurement and evaluation play an important role in demonstrating the success of the organization's communication efforts. A best-practices approach for program or campaign evaluation of attitudes and behavioral intention both before and after a campaign, using quantitative and qualitative research, was offered as a means to assess effectiveness. Effective measurement can help communication professionals better understand the communication problem, situation, issues, and target publics, set communication benchmarks, and inform decision-making. It also documents the value of communication programs and helps gain departmental resources and support from top management. This chapter addressed two fundamental questions in measuring the value of internal communication, namely, what should be measured and evaluated (what are the measurement criteria) and how to measure them.

Overall, internal communication can be measured at the outputs, outtakes, outcomes, and business impact levels. Output measures include counting the number of messages produced and channel effectiveness. Outtake measures include message reach, impressions, and how employees perceive the message content regarding understandability, relevance, clarity, and credibility, how much they could recall or retain the key messages, and their information satisfaction. Outcome measures include cognitive-level variables, such as knowledge and understanding of the organization's vision, mission, purposes, and core values, perceived internal reputation, ethical principles, transparency and authenticity; affective variables such as employee–organization relationships, job satisfaction, organizational identification, employee empowerment and engagement; and behavioral variables such as employee advocacy, employee communication behavior, organizational citizenship behavior, voice behavior, and employee alignment. Business impact measures include unit or organizational productivity, sales, revenue, employee retention, and customer satisfaction or retention.

Effective measurement and evaluation requires SMART communication objectives set up at the beginning of the program. Quantitative (e.g., survey, experiment, content analysis) and qualitative research methods (e.g., key informant interviews, focus groups, participant observation) can be used to gather data. "Big data" analytics, correlational analysis, and predictive modeling allow organizations to establish relationships between variables and use big data to its maximum value for the organization's success.

CHAPTER 10

The Future of Internal Communication

Companies today operate in an increasingly complex world. The fast-changing, competitive, diverse, and dynamic business environments are far less predictable than ever and cast both challenges and opportunities for organizations' communication practices. For organizations to keep up with the growing pace of change in the market, sustain a competitive advantage, and achieve business success, building an engaged, committed, and happy workforce and retaining talent is essential. Furthermore, in this increasingly connected, globalized, and transparent digital age, the line between internal and external is blurred. Internal stakeholders' voice is amplified and able to travel across borders in real time. Employees' roles as corporate ambassadors and brand advocates are far more salient than ever before. And more commonly than ever before, an engaged workforce is offering a competitive advantage to employers.

The evolving environment, technology, audiences, and macro- and micro-level issues are reshaping organizations' communication landscape and internal communication practices. Although anticipating what will happen tomorrow is often quite impossible, these attempts help us to plan for the changing expectations of employers and employees as well as the implications of such change for the workplace and society. In this chapter, we discuss the upcoming trends and issues that may alter internal communication practices in the upcoming years.

Trends and Issues Reshaping Internal Communication

The trends and issues affecting internal communication practices have been an ongoing discussion topic among professionals and scholars. People may hold different views on how the future will unfold for employees and workplace communication practices, but six major trends and issues that are happening or are about to happen are identified from our research and trade publications.

Digitized Workplace

The rapid growth and internal adaptation of digital technologies by organizations have transformed the workplace and the internal communication landscape. New media tools, such as blogs, social messengers, social networking sites (SNSs), and interactive videos, have not only altered how information can be transmitted inside organizations, but also how organizations and management listen to their employees, how content is created and shared, how employees are connected, and how internal communities are formed. These sweeping changes and disruptions, referred to as the "Digital Renaissance of Work" (Miller and Marsh 2014), have changed multiple aspects of an employee's life. On the one hand, interactive and human-centered digital tools enable organizations to personify themselves and to put a human face behind "cold" names. They also blur the communication hierarchies between top management and employees, foster direct leadership engagement and conversation with employees, and promote horizontal communication among peers. On the other hand, using social media platforms internally creates a democratic, equal, transparent, empowering, and open environment where employees may feel encouraged and safe to voice their opinions and share their thoughts, ideas, and talent with others. The rich data produced on internal social media provides organizations invaluable information to truly gauge what employees think, feel, or need. Despite the enormous and unparalleled opportunities to engage all internal stakeholders offered by the digitized workplace, it does not come without challenges. In addition to the fact that many organizations are not digitally equipped, or are unaware of how to set up an effective social media use policy, which tools to adopt and which not, and privacy and security issues all require organizations to exert efforts to resolve. Further, although communication is faster with digital media forms, it is also more fragmented and offers more chance for the introduction of inaccuracies that may be difficult to correct (Bowen 2013).

Generational Differences, Diversity, and Inclusion

The workforce in the United States and globally is growing increasingly diverse, as the world becomes flatter and more connected. Diversity and inclusion were suggested to be a top priority for businesses in 2016 (Bersin 2015). As Boomers leave the workforce, more influence will be asserted by Gen X, millennials, and Gen Z (identified as anyone born in 1998 or later). How to communicate effectively against this new theater of generational differences will be a new challenging issue for future organizations (Burton 2016). Indeed, diversity in the workplace not only refers to multigenerational or race, gender, and age differences, but it is also about the differences in employees' background, education, cultures, personalities, physical abilities or challenges, and so forth.

Research proves that companies with greater diversity outperform their peers by a significant margin. For instance, McKinsey's research (Hunt, Layton, and Prince 2015) showed that gender-diverse companies are 15 percent more likely to outperform their competitors; that ethnically diverse organizations are 35 percent more likely to outperform their peers. Inclusive teams outperform their peers by 80 percent in team-based assessment (Bersin 2015). Diversity and inclusion contribute to companies' increased adaptability, attraction to talent, broader range of skills and experiences, and innovation and creativity (Greenberg 2004), although challenges exist as well, such as language and cultural barriers, prejudice, stereotyping, and discrimination (Green et al. 2012). These challenges show where the importance of communication comes in. Internal communication initiatives, in relation to the diversifying workforce, can help maximize the benefits of diversity and overcome challenges by segmenting internal publics for more micro-targeted communication, developing a culture of genuine inclusion and openness, and fostering collaboration, mutual understanding, trust, and respect. Furthermore, the macro trends of globalization, technology, and an increasingly migratory workforce have offered companies opportunities to tap into the diverse talent pools that were hardly reachable before.

Globalized and Multicultural Workforces

Globalization has been an ongoing trend for decades. Today, the greater openness of economies, trade liberalization, growth of labor migration, and technology advancement have accelerated the global expansion of businesses. Many companies have stretched across borders to a point where they have larger operations and more employees in other parts of the world than in their home countries (The Economic Intelligence Unit 2015). At the same time, skilled and well-educated workers from developing countries seek higher wages and better opportunities across borders, thereby shaping a globalized, diverse, and multicultural workforce. Cultural diversity in general contributes to organizational success, with a positive effect on innovation and creativity. However, organizations face challenges in balancing corporate culture with societal culture. Management struggles to develop effective management and communication styles that are tailored to the needs of multicultural employees, who come from different backgrounds with diverse beliefs, values, and communication orientations and may react differently to news and information because of cultural, social, language, and historic differences (Burton 2016). As the changing demographics, changing patterns of mobility, and globalization continue to transform the nature of work and workers, how to engage and integrate a global and multicultural workforce is a new puzzle for modern organizations. Diversity also includes many other factors for inclusion such as physical limitations, thought diversity, veteran status, age and gender equality, religious liberties; these factors are further complicated by cultural differences. Communication is the key to overcoming such a challenge and to building cross-cultural understanding, although it requires cross-functional collaboration among management, human resources, technology, and communication.

Social Conscience and Impact

The future workforce will be led by millennials and Gen Z ers. Although the millennial generation was responsible for the disruption, Gen Z will be tasked with building a new social order. Recent research showed that 91 percent of Gen Z individuals were optimistic that their generation would build a better world. Both the millennial and Gen Z generations take into account a company's social responsibility (Bowen and Gallicano 2013; PwC 2011). In the era of greater demands for ethical accountability and transparency, organizations' stakeholders, including customers, investors, and employees, want to analyze the organizations' social behavior, not only their share price (Ignatius 2015). Thus, companies' ability to demonstrate a social conscience, show employees that they champion their causes and beliefs, and give them more influence, power, and opportunities to create meaningful changes has become a modern competitive advantage for organizations. Employees often express a greater commitment to the organization when that company expresses a clear and actionable set of ethical values (Bowen 2015, 2016a).

A *PR Week* study reported that by 2015, 85.7 percent of employers would be involved in their communities, 81.7 percent would offer employees time to take part in charitable work, and 49.3 percent would set aside a percentage of the revenue for charities or nonprofit organizations (Daniels 2015). As Jay Haines, founder of Grace Blue, noted:

> People have to understand on a day-to-day basis what they are coming to work to do; what they are expecting to achieve, and what the company is all about… That has become fundamental to whether people select to move or stay with a company. (Daniels 2015, 31)

Organizations need to identify a cause and find an area on which they can have the greatest influence, a cause that plays to a company's greatest strength, and incorporate such values into their vision, mission, and purposes, which are constantly communicated and reinforced to all company stakeholders. An established social conscience that is aligned with employee passion, meaning, and purposes not only sets the organization apart from its competitors, but also helps employees realize their values in life to build deeper connections and organizational identification. Internal communication professionals can help identify employee role models who live by organizational values, spotlight, and recognize their contributions, linking their efforts to the corporate values they hold sacrosanct and telling their stories to inspire and mobilize others (Burton 2016).

Work–Life Balance

Although technology has penetrated work life, the drivers of change in internal communication are not reliant on tools or technology—they come from the people. How people are treated and what they experience in the organization are at the center. Many authors have noted that competitive remuneration must be given to succeed with employee recruitment and retention, but what truly determines winning or losing the battle is whether or not the employer offers a great place to work (Daniels 2015). The issue of work–life balance is at the center of discussion on creating a pleasant work environment. *Flexibility* has become increasingly important for organizations, especially for attracting millennials and Gen Z, who place great emphasis on work–life balance, to enter the workplace. According to recent industry research, 92 percent of the employers today offer the ability to work from home, and more and more employers are striving toward more flexible work arrangements, providing employees with the skills and tools needed to work wherever they may be (Burton 2016).

Many companies provide clear paths to senior-level positions and offer cross-functional training, mentoring, and various career development opportunities, as good talent is constantly seeking for new experiences, opportunities, challenges, and responsibilities. Equally important, a collaborative, open, and fun work atmosphere and culture contribute to employees' perception of work–life balance. As Oscar Suris, Head of Corporate Communications at Wells Fargo noted, "Everyone wants the financial rewards and bonuses. They are important and we do them, but if you're still working in a climate that feels stoic, unappreciated, and not friendly, the value of those specific benefits gets undercut" (Daniels 2015, 31). Internal communication is irreplaceable in communicating the values and efforts of work–life balance of organization and in creating a supportive, appreciative, collaborative, and fun environment.

Radical Downsizing of Technology

The advent of *nanotechnology* and the myriad applications across numerous industries are set to revolutionize the entire technological world. *PR Week* offered nine separate industries that nanotech will revolutionize

(Bowen 2016b), from surgery to humanitarian relief to manufacturing. For example, one nanobot can replicate itself into thousands and then work to excise only potentially cancerous cells. But who controls it and how, what happens to the jobs of traditional surgeons, and which factors should determine access to the technology?

Additionally, neurotechnology has advanced to the point that brain-to-computer interfaces are now possible (Bowen 2016c). Artificial intelligence (AI), thought reading, and memory alteration are in development and have implications of all kinds for numerous industries. Manufacturing controls and efficiencies will soon be revolutionized in a manner just as dramatic as the industrial revolution, but this time it will be the nanorevolution. Human–machine interfaces will become so common in the workplace that many new work efficiencies and questions will emerge as both neurotechnology and nanotechnology revolutionize not only manufacturing, but also data gathering (Bowen 2016d). Perhaps the biggest challenges for both neurotechnology and nanotechnology are ethical questions that remain, as yet, unanswered (Bowen 2016d). Ethical questions of both the use of, control of, and access to nanotechnology will become a common challenge in public relations of the next years.

Mobile devices will become even more commonplace than they are today with nanotech, and their size and convenience will change how we interact with these devices. For example, mobile phone or data devices may be worn in contact lenses. They may also be implanted in the body, but who controls that data during work hours? How can we adapt these new technologies to speed the flow and efficiency of the internal workforce, without invading privacy or personal boundaries? Who has access to human and user-generated AI data, and what data will be tracked and stored? How will it be used in evaluating employees? The power of nanotech to radically alter workflow in manufacturing and numerous other functions is staggering. Nanotech and the far-reaching implications of neurotech and AI offer thousands of implementation issues and ethical questions for internal communications.

Future of Internal Communication Practices

The world is changing; the business environment is evolving and so do organizations and their internal stakeholders. The aforementioned macro trends and issues will inevitably change the practice of internal communication in the future. Although specific implementation will vary, the following transformation and trends of internal communication practices can be predicted.

Multimedia, Digitization, and Mobilization

With the day-to-day advancement of technology, companies will possess a greater variety of tools to reach and engage internal stakeholders. Although traditional channels, such as face-to-face communication, print media, videos, and e-mails, can hardly be replaced, the practice of internal communication is becoming digitized, multimedia, and multidimensional with the integration of online, social, and offline activities. As more and more digital "natives" will enter the workforce, organizations' embracing of new technology and social media in employee communication will become a must. Among the various emerging digital trends, mobile technology, especially social messaging apps, represent the new wave of digital communication and is expected to overtake SNSs in becoming the dominant platform (Ballve 2015). Mainly as a one-on-one communication channel, social messengers are naturally a more private, intimate, and personal communication tool. With the relational focus of mobile platforms, the internal adoption of social messaging enables companies to connect with employees virtually anytime and anywhere in a personable manner (Lien and Cao 2014). Furthermore, future workforces will demand greater flexibility and mobility, the way that employers communicate with employees will likely evolve and become more mobile. Accordingly, internal programs may gradually embrace the "mobile comes first" movement and design content suitable for mobile technologies, such as shorter, "snackable," and visual content. Eventually, these platforms can be used on AI and nanotechnology-based devices.

Personalized, Humanized, and Employee-Centric Communication

People are always at the heart of all communications. Along with the coming of the digital age, our voices are amplified and individual values are heightened. In the workplace, to build deeper employee connections and satisfy employees' higher-order and psychological needs, communication will become more humanized and personalized with an emphasis on employees' well-being, happiness, and development. Employers' efforts to promote work–life balance, such as flexible hours, unlimited vacation, paid maternity leave, and other career development opportunities, will become more prevalent, as it communicates the organization's employee-centric value and care about employees as individuals and addresses their real needs. Additionally, communication efforts will likely be more personalized by micro-targeting employee segments or one-on-one personalized communication, based on their own, real-time data. These targeted efforts will enable organizations to achieve specific outcomes with certain groups (e.g., mothers with children under five, international workers, early technology adopters, and so on) to connect with them on a regular basis with resonant information and activities.

Transparency and Authenticity

The open, transparent, and decentralized spirit of social media has escalated stakeholders' expectations of organizational transparency, including those of employees (Men and Stacks 2014). This trend will likely grow in the future with more organizational information made public and readily accessible. To improve employee trust in management and businesses, being ethical, transparent, and accountable is the first necessary step (Bowen, Hung-Baesecke, and Chen 2016). In addition, the quest for authenticity will continue. On the one hand, in the relentlessly commercialized world, people have learned to doubt, probe, and question anything and anyone they suspect of spinning them a line. An ethical organization is an authentic enterprise that values truthfulness, genuineness, transparency, and consistency; it is highly appreciated by all stakeholders. On the other hand, it requires the dedication and resources of the organization to support ongoing efforts in this area. The growing digitalization will offer organizations more invaluable opportunities to be authentic. As part of the personification process, the organization's social profile and social-mediated communication with employees can add a human touch, keep a human scale, and create a level of intimacy to balance the impersonal nature of many other traditional communication tools. Overall, transparency and authenticity are vitally important ethical attributes. The ethical consistency they create will go far in shaping the organization's future communication practice with employees and nurture quality and committed employee–organization relationships.

Symmetrical Communication, Empowerment, and Engagement

Over decades, the practice of internal communication has transformed from a one-way information dissemination model to a two-way symmetrical, dialogical communication approach. With the growing diversity of the workforce and the facilitation of interactive and conversational tools, two-way symmetrical and relational communication will continue to be a central theme in internal communication and employee engagement practices. Promoting dialogs involves management's willingness to listen, allowing employees to voice their genuine thoughts and even criticism, and providing them channels to do so. Employee meetings, town-hall meetings, and management one-on-one are all dialogical and potentially relational. Interactive features built in traditional newsletters, intranet, and social media tools also promote conversations. Another method is the suggestion box, which is a practice that originated hundreds of years ago and has been proven useful in soliciting ideas and opening up venues for innovation. Behind the idea of symmetrical communication are the employee-centric values and organizations' genuine care and concern for employees' interests. Eventually, employees will be more empowered with greater access to management, ability to share opinions, having their voice heard and valued, and finding deeper meaning in the workplace by exerting greater influence. Such a feeling of empowerment contributes to building an engaged future workforce, which is a constant theme for organizations and their internal communication practices.

Peer-to-Peer Communication and the Blurred Line Between Internal and External Communication

Organizations are gradually moving from hierarchical to horizontal communication. Employees constantly go to their peers to seek or verify information, especially in today's increasingly connected workplace with the aid of digital media. The importance of peer-to-peer communication is increasing, thereby transforming organizations' internal communication from a top–down or bottom–up dominant approach to a multidimensional model—information flow through employees' informal communication networks (with their peers) plays an increasingly important role. Furthermore, the line between internal and external communication is blurred. Anything internal can transcend boundaries and travel to external stakeholders in real time in this transparent and connected digital age. In other words, employee peer communication not only occurs internally with coworkers, but also externally with friends, family, and personal networks. Recognizing the powerful peer influence of employees, organizations may invest more resources to prepare employees to be better communicators, such as identifying opinion leaders, providing them with the correct information and messages, and offering communication training and easy tools for sharing internal communication content. However, employees have to tell the story in their own words, which are perceived to be more authentic. As Bradley (2016) noted, "If you want to work with influencers, you have to equip them and empower them to tell your story in their own words and have the guardrails in place so you can be comfortable letting them do it" (p. 30).

Internal Stakeholder-Generated Content, Sharing, and Collaboration

As stakeholder authentic voices and personal stories will be more greatly emphasized and valued, a shift will likely occur that enables employees to create internal communication content. Future internal communication programs may move from a centralized model of public relations department that creates the bulk of content to one that uses a citizen journalist model, in which employees create, publish, and share their own content or that of their peers. Employees will be more involved in the internal communication process as *storytellers* instead of information recipients. Additionally, fostering collaboration will be one of the foci of future internal communication programs, especially in the increasingly diverse and multicultural workplace. Collaboration will help promote innovation, mutual understanding, and overcome cultural barriers and prejudices. A participative, collaborative organizational culture will also bring together management and employees, reduce the power distance, and empower them by inviting their participation and free sharing of their thoughts. Ideally, a participative, collaborative, and inclusive cross-enterprise communication force that includes CEOs, all levels of leaders, and employees should be formed.

Emotion- and Behavior-Driven

Offering employees the information they need and keeping them informed and updated is only one of the basic goals of internal communication. A more important purpose of internal communication is to establish employees' deeper-level emotional connection with the organization. More and more companies today are striving to develop an emotional culture, which emphasizes how employees feel, such as experiencing joy, fun, happiness, and compassionate love at work, compared with the traditional cognitive culture that sets the tone for how employees think and behave at work, such as a customer-focused, innovative, and competitive culture (Barsade and O'Neill 2016). With the competition for talent continuing to be a top challenge facing global businesses, future internal communication efforts will be geared toward building emotional connections and cultivating a favorable organizational emotional culture. This culture may cast new challenges for internal communication professionals. Unlike cognitive culture, which is often conveyed verbally, emotional culture tends to be conveyed by nonverbal cues, such as body language and facial expressions, which may require new skill sets for communication practitioners. Ultimately, the cognitive- and emotional-level communication efforts will drive employees' behavior change. As the public relations profession is developing a new emphasis on *behavior change*, future internal communication programs are anticipated to have the same focus, that is, changing employee behavior such as increasing productivity, participating in prosocial activities, or engaging in positive communication behavior. Behavioral science, neuro-linguistic programming (Burton 2016), AI, and "big data" analytics can offer insights for internal communication managers to fulfill such purposes. The result will be communication practices that not only inform, involve, and inspire, but also build a community of efficient and engaged employees.

Future Internal Communication Research

Research guides and informs practices. Theory can help internal communication become more effective. Although internal communication is among the fastest-growing specializations in public relations and communication management, scholarship in this area has yet to keep pace with the initiatives from practitioners (Verčič, Verčič, and Sriramesh 2012). Considering future trends and issues, the ongoing transformation of internal communication practices, and the gaps in internal communication literature, we identified the following eight topics worthy of further scholarly investigation.

Internal Public and Audience Segmentation

Theories about stakeholders and publics in public relations have been well-established by previous scholars, such as Grunig's situational theory of publics (Grunig 1983; Grunig and Repper 1992). However, little empirical evidence exists on how these theories may hold when applied internally. In consideration of the growing sophistication of the workforce and the issues of multiple generations, diversity, and digitization, developing theories and knowledge to effectively analyze internal publics and segment employee audiences is important to attain better targeted communication. What criteria can be used for segmentation (e.g., demographics, psychographics, netgraphics, or behavioral characteristics)? Which factors will determine stakeholder level of activeness in internal issues (e.g., situational theory of internal stakeholders)? How can "big data" analytics inform the process of internal stakeholder analysis and audience segmentation? All these questions need to be addressed in the future. Theories from management, leadership, organizational behavior, and marketing will inform research in this arena.

Enterprise Social Media

As new technologies and social media tools begin to proliferate across organizations, we must develop a thorough theoretical understanding of how organizations can capitalize on the advantageous characteristics of enterprise social media to achieve positive employee and organizational outcomes. Research questions may tap into the aspects of motivations of employees' use of enterprise social media, how social media can influence internal communication issues such as interacting with new hires, community building, knowledge sharing and management, organization–employee relationship maintenance, social capital building, and so on (Leonardi, Huysman, and Steinfield 2013). In addition to building empirical linkages between social media use and various outcomes, theoretically deliberating how the process works is equally important (i.e., identifying the mediating or moderating factors and exploring in-depth and behind-the-scenes reasons why enterprise social media work or does not work for organizational success). Eventually, research should provide evidence that documents the investment on enterprise social media returns. In addition to building soft assets, such as employee social capital and relationships, does organizations' internal use of social media matter for the bottom line (Li and Stacks 2015), such as improving employee job performance, sales, or organizational productivity? Do any negative effects exist? How can internal social platforms be administered? Given that enterprise social media is still in its infancy, both exploratory and qualitative approaches (e.g., case studies, in-depth interviews, and focus groups) and quantitative methods (e.g., survey and model building) can help establish early theories.

Empowerment and Engagement

The concepts of internal stakeholder empowerment and engagement are intertwined. Neither is new, as many studies in the management arena have explored the antecedents, measures, processes, and consequences of employee empowerment and engagement. In internal communication, however, although empowerment and engagement have been buzzwords that often appear in trade publications and industry reports, research has been scarce on how exactly communication factors contribute to employees' feeling of competence, control, autonomy, and engagement in the organization. Future research should examine specifically how organizational culture, structure, management style, communication climate, strategies, messages, and channels (e.g., traditional vs. new media channels and interpersonal vs. mediated channels) could affect empowerment and engagement. Further, CEOs' and supervisors' communication effectiveness is speculated to affect stakeholder engagement. Establishing the linkages between leadership communication (e.g., styles, channels, and strategies) and employee empowerment and engagement could be another area of exploration. Additionally, with social media increasingly being implemented in work organizations as communication tools with and among employees, whether and how enterprise social media would affect empowerment and engagement would be an interesting topic for researchers.

Work–Life Integration

Work–life balance has been an ongoing discussion in the business world and has been recently brought to the spotlight by the media. A great volume of research has been devoted to the area in the past decade, which provides managerial implications on how to effectively balance employees' work and life roles to maximize business success. More recently, a modern concept of work–life integration has gained scholarly attention. Instead of emphasizing that work competes with life, work–life integration suggests employees could harness the passions and powers of the various parts of their lives and bring them together to achieve the "four-way wins" (i.e., work, home, community, and the private self)—actions that result in life being better in all four domains (Friedman 2014). How could internal communication factors play a role in helping internal stakeholders' achieve greater outcomes of work–life integration? How would the influence of internal communication on employees expand beyond the boundary into their personal lives? These are challenging but novel research questions that remain underexplored. Employees' knowledge, skills, and happy and positive emotions, as well as personal fulfillment, accomplishment, and success experienced at work, could all spill over to their personal lives (Haar 2013). Thus, management communication may help make employees' successful work–life integration happen.

Emotional Culture

Despite a renaissance of scholarship on the ways that emotions affect employees' behavior at work, emotional culture is rarely managed or studied as deliberately as cognitive culture (Barsade and O'Neill 2016). Barsade and O'Neil's exploratory research on emotional culture showed that positive emotions, such as joy, compassionate love, and fun, are consistently associated with better employee performance, quality, and customer service across industries and various organizations. Therefore, examining how internal communication practices can contribute to building a positive emotional culture in the organization is imperative. Subtopics such as which communication channels are most effective in communicating employee emotions (e.g., face-to-face, video, e-mail, or social media), what leadership communication styles and corporate communication strategies work the best for building an emotional culture, and how can emotional culture interact with communication factors to influence employee–organization relationships and employee engagement need to be further explored.

Change Communication

Organizations inevitably face and deal with change. With improving technology, keen market competition, and globalization of businesses and consumers, change is happening at a faster pace than ever before. Successful change management cannot be achieved without the support of effective communication (Elving 2005). Although consensus has been achieved on the vitality of communication in *strategic* change among internal communication scholars and professionals, specific communication actions, approaches, and effects remain unexplained (Elving 2005). Research should further investigate the topic by examining change in communication audiences (e.g., employees' psychological reaction to changes), messages and effectiveness (e.g., type of messages, message sources, and timing of messages), communication channels (e.g., which medium is most effective in communicating change at different stages), communication strategies (e.g., transparent, authentic, responsive, and upward communication), leadership involvement (e.g., CEO and supervisors' role in change communication), and so on. However, a realistic challenge faced by change communication researchers is accessing organizations that have recently undergone change. Given the sensitivity of the topic, companies are usually reluctant to share information about their change process. A collaborative approach between change communication professionals and scholars may help solve this problem.

Leadership Communication

Leadership communication has been recognized as a major component of an organization's internal communication system, along with corporate internal communication and peer (horizontal) communication. Despite the many studies that have been conducted examining supervisors' leadership communication with followers, including supervisor communication style, channels, competence, and quality, among others, a gap exists, particularly in CEO and executive communication (Men 2015). Growing demands for servant leadership, candor, virtue, and ethical accountability from leaders are evident (Bowen 2009, 2016a). Future research should examine the issue by investigating senior management's internal communication role, including CEO communication style, ethical values, channels, and social media engagement, and how these factors affect employee job satisfaction, relationship quality with the organization, and other outcomes, such as feeling of empowerment and engagement. Considering the transformation of the workforce into a more diverse, digitalized, globalized, and multicultural one, modern leaders need to equip themselves with an open mindset and develop unique communication competence and skill sets to adapt to the changing workplace. Leadership theories from the management arena should be informative and offer inspirational perspectives in developing research on leadership communication.

Measurement and Evaluation

Measurement strategies can help boost the effect of internal communication on organizations' bottom line. Data and metrics not only show the value of the internal communication team' work, but also provide foresight to guide future communication efforts. Effective measurement and evaluation have been a challenge for communication professionals. Knowing what to measure is not sufficient as the more important question is how to measure it. Empirical research is needed to reach a consensus on what should be the core set of criteria for internal communication effectiveness at the outputs, outtakes, outcomes, and business impact levels. A predictive, reliable model to measure the work in employee communication and engagement that is tied to behavioral outcomes is needed (Burton 2016). Furthermore, research on how to measure each type of result will provide invaluable insights for communication managers. Research on research methods and analytics is needed. Given that no industry standard presently exists to measure internal communication, future endeavors can take a stance toward developing a theory-informed and data-evidenced internal communication measurement standard (e.g., Stacks 2016).

Summary

Internal communication remains one of the fastest-growing communication practices. The rapidly changing business environment, workplace, and workforce have brought both opportunities for and challenges to internal communication practitioners. This chapter summarizes the macro trends and issues that aim to transform the practice of internal communication, such as digitization, globalization, diversity and inclusion, work–life balance, and growing concern for corporate social conscience. It predicts that internal communication in the future will be digitized, multimedia, mobile, and eventually, nano, AI, or neurotech-based, with blurred lines between internal and external, and will be emotionally and behaviorally driven. With the digitization of the organization and the workforce as well as the evolvement of the field, future internal communication practices will also emphasize more personalization, human touch, ethical accountability, transparency and authenticity, dialogs, employee participation, sharing, and collaboration to truly connect with, empower, and engage employees. To accelerate the development of the field, we suggest that scholars should keep pace and add to the body of knowledge on internal communication by tapping into the under-researched topics of internal public segmentation, enterprise social media, change communication, work–life integration, and measurement and evaluation issues. Indeed, the future is here.

Appendices: Measures

[1 = Strongly Disagree, 2 = Disagree, 3 = Undecided, 4 = Agree, 5 = Strongly Agree]

Appendix A

Internal Reputation

1. I have a good feeling about my company. (Emotional appeal)
2. I admire and respect my company. (Emotional appeal)
3. I trust my company. (Emotional appeal)
4. My company stands behind its products and services. (Products and services)
5. My company develops innovative products and services. (Products and services)
6. My company offers high-quality products and services. (Products and services)
7. My company offers products and services that are a good value for the money. (Products and services)
8. My company has excellent leadership. (Vision and leadership)
9. My company has a clear vision for its future. (Vision and leadership)
10. My company recognizes and takes advantage of market opportunities. (Vision and leadership)
11. My company is well-managed. (Work environment)
12. My company is a good company to work for. (Work environment)
13. My company has good employees. (Work environment)
14. My company supports good causes. (Social and environmental responsibility)
15. My company is an environmentally responsible company. (Social and environmental responsibility)
16. My company maintains high standards in the way it treats people. (Social and environmental responsibility)
17. My company has a strong record of profitability. (Financial performance)

18. Investing in my company entails low risks. (Financial performance)

19. My company tends to outperform its competitors. (Financial performance)

20. I believe my company has strong future growth prospects. (Financial performance)

Appendix B

Organizational Transparency

1. The company asks for feedback from people like me about the quality of its information. (Participative)

2. The company involves people like me to help identify the information I need. (Participative)

3. The company provides detailed information to people like me. (Participative)

4. The company makes it easy to find the information that people like me need. (Participative)

5. The company asks the opinions of people like me before making decisions. (Participative)

6. The company takes the time with people like me to understand who we are and what we need. (Participative)

7. The company provides information to people like me in a timely fashion. (Substantial)

8. The company provides information that is relevant to people like me. (Substantial)

9. The company provides information that can be compared with previous performance. (Substantial)

10. The company provides information that is complete. (Substantial)

11. The company provides information that is easy for people like me to understand. (Substantial)

12. The company provides accurate information to people like me. (Substantial)

13. The company provides information that is reliable. (Substantial)

14. The company presents more than one side of controversial issues. (Accountable)

15. The company is forthcoming with information that might be damaging to the organization. (Accountable)
16. The company is open to criticism by people like me. (Accountable)
17. The company freely admits when it has made mistakes. (Accountable)
18. The company provides information that can be compared with industry standards. (Accountable)

Appendix C

Organizational Authenticity

1. This organization always tells the truth.
2. I believe that this organization's actions are genuine.
3. I feel that this organization is willing to admit to mistakes when they are made.
4. I feel that this organization accepts and learns from mistakes.
5. I believe that this organization's behavior matches its core values.
6. The organization's beliefs and actions are consistent.
7. I think this organization matches the rhetoric with its action.

Appendix D

Employee–Organization Relationships

1. Whenever my organization makes an important decision, I know it will be concerned about people like me. (Integrity)
2. My organization can be relied on to keep its promises. (Dependability)
3. I believe that my organization takes the opinions of people like me into account when making decisions. (Dependability)
4. My organization has the ability to accomplish what it says it will do. (Competence)
5. I am happy with my organization. (Satisfaction)
6. Both my organization and people like me benefit from the relationship. (Satisfaction)

7. Most people like me are happy in their interactions with my organization. (Satisfaction)

8. Generally speaking, I am pleased with the relationship my organization has established with people like me. (Satisfaction)

9. I feel that my organization is trying to maintain a long-term commitment to people like me. (Commitment)

10. I can see that my organization wants to maintain a relationship with people like me. (Commitment)

11. There is a long-lasting bond between my organization and people like me. (Commitment)

12. Compared with other organizations, I value my relationship with my organization more. (Commitment)

13. My organization and people like me are attentive to what each other say. (Control mutuality)

14. My organization believes that the opinions of people like me are legitimate. (Control mutuality)

15. In dealing with people like me, my organization has a tendency to throw its weight around. (Control mutuality)

16. My organization really listens to what people like me have to say. (Control mutuality)

Appendix E

Organizational Identification

1. When someone criticizes my company, it feels like a personal insult.

2. I am very interested in what others think about my company.

3. When I talk about this company, I usually say "we" rather than "they."

4. This company's successes are my successes.

5. When someone praises this company, it feels like a personal compliment.

6. If a story in the media criticized the company, I would feel embarrassed.

Appendix F

Employee Empowerment

1. I believe I can make a difference in what happens in this company.
2. I am determined to be involved in the development of this company.
3. I believe I have a great deal of control over the decision-making process of this company.
4. I am confident about my abilities to improve the company.
5. I believe I can collaborate with this company as a valuable partner.

Appendix G

Employee Engagement

1. One of the most exciting things for me is getting involved with things happening in this company.
2. I am not really into the "goings-on" in this company.
3. Being a member of this company makes me come "alive."
4. Being a member of this company is exhilarating for me.
5. I am highly engaged in this company.
6. I am enthusiastic about this company.
7. I am proud of this company.
8. I am attentive to this company's activities.
9. I am actively involved with this company.

Appendix H

Employee Advocacy

1. I speak favorably about this company in public.
2. I recommend the company's brands, products, and services to others.
3. I defend the company when hearing criticism from others.

Appendix I

Employee Communication Behavior

Positive Megaphoning

1. I say good things to friends and neighbors about the positive aspects of the management and company.
2. I routinely recommend my organization and its services and products to people.
3. I attempt to persuade people who have negative opinions about my organization.
4. I refute prejudiced or stereotyped opinions about my organization.
5. In the past, I fought with those who criticized my organization and business.
6. I become upset and tend to speak up when encountering ignorant or biased opinions about my organization.

Negative Megaphoning

1. I talk about the mistakes and problems of our management to family and friends.
2. I state to friends and family that my organization is run more poorly than its competitors.
3. I talk to people about the problems of our services and products.

Scouting

1. I meet and check with suppliers and government officials to collect new information.
2. I voluntarily meet and check with those people who have grievances with the organization.
3. I voluntarily check people's feedback on organizational events.
4. I search for new information and subscribe to Listserv, newsletters, and publications for the organization.

5. Even after working hours, I contact strategic publics and stakeholders for their complaints and new information and share the information with my colleagues.
6. I make an extra effort to cultivate and maintain relationships with external stakeholders and strategic publics.
7. I meet people who work for similar businesses and check rumors and news about the organization or business.
8. I start conversations or give information to relevant colleagues about new trends or unusual signals related to work.

Appendix J

Organizational Citizenship Behavior

1. When the workload is most intense, I work extra hours by shortening usual breaks or staying at work later than usual.
2. I frequently suggest new ideas to improve my department.
3. I only have to do the job I am paid to do.
4. Even when it is not required, I try to guide the new members of my department.

Appendix K

Employee Voice Behavior

1. I develop and make recommendations to my supervisor concerning issues that affect my work.
2. I speak up and encourage others in my work unit to get involved in issues that affect our work.
3. I communicate my opinions about work issues to others in my work unit, even if their opinions are different and they disagree with me.
4. I keep well-informed about issues at work where my opinion can be useful.
5. I get involved in issues that affect the quality of life in my work unit.
6. I speak up to my supervisor to share ideas for new projects or changes in procedures at work.

Appendix L[1]

Ethical Behavior and Counsel

1. I feel well-prepared to engage in ethics counsel when my client or senior management faces a dilemma.
2. Communicators should play the role of ethical counsel to top management.
3. In my job, I counsel management on ethical decisions.
4. Communicators should advise management on ethical decisions rather than merely communicate the decisions of others.
5. I believe that I can act as the ethical conscience of my organization (or on behalf of clients).
6. My organization makes it clear to employees what is ethically acceptable and what is not.
7. Openness about ethical or unethical conduct is encouraged in my organization.
8. Managers in my company often engage in behavior that I consider unethical.
9. In order to succeed in my organization, it is often necessary to compromise my ethics.
10. Discussion of moral dilemmas and criticism of objectionable conduct is encouraged in my organization.

---

[1] Adapted from Bowen et al. (2006).

References

Appelbaum, S.H., S. Habashy, J.C. Malo, and H. Shafiq. 2012. "Back to the Future: Revisiting Kotter's 1996 Change Model." *Journal of Management Development* 31, no. 8, pp. 764–82.

Arthur W. Page Society. 2007. *The Authentic Enterprise*. New York: The Arthur W. Page Society.

Arthur W. Page Society. 2012. *Building Belief: A New Model for Activiting Corporate Character & Authentic Advocacy*. New York: The Arthur W. Page Society.

Avery, G.C. 2005. *Leadership for Sustainable Futures: Achieving Success in a Competitive World*. Northampton, MA: Edward Elgar.

Awamleh, R., and W.L. Gardner. 1999. "Perceptions of Leader Charisma and Effectiveness: The Effects of Vision Content, Delivery, and Organizational Performance." *The Leadership Quarterly* 70, no. 3, pp. 345–73.

Azanza, G., J.A. Moriano, and F. Molero. 2013. "Authentic Leadership and Organizational Culture as Drivers of Employees Job Satisfaction." *Journal of Work and Organizational Psychology* 29, no. 2, pp. 45–50.

Baker, E.L. 1980. "Managing Organizational Culture." *Management Review* 69, no. 7, pp. 8–13.

Bakker, A.B., J.J. Hakanen, E. Demerouti, and D. Xanthopoulou. 2007. "Job Resources Boost Work Engagement, Particularly When Job Demands Are High." *Journal of Educational Psychology* 99, no. 2, pp. 274–84.

Ballve, M. April 10, 2015. "Messaging Apps are Overtaking Social Networks to Become the Dominant Platforms on Phones." *Business Insider*. Retrieved on May 6, 2016 from www.businessinsider.com/messaging-apps-have-completely-overtaken-social-networks-to-become-the-dominant-platforms-on-phones-2015-4#ixzz3kz70NJRc

Barker, P. 2008. "How Social Media is Transforming Employee Communications at Sun Microsystems." *Global Business and Organizational Excellence* 27, no. 4, pp. 6–14. doi:10.1002/joe.20209

Barrett, D.J. 2002. "Change Communication: Using Strategic Employee Communication to Facilitate Major Change." *Corporate Communications: An International Journal* 7, no. 4, pp. 219–31.

Barsade, S., and O.A. O'Neil. 2016. "Managing Your Emotional Culture." *Harvard Business Review* 94, no. 1, pp. 58–66.

Bass, B.M. 1985. *Leadership and Performance Beyond Expectations*. New York: Free Press.

Bertalanffy, L. von. 1934. *Investigation of the Legality of the Growth. I. General Principles of Theory; Mathematical and Physiological Laws of Growth in Aquatic Animals.* Arch. Entwicklungsmech 131, pp. 613–53.

Bertalanffy, L. von. 1968. *General System Theory: Foundations, Developments, Applications.* New York: Braziller. Retrieved from www.panarchy.org/vonbertalanffy/systems.1968.html

Baum, J.R., E.A. Locke, and S.A. Kirkpatrick. 1998. "A Longitudinal Study of the Relation of Vision and Vision Communication to Venture Growth in Entrepreneurial Firms." *Journal of Applied Psychology* 83, no. 1, pp. 43–54.

Beck, N., J. Brüderl, and M. Woywode. 2008. "Momentum or Deceleration? Theoretical and Methodological Reflections on the Analysis of Organizational Change." *Academy of Management Journal* 51, no. 3, pp. 413–35.

Beer, M., and N. Nohria. 2000. *Breaking the Code of Change.* Boston, MA: Harvard Business School Press.

Bennett, T.E. February 1987. "How to Choose a Bank." *Inc. Magazine* 9, no. 2, pp. 110–112.

Berger, B. 2008. "Employee/Organizational Communications." Institute for Public Relations. Retrieved from www.instituteforpr.org/topics/employee-organizational-communications/

Berger, B. June 3, 2011. "What Employee engagement Means for New PR Pros." *PRWeek.* Retrieved from www.prweekus.com/what-employee-engagement-means-for-new-pr-pros/article/204277/

Beringer, C., D. Jonas, and H.G. Gemünden. 2012. "Establishing Project Portfolio Management: An Exploratory Analysis of the Influence of Internal Stakeholders' Interactions." *Project Management Journal* 43, no. 6, pp. 16–32.

Berry, L.L. 1981. "The Employee as Customer." *Journal of Retail Banking* 3, no. 1, pp. 25–28.

Bersin, J. 2015. "Why Diversity and Inclusion Will Be a Top Priority for 2016." *Forbes,* December 6. Retrieved on May 5 from www.forbes.com/sites/joshbersin/2015/12/06/why-diversity-and-inclusion-will-be-a-top-priority-for-2016/#612984a64bd4

Bledow, R., A. Schmitt, M. Frese, and J. Kuhnel. 2011. "The Affective Shift Model of Work Engagement." *Journal of Applied Psychology* 96, no. 6, pp. 1246–57.

Bordia, P., E. Hunt, N. Paulsen, D. Tourish, and N. DiFonzo. 2004. "Uncertainty During Organizational Change: Is it All About Control?" *European Journal of Work & Organizational Psychology* 13, pp. no. 3, 345–66.

Bormann, E.G. 1983. "Symbolic Convergence: Organizational Communication and Culture." In *Communication and Organizations: An Interpretative Approach,* eds. L.L. Putnam, and M.E. Pacanowsky, 99–122. Beverly Hills, CA: Sage.

Botero, I.C., and L.V. Dyne. 2009. "Employee Voice Behavior: Interactive Effects of LMX and Power Distance in the United States and Colombia." *Management Communication Quarterly* 23, no. 1, pp. 84–104.

Bowen, S.A. 2002. "Elite Executives in Issues Management: The Role of Ethical Paradigms in Decision Making." *Journal of Public Affairs* 2, no. 4, pp. 270–83.

Bowen, S.A. 2004a. "Organizational Factors Encouraging Ethical Decision Making: An Exploration Into the Case of An Exemplar." *Journal of Business Ethics* 52, no. 4, pp. 311–24.

Bowen, S.A. 2004b. "Expansion of Ethics as the Tenth Generic Principle of Public Relations Excellence: A Kantian Theory and Model for Managing Ethical Issues." *Journal of Public Relations Research* 16, no. 1, pp. 65–92.

Bowen, S.A. 2005a. "Internal Relations and Employee Communication." In *Effective Public Relations,* eds. S.M. Cutlip, A.H. Center, and G.M. Broom, 222–50. 9th ed. Upper Saddle River, NJ: Prentice Hall.

Bowen, S.A. 2005b. "A Practical Model for Ethical Decision Making in Issues Management and Public Relations." *Journal of Public Relations Research* 17, no. 3, pp. 191–216.

Bowen, S.A. 2006. "Autonomy in Communication: Inclusion in Strategic Management and Ethical Decision-Making, a Comparative Case Analysis." *Journal of Communication Management* 10, no. 4, pp. 330–52.

Bowen, S.A. 2008. "A State of Neglect: Public Relations as Corporate Conscience or Ethics counsel." *Journal of Public Relations Research* 20, no. 3, pp. 271–96.

Bowen, S.A. 2009. "What Communication Professionals Tell Us Regarding Dominant Coalition Access and Gaining Membership." *Journal of Applied Communication Research* 37, no. 4, pp. 427–52.

Bowen, S.A. 2010. "An Examination of Applied Ethics and Stakeholder Management on Top Corporate Websites." *Public Relations Journal* 4, no. 1, pp. 1–31.

Bowen, S.A. 2013. "Using Classic Social Media Cases to Distill Ethical Guidelines for Digital Engagement." *Journal of Mass Media Ethics: Exploring Questions of Media Morality* 28, no. 2, pp. 119–33.

Bowen, S.A. 2015. "Exploring the Role of the Dominant Coalition in Creating an Ethical Culture for Internal Stakeholders." *Public Relations Journal* 9, no. 1, pp. 1–23. www.prsa.org/Intelligence/PRJournal/Documents/2015v09n01Bowen.pdf

Bowen, S.A. 2016a. "Clarifying Ethics Terms in Public Relations from A to V, Authenticity to Virtue. BledCom Special Issue of PR Review Sleeping (with the) Media: Media relations." *Public Relations Review* 42, no. 4, pp. 564–72. http://dx.doi.org/10.1016/j.pubrev.2016.03.012

Bowen, S.A. 2016b. "Public Relations Professional Should Prepare to Tackle Nanotechnology." *PRWeek*, March 18. www.prweek.com/article/1388145/public-relations-professionals-prepare-tackle-nanotechnology

Bowen, S.A. 2016c. "Neurotechnology, Public Relations, and the Need for Answers." *PRWeek*, February 5. www.prweek.com/article/1382526/neuroethics-public-relations-need-answers

Bowen, S.A. 2016d. "Public Relations Professionals Should Prepare to Tackle Nanotechnology." *PRWeek*, March 18. www.prweek.com/article/1388145/public-relations-professionals-prepare-tackle-nanotechnology

Bowen, S.A. (in press). "Mission and Vision." In *The International Encyclopedia of Strategic Communication*, ed. R.L. Heath, pp. tbd. Hoboken, NJ: Wiley.

Bowen, S.A., R.L. Heath, J. Lee, G. Painter, F.J. Agraz, D. McKie, and M. Toledano. 2006. *The Business of Truth: A Guide to Ethical Communication Perspective*. San Francisco: International Association of Business Communicators Research Foundation.

Bowen, S.A., and E.V. Erzikova. 2013. "The International Divide in Public Relations Ethics Education: Advocacy Versus Autonomy." *Public Relations Journal* 7, no. 1, pp. 1–41. www.prsa.org/Intelligence/PRJournal/Documents/2013BowenErzikova.pdf

Bowen, S.A. and T.D. Gallicano. 2013. "A Philosophy of Reflective Ethical Symmetry: Comprehensive Historical and Future Moral Approaches in the Excellence Theory." In *Public Relations and Communication Management*, eds. K. Sriramesh, A. Zerfass, and J.N. Kim, 193–209. London: Taylor and Francis.

Bowen, S.A., C.J. Hung-Baesecke, and Y.R. Chen. 2016. "Ethics as a Pre-Cursor to Organization-Public Relationships: Building Trust Before and During the OPR Model." *Cogent Social Sciences* 2, no. 1, p. 1141467. http://dx.doi.org/10.1080/23311886.2016.1141467

Bowen, S.A., and C.J. Hung-Baesecke. 2013, May. "Is Ethics a Precursor to Authentic Organization-Public Relationships?" Paper presented at the 11th Annual International Conference on Communication and Mass Media (Atiner), Athens, Greece.

Bowen, S.A., and P. Prescott. 2015. "Kant's Contribution to the Ethics of Communication." *Ethical Space: The International Journal of Communication Ethics* 12, no. 2, pp. 38–44.

Bowen, S.A., and R.L. Heath. 2005. "Issues Management, Systems, and Rhetoric: Exploring the Distinction Between Ethical and Legal Guidelines at Enron." *Journal of Public Affairs* 5, no. 2, pp. 84–98.

Bowen, S.A., B.L. Rawlins, and T.M. Martin. 2010. *An Overview of the Public Relations Function*. New York: Business Expert Press.

Bowen, S.A., D.W. Stacks, and D.K. Wright. (in press). "Emissions Scandal: An Example of Bad Public Relations on a Worldwide Scale and the Defeat Device that Defeated a Worldwide Reputation." In *Public Relations Case Studies from Around the World*, eds. J.V. Turk, J. Paluszek, and J. Valin, 2nd ed, tbd. New York: Peter Lang Publishing.

Bradley, D. 2016. "The New Influencers." *PR Week*, February. pp. 29–31.

Breevaart, K., A. Bakker, J. Hetland, E. Demerouti, O.K. Olsen, and R. Espevik. 2014. "Daily Transactional and Transformational Leadership and Daily Employee Engagement." *Journal of Occupational and Organizational Psychology* 87, no. 1, pp. 138–57.

Broom, G.M., and D.M, Dozier. 1990. *Using Research in Public Relations: Applications to Program Management.* Englewood Cliffs, NJ: Prentice Hall.

Brown, M.E., L.K. Treviño, and D.A. Harrison. 2005. "Ethical Leadership: A Social Learning Perspective for Construct Development and Testing." *Organizational Behavior and Human Decision Processes* 97, no. 2, pp. 117–34.

Brownell, J. 1991. "Middle Managers: Facing the Communication Challenge." *The Cornell H.R.A. Quarterly* 31, no. 4, pp. 52–9.

Buckingham, M., and C. Coffman. 1999. *First, Break All the Rules.* New York: Simon & Schuster.

Bull, M., and T. Brown. 2012. "Change Communication: The Impact on Satisfaction With Alternative Workplace Strategies." *Facilities* 30, no. 3, pp. 135–51.

Burns, J.M. 1978. *Leadership.* New York: Harper & Row.

Burton, K. 2016, May 26. Personal Communication.

Christian, M.S., A.S. Garza, and J.E. Slaughter. 2011. "Work Engagement: A Quantitative Review and Test of its Relations with Task and Contextual Performance." *Personnel Psychology* 64, no. 1, pp. 89–136.

Clampitt, P.G. 2001. *Communicating for Managerial Effectiveness,* 2nd ed. Thousand Oaks, Calif: Sage Publications.

Clayton, S. November 10, 2015. *Change Management Meets Social Media.* Boston, MA: Harvard Business Press. Received on March 31, 2016 from https://hbr.org/2015/11/change-management-meets-social-media

Cooper, C.D., T.A. Scandura, and C.A. Schriesheim. 2005. "Looking Forward but Learning from Our Past: Potential Challenges to Developing Authentic Leadership Theory and Authentic Leaders." *Leadership Quarterly* 16, no. 3, pp. 475–93.

Crawford, E.R., J.A. LePine, and B.L. Rich. 2010. "Linking Job Demands and Resources to Employee Engagement and Burnout: A Theoretical Extension and Meta-Analytic Test." *Journal of Applied Psychology* 95, no. 5, pp. 834–48.

D'Aprix, R. 1996. *Communicating for Change: Connecting the Workplace with the Marketplace.* San Francisco: Jossey-Bass.

Daft, R. L., and R.H. Lengel. 1984. "Information Richness: A New Approach to Managerialinformation Processing and Organizational Design." In *Research in Organizational Behavior,* eds. B. Staw and L.L. Cummings, 191–233. 6 vols. Greenwich, CT: JAI Press.

Daft, R.L., and R.H. Lengel. 1986. "Organizational Information Requirements: Media Richness and Structural Design." *Management Science* 32, no. 5, pp. 554–71.

Dalal, B.S., M. Baysinger, B.J. Brummel, and J.M. Lebreton. 2012. "The Relative Importance of Employee Engagement, Other Job Attitudes, and Trait Affect as Predictors of Job Performance." *Journal of Applied Social Psychology* 42, no. S1, pp. E295–325.

Daniels, C. December 2015. "Best Places to Work 2015." *PR Week*, December, pp. 28–6.

De George, R.T. 2007. *Business Ethics*. 6th ed. Boston, MA: Prentice Hall.

De George, R.T. 2010. *Business Ethics*. 7th ed. Boston, MA: Prentice Hall.

de Vries, R.E., A. Bakker-Pieper, and W. Oostenveld. 2010. "Leadership = Communication? The Relations of Leaders' Communication Styles with Leadership Styles, Knowledge Sharing and Leadership Outcomes." *Journal of Business and Psychology* 25, no. 3, pp. 367–80.

Derue, D.S., J.G. Nahrgang, N. Wellman, and S.E. Humphrey. 2011. "Trait and Behavioral Theories of Leadership: An Integration and Meta-Analytic Test of their Relative Validity." *Personnel Psychology* 64, no. 1, pp. 7–52.

DiFonzo, N., and P. Bordia. 1998. "A Tale of Two Corporations: Managing Uncertainty During Organizational Change." *Human Resource Management* 37, no. 3–4, 295–305.

Dozier, D.M., L.A. Grunig, and J.E. Grunig. 1995. *Manager's Guide to Excellence in Public Relations and Communication Management*. Mahwah, NJ: Lawrence Erlbaum Associates.

Edelman Trust Barometer. 2015. New York: Edelman Public Relations. www.Edelman.com/insights/intellectual-property/2015-Edelman-trust-barometer/ (accessed October 12, 2015).

Eisenberg, E.M. and P. Riley. 2001. "Organizational Culture." In *The New Handbook of Organizational Communication: Advances in Theory, Research, and Method*, eds. F.M. Jablin, and L.L. Putnam, 291–322. Thousand Oaks: Sage.

Elving, W.J.L. 2005. "The Role of Communication in Organizational Change." *Corporate Communications: An International Journal* 10, no. 2, 129–38.

Falcione, R.L., L. Sussman, and R.P. Herden. 1987. "Communication Climate in Organizations." In *Handbook of Organizational Communication: An Interdisciplinary Perspective*, eds. F.M. Jablin, L.L. Putnam, K.H. Roberts, L.M. Porter, 195–227. Newbury Park: Sage.

Fayol, H. 1949. *General and Industrial Management*. New York: Pittman.

Feather, N.T., and K.A. Rauter. 2004. "Organizational Citizenship Behaviors in Relation to Job Status, Job Insecurity, Organizational Commitment and

Identification, Job Satisfaction and Work Values." *Journal of Occupational and Organizational Psychology* 77, no. 1, pp. 81–94.

Festinger, L. 1957. *A Theory of Cognitive Dissonance*. Stanford, CA: Stanford University Press.

Festinger, L. 1959. "Some Attitudinal Consequences of Forced Decisions." *Acta Psychologica* 15, pp. 389–90.

Festinger, L. ed. 1964. *Conflict, Decision, and Dissonance*. Vol. 3. Stanford, CA: Stanford University Press.

Festinger, L., and J.M. Carlsmith. 1959. "Cognitive Consequences of Forced Compliance." *The Journal of Abnormal and Social Psychology* 58, no. 2, pp. 203–10.

Finet, D. 2001. "Sociopolitical Environments and Issues." In *The New Handbook of Organizational Communication: Advances in Theory, Research, and Methods*, eds. F.M. Jablin, and L.L. Putnam, 270–90. Thousand Oaks: Sage.

Fombrun, C.J., N.A. Gardberg, and J.M. Sever. 2000. "The Reputation Quotient: A Multi-Stakeholder Measure of Corporate Reputation." *The Journal of Brand Management* 7, no. 4, pp. 241–55.

Frahm, J., and K. Brown. 2007. "First Steps: Linking Change Communication to Change Receptivity." *Journal of Organizational Change* 20, no. 3, pp. 370–87.

Friedl, J., and A.T. Verčič. 2011. "Media Preferences of Digital Natives' Internal Communication: A Pilot Study." *Public Relations Review* 38, no. 1, pp. 84–6.

Friedman, M. (1962) 2002. *Capitalism and Freedom*. Chicago, IL: University of Chicago Press.

Friedman, S. October 7, 2014. *What Successful Work and Life Integration Looks Like*. Boston, MA: Harvard Business Press. Retrieved on May 7 from https://hbr.org/2014/10/what-successful-work-and-life-integration-looks-like

Garbett, T. ed. 1988. *How to Build a Corporation's Identity and Project its Image*. Lexington, MA: Lexington Books.

George, W.R. 1977. "The Retailing of Services-a Challenging Future." *Journal of Retailing, Fall* 53, no. 3, pp. 85–98.

Gergs, H.H., and R. Trinczek. 2008. "Communication as the Key Factors to Change Management: A Sociological Perspective." In *Communication and Leadership in the 21ˢᵗ Century*, eds. S. Holger and B. Daniela, 141–56. Gutersloh: Verlag Bertelsmann Stiftung.

Giddens A. ed. 1991. *Modernity and Self-Identity: Self and Society in the Late Modern Age*. Cambridge: Polity Press.

Gillis, T. 2006. "Internal Communication Media." In *The IABC Handbook of Organizational Communication*, ed. T. Gillis, 257–67. San Francisco, CA: Jossey-Bass.

Goodman, M.B., C. Genest, D. Cayo, and S. Y. Ng. eds. 2009. *CCI Corporate Communication Practices and Trends Study.* New York: Corporate Communication International at Baruch College/CUNY.

Goodpaster, K.E. 2007. *Conscience and Corporate Culture.* UK: Blackwell.

Goyat, S. 2011. "The Basis of Market Segmentation: A Critical Review of Literature." *European Journal of Business and Management* 3, no. 9, pp. 45–54.

Graham, J.D. 1997. "Making the CEO the Chief Communication Officer: Counseling Senior Management." In *The Handbook of Strategic Public Relations & Integrated Communications,* eds. C.L. Caywood, 274–85. New York: McGraw-Hill.

Green, K.A., M. López, A. Wysocki, and K. Kepner. 2012. *Diversity in the Workplace: Benefits, Challenges, and the Required Managerial Tools,* 1–3. IFAS Extention: University of Florida. Retrieved on September 13, 2015 from https://edis.ifas.ufl.edu/hr022

Greenberg, J. 2004. "Workplace Diversity: Benefits, Challenges, and Solutions." Retrieved on September 13, 2015 from www.diversityworking.com/employerZone/diversityManagement/?id=9

Groysberg, B., and M. Slind. 2011. *Talk, inc.* Boston, MA: Harvard Business Press.

Grunig, J.E. 1978. "Defining Publics in Public Relations: The Case of a Suburban Hospital." *Journalism Quarterly* 55, no. 1, pp. 109–18.

Grunig, J.E. 1983. "Communication Behaviors and Attitudes of Environmental Publics: Two Studies." *Journalism Monographs Number Eighty-One.*

Grunig, J.E. 1992. "Symmetrical Systems of Internal Communication." In *Excellence in Public Relations and Communication Management,* ed. J.E. Grunig, 531–75. Hillsdale, NJ: Lawrence Erlbaum Associates.

Grunig, J.E., and T. Hunt. 1984. *Managing Public Relations.* New York: Holt Rhinehart and Winston.

Grunig, J.E., and F.C. Repper. 1992. "Strategic Management, Publics, and Issues." In *Excellence in Public Relations and Communication Management,* ed. J.E. Grunig, 117–58. Hillsdale, NJ: Lawrence Erlbaum Associates.

Grunig, L.A. 1992. "Activism: How it Limits the Effectiveness of Organizations and How Excellent Public Relations Departments Respond." In *Excellence in Public Relations and Communication Management,* ed. J.E. Grunig, 503–30. Hillsdale, NJ: Lawrence Erlbaum Associates.

Grunig, L.A., J.E. Grunig, and D.M. Dozier. 2002. "Excellent Public Relations and Effective Organizations: A Study of Communication Management in Three Countries." Mahwah, NJ: Lawrence Erlbaum.

Guttler, A., and T. Ullrich. 2008. "We Manage Your Damage: How Companies Effortlessly Master International Transformational Processes." In *Communication and Leadership in the 21st Century,* eds. S. Holger and B. Daniela, 141–56. Gutersloh: Verlag Bertelsmann Stiftung.

Haar, J.M. 2013. "Testing a New Measure of Work-Life Balance: A Study of Parent and Nonparent Employees from New Zealand." *The International Journal of Human Resource Management* 24, no. 17, pp. 3305–24.

Hackman, M.Z., and C.E. Johnson. 2004. *Leadership: A Communication Perspective* 4th ed. Waveland, IL: Long Grove.

Halpin, A.W., and D.B. Croft. 1963. *The Organizational Climate of Schools.* Chicago: Midwest Administration Center of the University of Chicago.

Harris, T.E. 1993. *Applied Organizational Communication: Perspectives, Principles, and Pragmatics.* Hillsdale, NJ: Erlbaum.

Harrison, R. 1972. "Understanding Your Organisation's Character." Harvard Business Review 50, pp. 119–28.

Harrison, L.H. 2015. "Managing Today's Multigenerational Workforce." Retrieved on September 13 from www.lhh.com/en-US/thought-leadership/ Documents/managing-todays-multigenerational-workforce.pdf

Harter, J.K., F.L. Schmidt, and T.L. Hayes. 2002. "Business-Unit Level Relationship Between Employee Satisfaction, Employee Engagement, and Business Outcomes: A Meta-Analysis." *Journal of Applied Psychology* 87, no. 2, pp. 268–79.

Hay, R.D. 1974. "A Brief History of Internal Organizational Communication Through the 1940s." *The Journal of Business Communication* 11, no. 4, pp. 6–10.

Heo, J., and C.H. Cho. 2009. "A New Approach to Target Segmentation: Media-Usage Segmentation in the Multi-Media Environment." *Journal of Targeting, Measurement and Analysis for Marketing* 17, no. 3, pp. 145–55.

Hewitt, P. 2006. "Electronic Mail and Internal Communication: A Three-Factor Model." *Corporate Communications: An International Journal* 11, no. 1, pp. 78–92.

Holmstrom, S. 2007. "Niklas Luhmann: Contingency, Risk, Trust and Reflection." *Public Relations Review* 33, no. 3, pp. 255–62.

Hon, L.C., and J.E. Grunig. 1999. *Guidelines for Measuring Relationships in Public Relations.* Gainesville, FL: Institute for Public Relations, Commission on PR Measurement and Evaluation.

House, R.J., P.J. Hangers, J. Javidan, P.W. Dorfman, V. Gupta, and Asssociatés. 2004. *Leadership, Culture, and Organizations: The GLOBLE Study of 62 Societies.* Thousand Oaks, CA: Sage.

Huang, J., J. Baptista, and R.D. Galliers. 2012. "Reconceptualizing Rhetorical Practices in Organizations: The Impact of Social Media on Internal Communications." *Information and Management* 50, nos. 2–3, pp. 112–24.

Hutton, J.G., M.B. Goodman, J.B. Alexander, and C.M. Genest. 2001. "Reputation Management: The New Face of Corporate Public Relations?" *Public Relations Review* 27, no. 3, pp. 247–61.

Hunt, V., D, Layton, and S. Prince. January 2015. "Why Diversity Matters." McKinsey & Company. Retrieved on October 24 from www.mckinsey.com/business-functions/organization/our-insights/why-diversity-matters

Huy, Q., and A. Shipilov. 2012. "The Key to Social Media Success Within Organizations." *MITSloan Management Review* 54, no. 1, pp. 73–81.

Ignatius, A. November 2015. "Leadership with a Conscience." *Harvard Business Review*, pp. 50–51.

Ilies, R., F.P. Morgeson, and J.D. Nahrgang. 2005. "Authentic Leadership and Eudaemonic Well-Being: Understanding Leader–Follower Outcomes." *Leadership Quarterly* 16, no. 3, pp. 373–94.

Institute for Public Relations 2016. *Organizational Clarity: The Case for Workforce Alignment and Belief.* Gainesville, FL: Institute for Public Relations. Retrieved from: www.instituteforpr.org/wp-content/uploads/Organizational-Clarity-White-Paper-05-06-16-Final-Online.pdf

IPG Media Lab. 2014. "Messaging Apps: The New Face of Social Media and What it Means for Brands." Retrieved on December 10 from http://ipglab.com/wp-content/uploads/2014/04/MessagingApps_Whitepaper_Final.pdf

Jablin, F.M. 1979. "Superior-Subordinate Communication: the State of the Art." *Psychological Bulletin* 86, no. 6, pp. 1201–22.

Jablin, F.M. 1987. "Formal Organizational Structure." In *Handbook of Organizational Communication: An Interdisciplinary Perspective,* eds. F.M. Jablin, L.L. Putnam, K.H. Roberts, L.M. Porter, 389–419. Newbury Park: Sage.

Jablin, F.M. 2001. "Organizational Intrigue, Assimilation, and Disengagement/Exit." In *The New Handbook of Organizational Communication: Advances in Theory, Research, and Methods,* eds. F.M. Jablin and L.L. Putnam, 732–818. Thousand Oaks: Sage.

Jablin, F.M., and P.M. Sais. 2001. "Communication Competence." In *The New Handbook of Organizational Communication: Advances in Theory, Research, and Methods,* eds. F.M. Jablin and L.L. Putnam, 819–64. Thousand Oaks: Sage.

Janis, I.L. 1972. *Victims of Groupthink: A Psychological Study of Foreign-Policy Decisions and Fiascoes.* Boston: Houghton Mifflin.

Jiang, H., and L.R. Men. 2015. "Creating an Engaged Workforce: The Impact of Authentic Leadership, Transparent Communication, and Work-Life Enrichment." *Communication Research.* doi:10.1177/0093650215613137

Jin, Y. 2010. "Emotional Leadership as a Key Dimension of Public Relations Leadership: National Survey of Public Relations Leaders." *Journal of Public Relations Research* 22, no. 2, pp. 159–81.

Johansson, C., and M. Heide. 2008. "Speaking of Change: Three Communication Approaches in Studies of Organizational Change." *Corporate Communications: An International Journal* 13, no. 3, pp. 288–305.

Johansson, C., V.D. Miller, and S. Hamrin. 2014. "Conceptualizing Communicative Leadership." *Corporate Communications: An International Journal* 19, no. 2, pp. 147–65.

Kahn, W.A. 1990. "Psychological Conditions of Personal Engagement and Disengagement at Work." *Academy of Management Journal* 33, pp. 692–724.

Kalla, H.K. 2005. "Integrated Internal Communications: A Multidisciplinary Perspective." *Corporate Communication* 10, no. 4, pp. 302–14.

Kalshoven, K., D.N. Den Hartog, and A.H.B. De Hoogh. 2011. "Ethical Leadership at Work Questionnaire (ELW): Development and Validation of a Multidimensional Measure." *The Leadership Quarterly* 22, no. 1, pp. 51–69.

Kant, I. (1785) 1964. *Groundwork of the Metaphysic of Morals*, ed. H.J. Paton, Trans. New York: Harper and Row.

Kant, I. (1793) 1974. *On the Old Saw: That May be Right in Theory But it Won't Work in Practice*, ed. E.B. Ashton, Trans. Philadelphia: University of Pennsylvania Press.

Kantabutra, S. 2008. "What Do We Know About Vision?" *Journal of Applied Business Research* 24, pp. 127–38.

Karanges, E., K. Johnston, A. Beatson, and I. Lings. 2015. "The Influence of Internal Communication on Employee Engagement: A Pilot Study." *Public Relations Review* 41, no. 1, 129–31.

Karanika-Murray, M., N. Duncan, H.M. Pontes, and M.D. Griffiths. 2015. "Organizational Identification, Work Engagement, and Job Satisfaction." *Journal of Managerial Psychology* 30, no. 8, pp. 1019–33.

Karatepe, O.M., and G. Karadas. 2015. "Do Psychological Capital and Work Engagement Foster Frontline Employees' Satisfaction?." *International Journal of Contemporary Hospitality Management* 27, no. 6, pp. 1254–78.

Kennedy, A. November 1983. "Back-Fence Conversations, New Tools for Quality Conversations." *Communication World*, p. 26.

Kim, J.N., and Y. Rhee. 2011. "Strategic Thinking About Employee Communication Behavior (ECB) in Public Relations: Testing the Models of Megaphoning and Scouting Effects in Korea." *Journal of Public Relations Research* 23, no. 3, pp. 243–68.

Kotter, J.P. 1995. *Leading Change: Why Transformation Efforts Fail*. Boston, MA: Harvard Business Press. Retrieved on February 29, 2016 from https://hbr.org/1995/05/leading-change-why-transformation-efforts-fail-2

Kotter, J.P. 1996. *Leading Change*. Boston, MA: Harvard Business School Press.

La Framboise, D., R.L. Nelson, and J. Schmaltz. 2002. "Managing Resistance to Change in Workplace Accommodation Projects." *Journal of Facilities Management* 1, no. 4, pp. 306–21.

Larkin, T.J., and S. Larkin. 1994. *Communicating change: Winning Employee Support for New Business Goals*. New York: McGraw-Hill.

Leonardi, P.M., M. Huysman, and C. Steinfield. 2013. "Enterprise Social Media: Definition, History, and Prospects for the Study of Social Technologies in Organizations." *Journal of Computer-Mediated Communication* 19, no. 1, pp. 1–19.

Lewis, L.K. 1999. "Disseminating Information and Soliciting Input During Planned Organizational Change: Implementers' Targets, Sources, and Channels for Communicating." *Management Communication Quarterly* 13, no. 1, pp. 43–75.

Lewis, L.K. 2000. "Communicating Change: Four Cases of Quality Programs." *Journal of Business Communication* 37, no. 2, pp. 128–56.

Li, C., and D.W. Stacks. 2015. *Is Social Media Needed to Profit in Business? A Fortune 500 Perspective.* New York: Peter Lang.

Li, Z. 2015. *Does Power Make Us Mean? An Investigation of Empowerment and Revenge Behaviors in the Cyberspace.* Unpublished doctoral [dissertation]. Florida: University of Miami.

Lien, C.H., and Y. Cao. 2014. "Examining WeChat Users' Motivations, Trust, Attitudes, and Positiveword-of-Mouth: Evidence from China." *Computers in Human Behavior* 41, pp. 104–11.

Likert, R. 1967. *The Human Organizations.* New York: MGraw-Hill.

Lin, C.F. 2002. "Segmenting Customer Brand Preference: Demographic or Psychographic." *Journal of Product and Brand Management* 11, no. 4, pp. 249–68.

Lindenmann, W.K. 1993. "An 'Effectiveness Yardstick' to Measure Public Relations Success." *Public Relations Quarterly* 38, no. 1, p. 7.

Lines, R. 2007. "Using Power to Install Strategy: the Relationships Between Expert Power, Position Power, Influence Tactics and Implementation Success." *Journal of Change Management* 7, no. 2, pp. 143–70.

Lipiäinen, H.S.M., H.E. Karjaluoto, and M. Nevalainen. 2014. "Digital Channels in the Internal Communication of a Multinational Corporation." *Corporate Communications: An International Journal* 19, no. 3, pp. 275–86.

Locke, E.A. 1976. "The Nature and Causes of Job Satisfaction." In *Handbook of Industrial and Organizational Psychology,* ed. M.D. Dunnette, 1297–349. Chicago: Rand McNally.

Luhmann, N. 1979. *Trust and Power.* Chichester, UK: John Wiley and Sons.

Luhmann, N. 1984. *Social Systems,* eds. J. Bednarz and D. Baecker, Trans, Stanford, CA: Stanford University Press.

Luo, Y., and H. Jiang. 2014. "Effective Public Relations Leadership in Organizational Change: A Study of Multinationals in Mainland China." *Journal of Public Relations Research* 26, no. 2, pp. 134–60.

Macey, W.H., and B. Schneider. 2008. "The Meaning of Employee Engagement." *Industrial and Organizational Psychology* 1, no. 1, pp. 3–30.

Macleod, D., and C. Brady. 2008. "The Extra Mile: How to Engage Your People to Win." Harllow, UK: Prentice Hall.

Madlock, P.E. 2008. "The Link Between Leadership Style, Communication Competence, and Employee Satisfaction." *Journal of Business Communication* 45, no. 1, pp. 61–78.

Mael, F., and B.E. Ashforth. 1992. "Alumni and their Alma Mater: A Partial Test of the Reformulated Model of Organizational Identification." *Journal of Organizational Behavior* 13, no. 2, pp. 103–23.

Morgan, G. 2006. *Images of Organization.* Beverly Hills, CA: Sage.

Mayfield, J., and M. Mayfield. 2012. "The Relationship Between Leader Motivating Language and Self-Efficacy: A Partial Least Squares Model Analysis." *Journal of Business Communication* 49, no. 4, pp. 357–76.

Mayfield, J., M. Mayfield, and W.C. Sharbrough III. 2015. "Strategic Vision and Values in Top Leaders' Communications: Motivating Language at a Higher Level." *International Journal of Business Communication* 52, no. 1, pp. 97–121.

McGregor, D. 1960. *The Human Side of Enterprise.* New York: McGraw-Hill.

McKinney, R., M. McMahon, and P. Walsh. 2013. *Danger in the Middle: Why Middle Managers aren't Ready to Lead.* Boston, MA: Harvard Business Publishing. Retrieved on September 10 from www.harvardbusiness.org/sites/default/files/PDF/17807_CL_MiddleManagers_White_Paper_March2013.pdf

McLuhan, M. 1964. *Understanding Media: The Extensions of Man,* 2nd ed. New York: McGraw-Hill Book Company.

McPhee, R.D., and M.S. Poole. 2001. "Organizational Structures and Configurations." In *The New Handbook of Organizational Communication: Advances in Theory, Research, and Methods,* eds. F.M. Jablin and L.L. Putnam, 503–43. Thousand Oaks: Sage.

Melcrum. 2013. "Could Big Data be a Game-Changer for Internal Communication?" Retrieved on April 29 from www.melcrum.com/research/intranets-digital-social-media/could-big-data-be-game-changer-internal-communication

Men, L.R. 2011. "CEO Credibility, Organizational Reputation, and Employee Engagement." *Public Relations Review* 38, no. 1, pp. 171–73.

Men, L.R. 2011a. "Exploring the Impact of Employee Empowerment on Organization-Employee Relationship." *Public Relations Review* 37, no. 4, pp. 435–37.

Men, L.R. 2011b. "How Employee Empowerment Influences Organization-Employee Relationships in China." *Public Relations Review* 37, no. 4, pp. 435–37.

Men, L.R. 2014a. "Internal Reputation Management: Effects of Authentic Leadership and Transparent Communication." *Corporate Reputation Review* 17, no. 4, pp. 254–72.

Men, L.R. 2014b. "Strategic Employee Communication: Transformational Leadership, Communication Channels, and Employee Satisfaction." *Management Communication Quarterly* 28, no. 2, pp. 264–84.

Men, L.R. 2014c. "Why Leadership Matters to Internal Communication: Linking Transformational Leadership, Symmetrical Communication, and Employee Outcomes." *Journal of Public Relations Research* 26, no. 3, pp. 256–79.

Men, L.R. 2015a. "The Internal Communication Role of the Chief Executive Officer: Communication Channels, Style, and Effectiveness." *Public Relations Review* 41, no. 4, pp. 461–71.

Men, L.R. 2015b. "Employee Engagement in Relation to Employee–Organization Relationships and Internal Reputation: Effects of Leadership Communication." *Public Relations Journal* 9, no. 2. www.prsa.org/Intelligence/PRJournal/Documents/2015v09n02Men.pdf

Men, L.R. 2015c. "The Role of Ethical Leadership in Internal Communication: Influence on Communication Symmetry, Leader Credibility, and Employee Engagement." *Public Relations Journal* 9, no. 1. www.prsa.org/Intelligence/PRJournal/Documents/2015v09n01Men.pdf

Men, L.R., and W.S. Tsai. 2014. "Perceptual, Attitudinal, and Behavioral Outcomes of Organization—Public Engagement on Corporate Social Networking Sites." *Journal of Public Relations Research* 26, no. 5, pp. 417–35.

Men, L.R., and C.F. Hung-Baesecke. 2015. "Engaging Employees in China." *Corporate Communications: An International Journal* 20, no. 4, pp. 448–67.

Men, L.R., and D.W. Stacks. 2013. "Measuring the Impact of Organizational Leadership Style and Employee Empowerment on Perceived Organizational Reputation." *Journal of Communication Management* 17, no. 2, pp. 171–92.

Men, L.R., and D.W. Stacks. 2014. "The Effects of Authentic Leadership on Strategic Internal Communication and Employee-Organization Relationships." *Journal of Public Relations Research* 26, no. 4, pp. 301–24.

Meng, J., and B.K. Berger. 2012 "Measuring Return on Investment (ROI) of Organizations' Internal Communication Efforts." *Journal of Communication Management* 16, no. 4, pp. 332–54.

Menguc, B., S. Auh, M. Fisher, and A. Haddad. 2013. "To be Engaged or Not to be Engaged: The Antecedents and Consequences of Service Employee Engagement." *Journal of Business Research* 66, no. 11, pp. 2163–70.

Michaelson, D., and D.W. Stacks. 2014. *A Professional and Practitioner's Guide to Public Relations Research, Measurement, and Evaluation.* 2nd ed. New York: Business Expert Press.

Michaelson, D., and D.W. Stacks. 2014. *A Professional and Practitioner's Guide to Public Relations Research, Measurement, and Evaluation.* 2nd. ed. New York: Business Expert Press.

Miller, P., and E. Marsh. 2014. *The Digital Renaissance of Work: Delivering Digital Workplaces Fit for the Future*. New York: Routledge.

Mintzberg, H. 1983. *Power in and Around Organizations*. Englewood Cliffs, NJ: Prentice-Hall.

Molleda, J. 2010. "Authenticity and the Construct's Dimensions in Public Relations and Communication Research." *Journal of Communication* 14, no. 3, pp. 223–36.

Molleda, J., and M. Roberts. 2008. "The Value of Authenticity in Global Strategic Communication: The New Juan Valdez Campaign." *International Journal of Strategic Communication* 2, no. 3, pp. 154–74.

Morgan, G. 2006. *Images of Organization*. Beverly Hills, CA: Sage.

Moroko, L., and M.D. Uncles. 2009. "Employee Branding and Market Segmentation." *Journal of Brand Management* 17, pp. 181–96.

Munn, S.L. 2013. "Unveiling the Work-Life System: The Influence of Work-Life Balance on Meaningful Work." *Advances in Developing Human Resources* 15, no. 4, pp. 401–17.

Naslund, A. 2010. "Social Media from the Inside Out." *Communication World* 27, no. 5, pp. 36.

Neufeld, D.J., Z. Wan, Y. Fang. 2010. "Remote Leadership, Communication Effectiveness and Leader Performance." *Group Decision and Negotiation* 19, no. 3, pp. 227–46.

Ng, T.W.H., and D.C. Feldman. 2012. "Employee Voice Behavior: A Meta-Analytic Test of the Conversation of Resources Framework." *Journal of Organizational Behavior 33*, no. 2, 216–34.

Northouse, P.G. 2007. *Leadership: Theory and Practice,* 4th ed. Thousand Oaks, CA: Sage.

Ovaitt, F. 2014. "Where Sharing can Shape Strategy." *PR News,* March, pp. 1, 7.

Park, D., and B.K. Berger. 2004. "The Presentation of CEOs in the Press, 1990–2000: Increasing Salience, Positive Valuence, and a Focus on Competency and Personal Dimensions of Image." *Journal of Public Relations Research* 16, no. 1, pp. 93–125.

Penley, L.E., and B. Hawkins. 1985. "Studying Interpersonal Communication in Organizations: A Leadership Application." *Academy of Management Journal* 28, no. 2, pp. 309–26.

Pincus, J.D., R.E. Rayfield, and M.D. Cozzens. 1991. "The Chief Executive Officer's Internal Communication Role: A Benchmark Program of Research." *Journal of Public Relations Research 3*, nos. 1–4, pp. 1–35.

Podsakoff, P.M., S.B. MacKenzie, J.B. Paine, and D.G. Bachrach. 2000. "Organizational Citizenship Behaviors: A Critical Review of the Theoretical and Empirical Literature and Suggestions for Future Research." *Journal of Management* 26, no. 3, pp. 513–63.

Porter, H., J.S. Wrench, and C. Hoskinson. 2007. "The Influence of Supervisor Temperament on Subordinate Job Satisfaction and Perceptions of Supervisor Socio communicative Orientation and Approachability." *Communication Quarterly* 55, no. 1, pp. 129–53.

Porter, M.E. 1996. "What is Strategy?." *Harvard Business Review* 74, no. 6, pp. 61–83.

PWC (PricewaterCooper's). 2011. "Millennials at Work Reshaping the Workplace." Retrieved on September 13 from www.pwc.com/m1/en/services/consulting/documents/millennials-at-work.pdf

Rauch, C.F., and O. Behling. 1984. "Functionalism: Basis for an Alternate Approach to the Study of Leadership." In *Leaders and Managers: International Perspectives on Managerial Behavior and Leadership,* eds. J.G. Hunt, D.M. Hosking, C.A. Schriesheim, and R. Stewart, 45–62. Elmsford, NY: Pergamon Press.

Rawlins, B. 2009. "Give the Emperor a Mirror: Toward Developing a Stakeholder Measurement of Organizational Transparency." *Journal of Public Relations Research* 21, no. 1, pp. 71–99.

Raywood, G. 2015. "Engaging Frontline Employees: Six Principles for Maximizing the Two-Minute Window." Retrieved on September 10 from www.edelman.com/post/engaging-frontline-employees

Redding, W.C., and G.A. Sanborn. 1965. *Business and Industrial Communication.* Verlag: Joanna Cotler Books.

Resick, C.J., D.S. Whitman, S.M. Weingarden, and N.J. Hiller. 2009. "The Bright-Side and the Dark-Side of CEO Personality: Examining Core Self-Evaluations, Narcissism, Transformational Leadership, and Strategic Influence." *Journal of Applied Psychology* 94, no. 6, pp. 1365–81.

Rice, A.K. 1963. *The Enterprise and its Environment.* London: Tavistock.

Rich, B.L., J.A. LePine, and E.R. Crawford. 2010. "Job Engagement: Antecedents and Effects of Job Performance." *Academy of Management Journal* 53, no. 3, pp. 617–35.

Richards, D., and S. Engle. 1986. "After the Vision: Suggestions to Corporate Visionaries and Vision Champions." In *Transforming leadership,* ed. J.D. Adams, 199–214. Alexandria, VA: Miles River Press.

Robinson, D., S. Perryman, and S. Hayday. 2004. *The Drivers of Employee Engagement.* Brighton, UK: Institute for Employment Studies.

Rodgers, V. 2006. "The Future of Measurement in Corporate Communication." In *The IABC Handbook of Organizational Communication: A Guide to Internal Communication, Public Relations, Marketing, and Leadership,* ed. T.L. Gillis, 2 vols. San Francisco, CA: Jossey-Bass.

Ryan, M., and D.L. Martinson. 1983. "The Public Relations Office as Corporate Conscience." *Public Relations Quarterly,* Summer, 20–23.

Sager, K.L. 2008. "An Exploratory Study of the Relationships Between Theory X/Y Assumptions and Superior Communicator Style." *Management Communication Quarterly* 22, no. 2, pp. 288–312.

Saks, A.M. 2006. "Antecedents and Consequences of Employee Engagement." *Journal of Managerial Psychology* 21, pp. 600–18.

Saks, A.M., and J.A. Gruman. 2011. "Getting Newcomers Engaged: The Role of Socialization Tactics." *Journal of Managerial Psychology* 26, no. 5, pp. 383–402.

Saks, A.M., and J.A. Gruman. 2014. "What do we Really Know About Employee Engagement?." *Human Resource Development Quarterly* 25, no. 2, pp. 155–82. doi:10.1002/hrdq.21187

Schaufeli, W.B., M. Salanova, V. Gonzalez-Roma, and A.B. Bakker. 2002. "The Measurement of Engagement and Burnout: A Two Sample Confirmatory Factor Analytic Approach." *Journal of Happiness Studies* 3, no. 1, pp. 71–92.

Seeger, M.W. 1997. *Ethics and Organizational Communication.* Cresskill, NJ: Hampton.

Seeger, M.W., R.R. Ulmer, J.M. Novak, and R. Sellnow. 2005. "Post-Crisis Discourse and Organizational Change, Failure and Renewal." *Journal of Organizational Change Management* 18, no. 1, pp. 78–95.

Shen, H., and J.N. Kim. 2012. "The Authentic Enterprise: Another Buzz Word, or a True Driver of Quality Relationships?" *Journal of Public Relations Research* 24, no. 4, pp. 371–89.

Sims, R.R. 1994. *Ethics and Organizational Decision Making: A Call for Renewal.* Westport, CT: Quorum.

Smircich, L., and M.B. Calas. 1987. "Organizational Culture: A Critical Assessment." In *Handbook of Organizational Communication: An Interdisciplinary Perspective,* eds. F.M. Jablin, L.L. Putnam, K.H. Roberts, and L.M. Porter, 228–63. Newbury Park: Sage.

Smith, L., and P. Mounter. 2008. *Effective Internal Communication,* 2nd ed. London: CIPR.

Smith, P.C., L.M. Kendall, and C.L. Hulin. 1969. *The Measurement of Satisfaction in Work and Retirement.* Chicago: Rand McNally.

Smith, A.L. 1991.*Innovative Employee Communication: New Approaches to Improving Trust, Teamwork, and Performance.* Englewood Cliffs, NJ: Prentice Hall.

Sonnenfeld, J.A. 1985. "Shedding Light on the Hawthorne Studies." *Journal of Occupational Behavior* 6, no. 2, pp.111–30.

Sorenson, S. 2013. "How Employee Engagement Drives Growth." *Gallup Business Journal.* Retrieved on January 14, 2016 from www.gallup.com/businessjournal/163130/employee-engagement-drives-growth.aspx

Sriram, P. April 2014. "The Art of Leadership Communication: 6 Rules for Effective Communication." *Leadership Excellence.* Retrieved on September 23 from www.hr.com/en/magazines/leadership_excellence_essentials/april_2014_leadership/the-art-of-leadership-communication-6-rules-for-ef_hubbvic4.html

Sriramesh, K., J.E. Grunig, and J. Buffington. 1992. "Corporate Culture and Public Relations." In *Excellence in Public Relations and Communication Management,* ed. J.E. Grunig, 577–96. Hillsdale, NJ: Lawrence Erlbaum Associates.

Stacks, D.W. 2002. *Primer of Public Relation Research.* New York: Guilford.

Stacks, D.W. 2010. *Primer of Public Relations Research,* 2nd ed. New York: Guilford.

Stacks, D.W. July 2016. "Strategic Standardization in Public Relations/Corporate Communication Research: Why It Matters and Where We Are." Paper presented at Bledcom2016, Bled, Slovenia.

Stacks, D.W. 2017. *Primer of Public Relations Research,* 3rd ed. New York: Guilford.

Stacks, D., and S.A. Bowen. 2013. *Dictionary of Public Relations Measurement and Research,* 3rd ed. Gainesville, FL: Institute for Public Relations. Reprinted (2013) by the International Association for the Measurement and Evaluation of Communication (AMEC). Translated into Chinese, Mandarin, Spanish, Arabic, Italian, Portuguese, Russian and Korean. www.instituteforpr.org/dictionary-public-relations-measurement-research-third-edition

Stacks, D.W., and D. Michaelson. 2010. *A Practitioner's Guide to Public Relations Research, Measurement, and Evaluation.* New York: Business Expert Press.

Stacks, D.W., M. Dodd, and L.R. Men. 2011. "Public Relations Research and Planning." In *The IABC Handbook of Organizational Communication Public Relations, Marketing and Leadership,* eds. T. Gillis, 287–300. 2nd ed. San Francisco: Jossey-Bass, Inc.

Stacks, D.W., D.K. Wright, and S.A. Bowen. 2014. "IBM's Smart Planet Initiative: Building a More Intelligent World." In *Public Relations Cases from Around the World,* eds. J. Turk, J. Valin, and J. Paluszek, 1–22. New York: Peter Lang.

Stensaker, I., and J. Falkenberg. 2007. "Making Sense of Different Responses to Corporate Change." *Human Relations* 60, no. 1, pp. 137–77.

Stephens, K.K., A.K. Barrett, and M.J. Mahometa. 2013. "Organizational Communication in Emergencies: Using Multiple Channels and Sources to Combat Noise and Capture Attention." *Human Communication Research* 39, no. 2, pp. 230–51.

Stoffels, J.D. 1994. *Strategic Issues Management: A Comprehensive Guide to Environmental Scanning.* Milwaukee, WI: Pergamon.

Stogdill, R.M. 1974. *Handbook of Leadership: A Survey of the Literature.* New York: Free Press.

The Economic Intelligence Unit. 2015. "Engaging and Integrating a Global Workforce." Retrieved on May 6, 2016 from www.shrm.org/about/foundation/documents/3-15%20eiu%20theme%202%20report-final.pdf

The Economist Intelligence Unit Limited. 2014. "What's Next: Future Global Trends Affecting your Organization." Retrieved on September 13, 2015 from www.shrm.org/about/foundation/shapingthefuture/documents/2-14%20 theme%201%20paper-final%20for%20web.pdf

Thomas, C.E., V.P. Richmond, and J.C. McCroskey. 1994. "The Association Between Immediacy and Sociocommunicative Style." *Communication Research Reports* 11, no. 1, pp. 107–15.

Towers Watson. 2014. "How the Fundamentals Have Evolved and the Best Adapt: Change and Communication ROI Report." Retrieved on August 14 from file:///Users/cicirita/Downloads/change-and-communication-roi-study-2013-2014-UK.pdf

Treem, J.W., S.L. Dailey, C.S. Pierce, and P.M. Leonardi. 2015. "Bringing Technological Frames to Work: How Previous Experience with Social Media Shapes the Technology's Meaning in an Organization." *Journal of Communication* 65, no. 2, pp. 396–422.

Trevino, L.K., R.L. Daft, and R.H. Lengel. 1990. "Understanding Manager's Media Choices: A Symbolic Interactionist Perspective." In *Organizations and Communication Technology,* eds. J. Fulk and C. Steinfield, 71–94. Newburry Park, CA: Sage.

Trevino, L.K., G.R. Weaver, and S.J. Reynolds. 2006. "Behavioral Ethics in Organizations: A Review." *Journal of Management* 32, no. 6, pp. 951–90. doi:10.1177/0149206306294258

Turner, Z. 2016, May 24. "In Germany, an Epidemic of Stress, or 'Das Burnout." *The Wall Street Journal,* pp. D1–D2.

van Riel, C.B., G. Berens, and M. Dijkstra. 2005. *The Influence of Employee Communication on Strategic Business Alignment.* Report of the Erasmus Research Institute of Management: Erasmus University, Rotterdam, the Netherlands.

Verčič, A.T., D. Verčič, and K. Sriramesh. 2012. "Internal Communication: Definition, Parameters, and the Future." *Public Relations Review* 38, no. 2, pp. 223–30.

Verčič, D., L.A. Grunig, and J.E. Grunig. 1996. "Global and Specific Principles of Public Relations: Evidence from Slovenia." In *International Public Relations: A Comparative Analysis,* eds. H. M. Culbertson and N. Chen, 31–65. Mahwah, NJ: Lawrence Erlbaum Associates.

Vidgen, R., J.M. Sims, and P. Powell. 2013. "Do CEO Bloggers Build Community?" *Journal of Communication Management* 17, no. 4, pp. 364–85.

Vogelgesang, G.R., H. Leroy, and B.J Avolio. 2013. "The Mediating Effects of Leader Integrity with Transparency and Communication at Work and Gauge/ Performance." *The Leadership Quarterly* 24, no. 3, pp. 405–13.

Vnmanpower.com. January 14, 2016. "Why Your Business Needs to Consider Blue Collar Work Engagement." Retrieved on August 27, 2016 from http://vnmanpower.com/en/why-business-needs-consider-blue-collar-worker-engagement-bl242.html

Walumbwa, F.O., B.J. Avolio, W.L. Gardner, T.S. Wernsing, and S.J. Peterson. February 2008. "Authentic Leadership: Development and Validation of a Theory-Based Measure." *Journal of Management* 34, no. 1, pp. 89–126.

Washington, M., and M. Hacker. 2005. "Why Change Fails: Knowledge Counts." *Leadership and Organization Development Journal* 26, no. 5, pp. 400–11.

Wayne, J.H., J.G. Grzywacz, D.S. Carlson, and K.M. Kacmar. 2007. "Work-Family Facilitation: A Theoretical Explanation and Model of Primary Antecedents and Consequences." *Human Resource Management Review* 17, no. 1, pp. 63–76.

Weber Shandwick, Inc. 2013. "Socializing Your CEO III: From Marginal to Mainstream." Retrieved on September 24, 2015 from www.webershandwick.com/uploads/news/files/socializing-your-ceo-iii-exec-summary.pdf

Weber, M. 1930. *The Protestant Ethic and the Spirit of Capitalism*. New York: Routledge (T. Parsons, Trans).

Weber, M. 1947. "The Theory of Social and Economic Organizations." eds. A.M. Henderson and T. Parsons, Trans. New York: Free Press.

Wedel, M., and W.A. Kamakura. 1999. *Market Segmentation: Conceptual and Methodological Foundations*, Boston, MA: Kluwer Academic Publishers.

Weick, K.E. 1979. "The Social Psychology of Organizing." 2nd ed. New York: Addison-Wesley.

Weick, K.E. 1987. "Theorizing About Organizational Communication." In *Handbook of Organizational Communication: An Interdisciplinary Perspective*, eds. F.M. Jablin and L.L. Putnam and K.H. Roberts and L.W. Porter, 97–122. Newbury Park, CA: Sage.

Weiss, D.J., R.V. Dawis, G.W. England, and L.H. Lofquist. 1967. *Manual for the Minnesota Satisfaction Questionnaire*. Minneapolis: Industrial Relations Center, University of Minnesota.

Welch, M., and P.R. Jackson. 2007. "Rethinking Internal Communication: A Stakeholder Approach." *Corporate Communications* 12, no. 2, pp. 177–98.

Westley, F., and H. Mintzberg. 1989. "Visionary Leadership and Strategic Management." *Strategic Management Journal* 10, no. S1, pp. 17–32.

White, C., A. Vanc, and G. Stafford. 2010 "Internal Communication, Information Satisfaction, and Sense of Community: The Effect of Personal Influence." *Journal of Public Relations Research* 22, no. 1, pp. 65–84.

Whitworth, B. 2011. "Internal Communication." In *The IABC Handbook of Organizational Communication*, ed. T. Gillis, 195–206. 2nd ed. Jossey-Bass, Inc.

Wright, D.K., R. Gaunt, B. Leggetter, M. Daniels, and A. Zerfass. 2009. "Global Survey of Communications Measurement 2009-Final Report." Retrieved on April 29 from www.benchpoint.com/summit.pdf

Wu, J. 2014. "How WeChat, the Most Popular Social Network in China, Cultivates Wellbeing." Scholarly Commons. Received on December 10 from http://repository.upenn.edu/mapp_capstone/65

Yammarino, F.J., and T.N. Naughton. 1988. "Time Spent Communicating: A Multiple Levels of Analysis Approach." *Human Relations* 41, pp. 655–76.

Yukl, G. 2006. *Leadership in Organizations*, 6th ed. Upper Saddle River, NJ: Prentice Hall.

Yukl, G., and D.D. Van Fleet. 1992. "Theory and Research on Leadership in Organizations." In *Handbook of Industrial and Organizational Psychology*, eds. M.D. Dunnette and L.M. Hough, 147–197. 3 vols. Palo Alto, CA: Consulting Psychologists Press.

Index

OTHER TITLES IN OUR PUBLIC RELATIONS COLLECTION

Don W. Stacks and Donald K. Wright, Editors

- *Public Relations Ethics: How To Practice PR Without Losing Your Soul* by Dick Martin and Donald K. Wright
- *MetricsMan: It Doesn't Count Unless You Can Count It* by Don Bartholomew and Zifei Fay Chen
- *Public Relations for the Public Good: How PR Has Shaped America's Social Movements* by Shelley Spector and Louis Capozzit

Announcing the Business Expert Press Digital Library

Concise e-books business students need for classroom and research

This book can also be purchased in an e-book collection by your library as

- a one-time purchase,
- that is owned forever,
- allows for simultaneous readers,
- has no restrictions on printing, and
- can be downloaded as PDFs from within the library community.

Our digital library collections are a great solution to beat the rising cost of textbooks. E-books can be loaded into their course management systems or onto students' e-book readers.
The **Business Expert Press** digital libraries are very affordable, with no obligation to buy in future years. For more information, please visit **www.businessexpertpress.com/librarians**. To set up a trial in the United States, please email **sales@businessexpertpress.com.**